SOCCER FIRSTS

SOCCER FIRSTS

John Robinson

Jock Stein's all-conquering Celtic team, pictured above their 'haul' of trophies in their best ever season. (Gus Christie)

Editor: Beatrice Frei
Design and Layout: David Roberts
Picture Editor: Alex Goldberg

© **John Robinson and Guinness Publishing Ltd,
1986, 1989**
First published in 1986
Second edition 1989

Published in Great Britain by
Guinness Publishing Ltd,
33 London Road, Enfield, Middlesex

Phototypeset in 9½/10½pt Melior Roman and
9½/10½pt Rockwell by
Ace Filmsetting Ltd, Frome, Somerset
Printed and bound in Great Britain by
Butler & Tanner Ltd, Frome, Somerset

British Library Cataloguing in Publication Data

Robinson, John, 1947–
Soccer firsts. — 2nd ed.
1. Association football
I. Title   II. Robinson, John, 1947–.
Guinness soccer firsts
796.334

ISBN 0-85112-367-8

The publishers have endeavoured to credit
photograph sources where known. We would be
interested to hear from any readers who may have
photographic or illustrative material in their
possession which might be considered for use in
any future edition of this book.

CONTENTS

The World's earliest football photograph
This photograph, featuring the '4th Team Football
Squad' of the Addiscombe Military College, East
Croydon, was taken in 1855 by Aaron Penley, the
noted artist. Although 16 players were pictured, we
know from contemporary reports that a form of
soccer was played at the college. The playing pitch
at the college had two 'stout' goalposts at either
end and the purpose of the game was to get the ball
between the adversary's posts.
(Hulton Picture Company)

INTRODUCTION

When Wimbledon's goalkeeper Dave Beasant dived to his left to keep out John Aldridge's penalty kick in the 1988 FA Cup Final, he inadvertently committed John Robinson and Guinness Books to a new edition of *Soccer Firsts*.

How could they continue to market the popular first volume, published in 1986, when such compelling new material demanded inclusion? Not only was it the first time a penalty had been missed in the FA Cup Final at Wembley, but Beasant became the first goalkeeper to go up the steps to receive the trophy as captain of the winning side.

Football history is being rewritten all the time. Just a few weeks after Wimbledon's achievement in rising from the Southern League to the First Division and the FA Cup Final in just 11 years, and with Beasant now on his way to Newcastle, there was another 'first' in the European Championship — Holland winning an international tournament for the first time.

By then, John Robinson had already decided to widen the European Championship coverage in *Soccer Firsts*, to include a comprehensive country-by-country results section. The tournament now ranks alongside, rather than behind, the World Cup, so it is appropriate it should be chronicled accordingly.

Also on the increase in the pages which follow is the list of individual club 'firsts', and here again this 1989 edition is high on topicality. Aston Villa's presence in this section reflects their return to the First Division, and surely no premier publication should be without them.

The same can be said of Sheffield Wednesday and Manchester City — two other stalwart members of the football establishment. Clubs with such a towering tradition command a rightful place in any respectable review of the English game.

Neither should the Scottish League section be overlooked. Heart of Midlothian are right on cue in 1989 with their 'first' appearance in the quarter finals of a European competition. A quick flick through the first edition confirmed Hearts' original place in *Soccer Firsts* — they were the first Scottish club to install video cameras at their ground.

Talking of cameras, the chapter on television (for obvious reasons) always catches my eye. Only by that did I learn that the 'first' football match to be televised live was the Italy v West Germany international in 1936. By coincidence,

the same two nations met in this commentator's 'first' World Cup Final in 1982.

Just a few months before the publication of this second edition, I took part in another television 'first'. Appropriately, the first round proper of the FA Cup was covered in depth by the BBC. So I suppose you could say that Enfield and Southport, closely followed in the next round by Altrincham and Kettering, were the 'first' non-league clubs to host the full range of outside broadcast cameras at that stage of the competition.

All of which makes me realize that the major headache facing the author and publishers of this volume is not so much what to include — as what to leave out!

The material which has forced its way in has done so on its own merit, complementing the book's neat, compact style. What a crutch it is at times to lean on such as the 'catch me out if you can' quiz sessions at yours or my local club or pub; what a ready reference when it comes to settling an argument; what a comfortable companion on the train journey to the next match.

I confidently recommend this second edition to any new readers, knowing full well that a third is surely inevitable early in the 1990s. However, the beauty of *Soccer Firsts* is that it can never really be out of date.

A 'first', in football as in anything else, always remains a first.

John Motson

1 MILESTONES

1848 The first rules were drawn up at Cambridge University.

1857 The first of all the existing football clubs (Sheffield FC) was founded. Certain records state the date of its foundation to be 1855 and others show it to have been 24 October 1857.

1860 The first foreign football club, Harvard University, was founded.

1862 The first Football League club, Notts County, was founded.

1863 The English Football Association was formed.

1865 The first South American club, Buenos Aires of Argentina was founded.

The first 'tape' stretched between goal posts eight feet from the ground (to restrict the height of the goal) was introduced.

1866 The first 'inter-city' match was played at Battersea Park, London, between London and Sheffield—London won by 2 goals to nil.

1867 The first Scottish club, Queens Park, was founded.

1869 The first army football team, Royal Engineers, joined the Football Association.

1870 The first Welsh club, Druids, was founded.

1871 The first Football Association Challenge Cup was contested.

Goalkeepers were first mentioned in the rules.

1872 The first official international match between Scotland and England took place.

Corner kicks were first introduced.

1873 The first Welsh Football League club, Wrexham, was founded.

The Royal Engineers became the first team to go on a tour and won all three of their games against North Midlands teams.

The Scottish Football Association was formed and the first Scottish FA Cup contested.

1874 Samuel Widdowson invented shinguards and became the first player to wear them when playing for Nottingham Forest.

1875 The first cross-bars were used.

Oxford University used an educational tour of Germany to embark upon the first overseas tour by a British club.

1876 The Welsh Football Association was formed.

1877 The Welsh Cup was first contested.

1878 A whistle was first used by the referee of a match between Nottingham Forest and Sheffield Norfolk.

1879 The first Irish club, Cliftonville, was founded.

1880 The Irish Football Association was formed and the Irish Cup first contested.

Australian soccer commenced.

1881 The first football special was organized to take Dumbarton fans by rail to the 1881 Scottish Cup final with Queens Park.

1882 The International Football Association Board was set up.

1883 The first British Home International Championship was contested.

1886 International caps were first awarded.

1888 The Football League was formed.

1889 Preston North End won the first Football League championship and completed the first double.

The Dutch Football Association was formed.

The Danish Football Association was formed.

1890 The Scottish League was formed.

The Irish League was formed.

The first goal nets were used by Old Etonians.

1891 Referees and linesmen replaced umpires.

Penalty kicks were first introduced.

The first inter-league game was contested.

1892 The Football League Second Division was formed from Football Alliance members.

1893 The Argentinian Metropolitan League commenced (First winners: Lomas).

The Scottish League Second Division was formed.

The FA Amateur Cup was first contested.

1894 Celtic FC constructed the first press box at Celtic Park.

1895 The FA Cup was stolen, never recovered.

The Belgian Football Association was formed and the Belgian League commenced (first winners FC Liege).

The Swiss Football Association was founded.

1896 The Swedish Football Association was formed and the Swedish League commenced (first winners Oergryte).

MILESTONES

Celtic FC installed the first crush barriers for the Scotland v England international.

1897 Corinthians became the first British club to tour South America and the first to play outside Europe.

1898 The Player's Union was formed.

Queens Park became the first Scottish club to play abroad when they toured Denmark.

Grasshoppers win the first Swiss Championship.

The Italian Football Association was formed and Genoa win the first Italian Championship.

RAP win the first Dutch Championship.

The FA Charity Shield was first contested between Sheffield United FC and Corinthians.

1899 RAP win the first Dutch Cup competition.

1900 The Hungarian Football Association was formed and the Hungarian League commenced (first winners BTC).

The Maltese Football Association was formed.

The German Football Association was formed.

The Uruguayan League commenced and Penarol won the first championship.

1901 Tottenham Hotspur won the FA Cup whilst still in the Southern League.

1902 Terracing collapsed at Ibrox Park causing the first football disaster with 25 spectators dead and hundreds injured.

The Norwegian Football Association was formed and Grane Arendal won the first Norwegian Cup.

The Spanish Football Association was formed and Vizcaya Bilbao won the first Spanish Cup.

The Brazilian Sao Paulo League was formed and Sao Paulo AC won the first championship.

Middlesbrough erected the first half-time scoreboard.

1903 VfB Leipzig won the first German championship.

1904 FIFA was formed.

The Austrian Football Association was formed.

1905 The first international match in South America was played between Uruguay and Argentina.

1906 The Rio de Janeiro League was formed in Brazil (first champions Fluminese).

Guarani won the first Paraguayan League championship.

1907 The Professional Footballers Association (PFA) was formed.

The Finnish Football Association was formed and the Finnish League commenced (first champions Unitas Helsinki).

1908 The first official Olympic soccer tournament was played in London.

The Luxembourg Football Association formed.

The Rumanian Football Association was formed.

1910 Racing Luxembourg won the first Luxembourg League championship.

Floriana won the first Maltese League championship.

MTK won the first Hungarian Cup competition.

Olimpia Bucharest won the first Rumanian League championship.

1911 The Icelandic Football Association was formed and the Icelandic League commenced (first champions KR Reykjavik).

1912 The Rules were altered to prevent goalkeepers handling the ball outside their own penalty area.

The Russian Football Association was formed.

Rapid Vienna won the first Austrian League championship.

Sparta Prague won the first Czechoslovakian League championship.

RC Brussels won the first Belgian Cup competition.

1913 The United States of America's Football Association was formed.

KB Copenhagen won the first Danish Championship.

'10 yards' rule introduced for free kicks.

1914 '10 yards' rule extended to cover corners.

The Portuguese Football Association was formed.

'The Strongest' won the first Bolivian League championship.

1915 The Chilean Football Association formed.

1916 The South American Championship was first contested.

1918 The French Football Association was formed and Olympique de Pantin won the first French Cup competition.

1919 The Yugoslavian Football Association was formed.

Rapid Vienna won the first Austrian Cup competition.

1920 The Football League, Third Division was formed from Southern League clubs.

1921 The Football League, Third Division North, was formed.

MILESTONES

The Eire Football Association was formed and the League of Ireland commenced (first champions St James Gate).

The Polish Football Association was formed and the Polish League commenced (first champions Cracovia).

1922 Racing Luxembourg won the first Luxembourg Cup competition.

FC Porto won the first Portuguese Cup competition.

St James Gate won the first Eire Cup competition.

1923 The first Wembley FA Cup Final was played.

The Bulgarian Football Association was formed.

The Turkish Football Association was formed and the Turkish League commenced (first champions Harbuje).

Gradjanski Zagreb won the first Yugoslavian League championship.

Littlewoods distributed the first football pool coupons outside of Old Trafford, Manchester.

1924 The rules were changed to allow goals to be scored directly from corner kicks.

1925 The offside rule was changed to require only two defenders between an attacker and the goal.

Vladislav Varna won the first Bulgarian League championship.

1926 The Greek Football Association was formed.

CS Progreso won the first Peruvian League championship.

Artur Friedenreich became the first player to score 1000 goals in Brazilian football.

1927 The Mitropa Cup was first contested.

JC Clegg, the president of the FA, was knighted.

1928 The British associations withdrew from FIFA over broken-time payments to amateurs.

Aris Salonika won the first Greek League championship.

1929 Barcelona won the first Spanish League championship.

England lost an international against a foreign team for the first time when Spain beat them 4–3 in Madrid.

1930 The first World Cup competition was contested in Uruguay.

The Albanian Football Association was formed and the Albanian League commenced (SC Tirana became the first champions).

1931 Aberdeen FC constructed the first trainers' dugout at their ground.

1932 AEK Athens won the first Greek Cup competition.

1933 Magallanes won the first Chilean League championship.

The Liechtenstein Football Association was formed.

Lille OSC won the first French League championship.

1934 The Cypriot Football Association was formed and the Cyprus League commenced (the first champions were Trust).

Ripensia Timisoara won the first Rumanian Cup competition.

1935 Trust won the first Cyprus Cup competition.

IFC Nürnberg won the first German Cup competition.

Sliema Wanderers won the first Maltese Cup competition.

FC Porto won the first Portuguese League championship.

1936 Dynamo Moscow won the first Russian League championship.

Lokomotiv Moscow won the first Russian Cup competition.

Torino won the first Italian Cup competition.

The BBC first televised a football match—a film of an Arsenal v Everton game.

1938 Fredrikstad won the first Norwegian League championship.

The Ecuador Football Association was formed.

1941 IF Hälsingborg won the first Swedish Cup competition.

1946 The British associations rejoined FIFA.

Levski Sofia won the first Bulgarian Cup competition.

The Scottish League Cup was first contested.

1947 Partizan Belgrade won the first Yugoslavian Cup competition.

1948 Independiente Santa Fe won the first Colombian League championship.

SG Planitz won the first East German League championship.

Partizan Tirana won the first Albanian Cup competition.

Franz 'Bimbo' Binder became the first European to score 1000 goals whilst playing for Vienna Rapide, Austria and Germany.

1949 Torino were decimated when their plane crashed, killing everyone on board.

Rangers achieved the first 'Treble'.

MILESTONES

Stanley Matthews in understandably cheerful mood following news that he is to be knighted. (Syndication International)

Wag'nbaun-Dessau won the first East German Cup competition.

1951 Ruch Chorzow won the first Polish Cup competition.

1952 The Venezuelan Football Association was formed.

1954 UEFA was formed.

1955 The European Cup competition commenced.

Aarhus GF won the first Danish Cup competition.

Valkeakosken Haka won the first Finnish Cup competition.

The Inter-Cities Fairs Cup competition commenced.

1956 Lasalle won the first Venezuelan League championship.

The first floodlit Football League game took place.

1957 Emelec won the first League championship in Ecuador.

1958 The Munich air crash decimated the 'Busby Babes'.

1959 Billy Wright became the first Briton to win 100 caps.

1960 The first European Nations Cup Final was contested in Paris, France.

KR Reykjavik won the first Icelandic Cup competition.

The Football League Cup was first contested.

The World Club Championship was first contested.

The South American club championship was first contested.

1961 The first European Cup-Winners Cup Final was contested.

Dukla Prague won the first Czechoslovakian Cup competition.

1963 Galatasaray won the first Turkish Cup competition.

1965 Stanley Matthews became the first soccer player to be knighted.

The Football League first allowed substitutes in cases of injury.

ENGLAND 3 GERMANY W. 2

Hurst blasts a fourth goal and captain Bobby Moore celebrates with the trophy as England win the World Cup for the first and so far only time in 1966. (Syndication International)

MILESTONES

1966 England won the World Championship.

1967 The Argentinian National League commenced and Independiente won the first championship.

The Brazilian National League commenced and Palmeiras won the first championship.

In the USA both the United Soccer Association (first champions Los Angeles Wolves) and the National Professional Soccer League (first champions Oakland Clippers) commenced.

Celtic became the first British club to win the European Cup.

1968 In the USA, the North American Soccer League was formed, replacing the US Association and the NPSL, and the first champions were Atlanta Chiefs.

1970 Brazil won the Jules Rimet trophy outright.

In New Zealand, the National League was formed.

1971 The Super Cup competition commenced.

1975 The Football League began to use 'goal difference' in place of 'goal average'.

1977 The first World Youth Cup was played in Tunisia and was won by the USSR.

In Australia, the National League was formed (the first champions were Sydney City).

1978 Aberdeen made Pittodrie into the first all-seater stadium in Britain.

1983 Pat Jennings became the first British player to make over 1000 first-class appearances.

1985 The first Wembley final exclusively for Third and Fourth Division clubs (the Freight Rover Trophy) ended in victory for Wigan Athletic.

France beat Uruguay in the first Inter-continental Cup match.

1986 Mexico became the first country to host the World Cup Finals for a second time.

1987 Introduction of automatic promotion to the Fourth Division of the Football League (Scarborough became the first club to be promoted in this way).

Scarborough's promotion-winning team.
(Colorsport)

The Football League is the oldest competition of its kind and was the conception of William McGregor of Aston Villa FC who arranged a preliminary meeting at Anderton's Hotel in Fleet Street on 22 March 1888. A formal meeting followed on 17 April 1888 and the League came into existence with 12 member clubs: Accrington FC, Aston Villa FC, Blackburn Rovers FC, Bolton Wanderers FC, Burnley FC, Derby County FC, Everton FC, Notts County FC, Preston North End FC, Stoke FC, West Bromwich Albion FC and Wolverhampton Wanderers FC. A year later, the Football Alliance was formed, and in 1892 this was absorbed to become the Second Division of the Football League.

In 1920, in what amounted to a mass defection, the Southern League clubs were incorporated to form a Third Division of associate members and, a year later, 20 senior northern clubs came in to form the Third Division (North) (the previous Third Division being redesignated 'South'). Except for the addition of four more clubs in 1950, the only other change that the League has seen occurred in 1958 when the bottom 12 clubs in the old Third Divisions were formed into a deregionalized Fourth Division and the top 12 clubs into the Third Division.

The first player to score a goal in the Football League

On the opening day of the 1888/9 season five games were played and a total of 23 goals were scored. George Cox of Aston Villa FC achieved the 'distinction' of becoming the first player to score an own goal although his club managed to draw 1–1 with Wolverhampton Wanderers FC. The first goal was scored by Gordon of Preston North End.

The first player to score a hat-trick in the Football League

On the second Saturday of the first season (15 September 1888), Walter Tait of Burnley FC scored three of his club's four goals to notch up the first League hat-trick. Burnley won the game 4–3 against Bolton Wanderers FC.

The first Football League champions

Preston North End FC were in devastating form in the 1888/9 season and won both the League championship and the FA Cup without losing a single game.

Thus they achieved not only the first championship win, but also the first 'double' and did so with a league points tally of 40 out of 44, a percentage never again equalled.

The first club to score double figures in a Football League game

On 14 September 1889 Preston North End FC started the second season of the League in the same form as they finished the previous season. Their unfortunate opponents, Stoke FC, had finished the previous season at the bottom of the table and Preston's 10–0 victory set them on course for a similar final placing. J Ross scored five of the goals and went on to become Preston's top scorer with 24 League goals in the season.

The first club to retain the League championship

Although unable to achieve the same margin of success as they achieved in the 1888/9 season, Preston won the championship once again in 1889/90 with 33 points from 22 games and became the first club to retain the championship.

The first club to fail to be re-elected to the Football League

Stoke, who finished bottom for the second consecutive time in 1889/90, were not re-elected at that year's AGM although they were in fact elected again in 1891/2 along with Darwen. Sunderland, who replaced them, were the first team to be elected into the League and proved themselves to be worthy replacements. However, they were soon in hot water and became the first club to have points deducted as a result of disciplinary action when fielding an ineligible player in their 4–0 defeat of West Bromwich Albion on 20 September 1890.

The first player to score from a penalty in the Football League

The penalty kick was first introduced at the start of the 1891/2 season and Wolverhampton Wanderers' player John Heath scored the first penalty goal in his side's 5–0 victory over Accrington on 14 September 1891. This was also the first penalty to be awarded in the Football League.

The first clubs to play for a full season in the Football League without drawing a game

In Sunderland's second season in the League they comfortably won the championship with 42 points and shared with Aston Villa the distinction of not drawing a single League game. At the foot of the table, Darwen became the first club to concede a century of goals, letting in 112 in 26 games, then, thanks to the formation of the Second Division, became the first club to be relegated. They must have felt a little aggrieved that they were not kept in the First Division, which was increased in size to 16 clubs with the election of Nottingham Forest, The Wednesday (Sheffield Wednesday) and Newton Heath (Manchester United)!

The first away team to score double figures in the Football League

Sheffield United achieved the first double-figure away victory, against Burslem Port Vale (Port Vale) on 10 December 1892, with a 10–0 scoreline. Their top scorer, Hammond, got four of the goals but could count himself fortunate that the Port Vale keeper had lost his spectacles in the mud!

The first Football League Second Division champions

Small Heath (Birmingham City) won the first Second Division championship, but playing against Newton Heath (Manchester United) in the end-of-season test matches, could only manage to draw one game and were not, therefore, promoted to the First Division.

Ironically, Darwen who were the first club to be relegated, finished third in the Second Division but were promoted after winning their test match against Notts County (who were the first League club to be founded in 1862). Darwen thus became the first relegated club to be promoted the following season and, going down again the next year, went on to beome the first promoted club to be relegated!

The first British club to score a century of League goals in a season

Having won the 1891/2 championship convincingly, Sunderland registered an even more emphatic triumph in 1892/3 when they won by 11 clear points and became the first club to score 100 League goals in the process. Remarkably, they did not lose a home game in either season—still a record.

The first player to score a double hat-trick in the Football League

Southworth, Everton's and the League's top scorer in the 1893/4 season, scored six of his club's goals in their 7–1 victory over West Bromwich Albion on 30 December 1893, to record the first double hat-trick.

The first Football League club to play a complete season without taking a single away point

Northwich Victoria lost all 14 of their away fixtures during the 1893/4 season and failed to be re-elected when they finished bottom of the Second Division with only nine points. This was the first time that any club had failed to reach double figures!

The first club to win the Football League championship three times

Having won the championship in 1891/2 and 1892/3, Sunderland 'only' achieved the runners-up place in 1893/4 but in 1894/5 they came back for their third win in four years.

The first club to win the Second Division championship on goal average/difference

Both Liverpool and Manchester City finished the 1895/6 season on 46 points but Liverpool's superior goalscoring record (F106: A32), far excelled City's (F63: A38) and they were awarded the championship and went on to win promotion in the test matches.

The first club to score 1000 goals in the Football League

Aston Villa became the first club to reach this total in the 1903/4 season after only 450 League games.

The first club to win the Second Division championship and the League championship in consecutive seasons

At the end of the 1903/4 season, Liverpool were relegated from the First Division for the second time. The following season they powered back to win the Second Division championship (just as they had when they were first relegated) and, the following year, went on to become the first club to win the two championships in consecutive years.

The first meeting of London clubs in the Football League

The Football League was, with the exception of Woolwich Arsenal (Arsenal), comprised solely of northern and Midlands clubs until the 1905/6 season. That year, both Chelsea and Clapton Orient (Orient) joined and that season saw the first ever League meeting between two London clubs. The first meeting in the First Division took place on 2 November 1907 when Woolwich Arsenal (Arsenal) met Chelsea at Stamford Bridge.

The first foreign player to appear in the Football League

Max Seeburg, a German, whose first appearance in the Football League was for Tottenham Hotspur in the 1908/9 season, is reputed to have been the first overseas player.

The first goalkeeper to save three penalties in a game

Grimsby Town's Walter Scott saved three out of

four penalties awarded against his team at Burnley on 13 February 1909 and Burnley became the first side to miss three penalties in one game.

The first Football League club to have its ground bombed

In November 1916, a German Zeppelin dropped its bombs on Hartlepool United's ground causing structural damage. The club known by their former name of Hartlepools Utd were not then in the Football League.

The first occasion that father and son played together for the same club in first-class football

During the First World War, although the Football League was officially suspended, most clubs still participated in various competitions and in the 1916/7 'Midland Subsidiary tournament' J Butler and W Butler, father and son, both appeared in the same Grimsby Town team.

The first Football League club to be expelled

Leeds City (no connection with Leeds United) were wound up in October 1919 for 'irregular practices' and expelled from the League. Port Vale stepped into their place and fulfilled the remaining fixtures.

The first champions of the Football League Third Division

The Third Division was formed at the beginning of the 1920/1 season when practically the whole of the Southern League joined as 'Associate' members. Crystal Palace won the first championship and the next season the Third Division was regionalized into North and South.

The first Football League club to be relegated in consecutive seasons

Bradford Park Avenue were relegated to the Second Division at the end of the 1920/21 season and, the following year, finishing second from bottom, went on to become the first club to make the 'double drop'.

The first player to score ten penalties in a season in the Football League

Jimmy Evans of Southend United became the first player to achieve double figures in penalty goals in the 1921/2 season and Billy Walker of Aston Villa scored the first hat-trick of League penalties on 12 November 1921 against Bradford City.

The first club to win three consecutive League championships

Huddersfield Town dominated the mid-twenties and, after becoming the first club to win the championship on goal average in 1923/4, went on to win both the 1924/5 and 1925/6 championships by a clear margin. On 11 October 1924 their player, Billy Smith, scored a goal directly from a corner-kick—the first such goal in the Football League.

The first Football League match to be broadcast

The First Division encounter between Arsenal and Sheffield United at Highbury on 22 January 1927 was the first game to be broadcast over the radio. The match ended 1–1.

The first clubs to have numbered shirts for a Football League game

On 25 August 1928 both Arsenal and Chelsea decided to number their shirts for their games with Sheffield Wednesday and Swansea Town respectively.

The first player-manager to appear for a First Division Football League club

Andy Cunningham who managed Newcastle United during the 1929/30 season became the first player-manager of a First Division club.

The first 6–6 draw in the Football League

Leicester City and Arsenal, two sides not noted for conceding goals, played the first 6–6 draw at Filbert Street on 21 April 1930.

The first Football League fixture to be played at Wembley

Two London clubs, Clapton Orient (Orient) and Brentford met at Wembley on 22 November 1930 in a Third Division (South) fixture. Clapton Orient won 3–0 and it was perhaps fortunate for them that the fixture was not Brentford's home tie as Brentford, that year, became the first Third Division club to win all (ie 21) of its home matches.

The first London club to win the Football League championship

Such was the domination of the northern and Midlands clubs that it was not until 1930/1 that Arsenal became the first London club to achieve this feat, although winning a further three out of the next four titles no doubt redressed the balance a little! Their mastermind, manager Herbert Chapman who had already achieved great success with Huddersfield Town, became the first person to manage two different championship-winning teams.

The first Football League match to be completed without a corner being awarded

On 5 December 1931 Newcastle United met

THE FOOTBALL LEAGUE

Soccer genius Herbert Chapman pictured during his all-conquering Arsenal days. (D C Thomson Ltd)

The first player to score a triple hat-trick in a Football League game

Robert (Bunny) Bell of Tranmere Rovers scored nine goals against Oldham in Division Three (North) on 26 December 1935. His club won the game 13–4 and he even missed a penalty!

The first club to gain promotion from the Third to the First Division in successive seasons

Proving that movement upwards is more difficult than downwards, it was 16 seasons before a club (Charlton Athletic) managed to achieve the first 'double promotion' although Bradford Park Avenue had achieved the 'double drop' in only two seasons! Charlton won the Division Three (South) championship in 1934/5 and were runners-up in the Second Division in 1935/6.

Eddie Hapgood, the Arsenal player, credited by some contemporary reporters with scoring a penalty with a header! (Pattrieoux)

Portsmouth in what must have been a boring match! Records show that no corners were awarded and no goals were scored by either side.

The first Football League club to resign in mid-season

Wigan Borough (no connection with Wigan Athletic) resigned from the League on 26 October 1931 and their fixtures were expunged from the final table.

The first player to be flown to a Football League match

Vivian Gibbons, a schoolteacher working in London, was refused time off to play for his club, Bristol Rovers, on 7 September 1932 and a member of the Rovers board decided to find a way around the refusal. The solution was to fly him from Romford to Filton after school and he duly arrived in time for the 6.15 pm kick-off against Southend United.

The first player to head a goal after a penalty kick

Contemporary reporting declared Arsenal's Eddie Hapgood to have scored a penalty with his head during his club's game with Liverpool on 5 January 1935! This was of course not so, as the penalty kick was in fact saved by the Liverpool keeper and Hapgood headed in the clearance.

THE FOOTBALL LEAGUE

The first player to score ten goals in a Football League game

Joe Payne of Luton Town, playing his first game at centre-forward, scored ten of his club's goals in their Third Division (South) 12–0 defeat of Bristol Rovers on 13 April 1936. No other player has ever scored more than nine goals in a Football League match.

The first club to win the League title and then to be relegated the following season

Manchester City who won the 1936/7 League

Joe Payne—the first and only player to score ten goals in a Football League game. (Colorsport)

championship with 57 points finished the next season second from bottom and were relegated to the Second Division.

The first club to win the Football League championship having been promoted from the Third Division.

When Portsmouth won the League title in 1948/9, it would have been difficult to describe them as being anything but a First Division club, having spent the previous 14 seasons in that division. However, a former member of the Southern League, they did not join the Football League until 1920 and, progressing from the Third Division, they were the first of the 'new boys' to win the championship. Ironically, they went on to become the first champions to fall back into the Third Division in 1961.

Ray Straw—the first player to play in all six divisions of the Football League (including Third Division North and Third Division South). (Colorsport)

The first person to play for and later manage Football League championship-winning sides

Arsenal's Ted Drake played in the title-winning sides of 1933/4, 1934/5 and 1935/6 and went on to manage Chelsea's 1954/5 championship team.

The first club in the Football League to field a full side of Scottish players

Although Sunderland's extremely successful team of the 1890s was largely comprised of Scots, it fell to Accrington Stanley to field the first 'all-Scots' side in the Third Division (North) in 1955.

The first ex-professional Football League player to become a Football League referee

Although a number of football's early stalwarts, including Lord Kinnaird and J C Clegg, went on to referee at the highest levels when their playing careers were over, it was not until 1955 that the first ex-professional Football League player did so. Jack Swain, who made First Division appearances for Grimsby Town between 1937 and 1939, achieved this distinction when he was put on to the Football League list for the 1955/6 season.

The first floodlit Football League match

This took place at Fratton Park, Portsmouth on 22 February 1956 when Portsmouth lost 2–0 to Newcastle United.

The first British club to score and concede 100 League goals during a season

In 1957/8 Manchester City achieved the dubious distinction of becoming the first club to mark up this 'double century' with 104 goals for and 100 against. No other club has 'achieved' this feat.

The first winners of the Football League Fourth Division

With the deregionalization of the Third Divisions of the Football League in 1958/9, a new four-up four-down promotion/relegation system was

THE FOOTBALL LEAGUE

adopted between the Third and Fourth Divisions. Port Vale won the first Fourth Division championship with 64 points.

The first Football League match to be televised live

The first game televised live on Friday 9 September 1960 between Blackpool and Bolton was intended to be the forerunner of a regular Friday night televised soccer programme. Bolton won the game 1–0 but the match itself was a dreary affair and the plan for further games was dropped.

The first person to play in all six divisions of the Football League

Playing for Derby County and Coventry City, Ray Straw became the first player to appear in all six divisions in 1960.

The first club to win the Fourth Division championship in the season that it was elected

Peterborough, elected to the League in 1960/1 in place of Gateshead took the Fourth Division by storm. Terry Bly hammered in 52 goals to set the division's individual goalscoring record and their overall goal tally (134) still stands as a record for a Football League club. Their championship win crowned a remarkable year for the club in their first League season.

Charlton Athletic's Keith Peacock in 1967. (Photosource)

The first person to play for and later manage the same club to the Football League championship

Bill Nicholson who was a member of the championship-winning Spurs team of 1950/1, went on to manage the club exactly ten years later when they next won the championship.

The first promoted club to win the Football League championship in its first season in the First Division

Ipswich Town, having won the Second Division title in 1960/1, went on to win the First Division championship in 1961/2, their first season in the top division.

The first club to rise from the Fourth Division to the First Division of the Football League

In 1960/1 Northampton Town began their meteoric rise from the Fourth Division which, by 1965/6, took them right up to the First Division. Unfortunately for them, within four seasons they were back in the Fourth Division once again—another first.

The first substitute to appear in the Football League

Substitutes were first allowed for Football League matches at the commencement of the 1965/6 season and it fell to Keith Peacock of Charlton Athletic to become the first actually to play. His substitution was made on 21 August 1965 during his club's Second Division game against Bolton Wanderers. On the same day in a Fourth Division match between Barrow and Wrexham, Bobby Knox became the first substitute to score a goal when he helped his club to achieve a 4–2 victory.

The first match to be shown 'live' on closed-circuit television

The Second Division game between Cardiff City and Coventry City which was played on 7 October 1965 at Ninian Park was the first to be shown live on closed-circuit television. It was actually beamed onto four large screens at Coventry's Highfield Road Stadium.

The first League match in Britain to be televised in colour

The First Division game at Anfield between Liverpool and West Ham United on 15 November 1969 was the first fixture to be televised in colour. However, since colour receiver sets were few and far between at that time, the bulk of the audience saw it in glorious black and white!

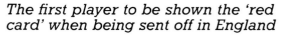

THE FOOTBALL LEAGUE

The first player to appear before a disciplinary tribunal in England

Liverpool's Larry Lloyd became the first player to appear before a disciplinary tribunal on 9 November 1982.

The first Football League match to be played on a Sunday

On Sunday 20 January 1974, Millwall met Fulham at The Den in the first Sunday League match and Millwall's Brian Clark scored the first Sunday League goal, the only goal of the match. The following weekend Darlington became the first club to play two League fixtures over a weekend when, having met Stockport County on the Saturday, they played Torquay United on the Sunday.

(Below) Liverpool's stalwart defender Larry Lloyd pictured during his heyday with the Merseyside club. (ASP)

(Below right) Malcolm MacDonald during his playing days with Newcastle United. (ASP)

The first player to be shown the 'red card' when being sent off in England

David Wagstaffe of Blackburn Rovers, who was sent off during his club's Second Division away game against Orient on 2 October 1976, was the first player to be shown the red card to signify that he was being sent off.

The first paid director of a Football League club

Malcolm MacDonald, the former England striker, became the first paid director when he was appointed to the Fulham board in November 1981.

The first club outside the United States to play their domestic League fixtures on artificial turf

Queens Park Rangers' ground, 'The Rangers Stadium' in South Africa Road, had an 'astroturf' playing surface laid before the commencement of the 1981/2 season and, after a trial period, this proved so successful, that other clubs are now following the Rangers lead.

(Above) David Wagstaffe made his name with Wolves, but his most dubious achievement came while at Blackburn Rovers. (ASP)

The first promoted club (other than the reigning Second Division champions) to win the Football League championship in its first season back in the First Division

Nottingham Forest, who were promoted to the First Division at the end of the 1976/7 season, having finished in third place in the Second Division, went on to win the Football League championship in 1977/8, their first season back in the higher sphere. In that season they also won the Football League Cup and, in doing so, became the first winners of the League/League Cup 'double'.

The first Football League club to be relegated in three consecutive seasons

Bristol City slipped from the First Division to the Fourth Division in successive seasons between 1979 and 1982 winning only 27 of their 130 games in the process.

The first Football League club to play a match in a prison

An obscure first was recorded on 18 February 1982 when Bristol Rovers defeated a team comprised of prisoners at Erlestoke Prison in Wiltshire. The score was 11–0.

The first player to be on the books of three Football League clubs in one day

Mick Harford was signed by Bristol City from Newcastle United in August 1981 but the £160 000 fee was not fully paid due to City's near bankruptcy. In March 1982, because of their financial difficulties, his transfer to Birmingham was arranged, but because of the amount outstanding to his original club, he had to re-sign

THE FOOTBALL LEAGUE

Jim Smith receives his 92 Club trophy from Olie Pardo, the club's publicity officer. (Steve Ellis)

for them before being immediately transferred to Birmingham.

The first player to be sent off for a 'Professional Foul' in the Football League

A clampdown on deliberate fouls which would previously have merited no more than a free kick and a warning began at the start of the 1982/3 season. Many players and spectators considered such a clampdown to be both unfair and undesirable but such views were of no consequence to Leicester City's Eddie Kelly who was the first to be given his marching orders for a deliberate hand-ball (against Rotherham United on 31 August 1982).

The first player to appear in over 1000 first class matches in England

Pat Jennings, the Northern Ireland goalkeeper, achieved this feat on 26 February 1983 whilst playing for Arsenal against West Bromwich Albion at the Hawthorns. Whilst the bulk of the games that he played were Football League games, the tally included cup games and international appearances also.

The first Sunday League fixture to be televised live

When Tottenham Hotspur (which had become

the first club to go 'public' with a Stock Exchange flotation on 13 October 1983) met Nottingham Forest at White Hart Lane on 2 October 1983, the game became the first Sunday League fixture to be televised. Spurs won the game 2–1.

The first player to score a century of goals for a Scottish League club and a Football League club

Having already notched up a hundred goals for Celtic, Kenny Dalglish transferred to Liverpool and completed his century of goals for them too on 26 November 1983 against Ipswich Town at Portman Road.

The first club to accumulate 100 League points during a season in the Football League

With the introduction of three points for a win at the start of the 1981/2 season, the maximum number of points which could be scored in the Third and Fourth Divisions increased from 92 to 138. In the 1983/4 season, York City topped the Fourth Division, winning the championship by 16 clear points with a points aggregate of 101— the first three-figure points total.

The first British club to install a video screen at their ground

Following in the footsteps of NASL clubs, Arsenal became the first British club to install a video screen at their ground late in 1984. The screen was

THE FOOTBALL LEAGUE

first used on 20 October 1984 for their fixture against Sunderland.

The first club to win the Third and Second Division championships in consecutive seasons

Under the guiding eye of manager Jim Smith, Oxford United were determined not to miss promotion for a third time after finishing fifth in 1981/2 and 1982/3, and in 1983/4 they made no mistake in winning the Third Division championship by eight clear points. The following season, they went on to dumbfound critics by winning the Second Division championship in an equally convincing manner to become the first club to record this 'double-championship' win.

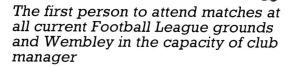

The first person to attend matches at all current Football League grounds and Wembley in the capacity of club manager

Jim Smith, who became a manager on 26 October 1972, when he took over at Colchester United, subsequently managed Blackburn Rovers, Birmingham City, Oxford United, QPR and Newcastle United and travelled to every single Football League ground for first-team fixtures between 1972 and 1986.

On 8 April 1986 at Sheffield Wednesday's Hillsborough ground, he was enrolled as a member of 'The 92 club' for this achievement.

The first player-manager of a Football League championship-winning side

Kenny Dalglish took over as the player-manager of Liverpool in 1985/6, and pulled off a remarkable feat by becoming, not only the first player-manager to win the Football League championship but also the first player-manager to achieve the 'double'. Unlike many player-managers, his appearances as a player were frequent and, indeed, he scored Liverpool's winning goal at Chelsea on the final day of the season!

The first club to be automatically relegated from the Football League

Lincoln City, who only dropped to the bottom place in the Fourth Division of the Football League on the final day of the 1986/7 season, were the first team to be automatically relegated to the GM Vauxhall Conference.

The following season, under manager Colin Murphy, they stormed back to win the title and became the first relegated club to regain their Football League status at the first time of asking.

(Top) Kenny Dalglish became the first Scot to win 100 caps. (ASP)
(Above) Colin Murphy, Lincoln City's manager, in his moment of triumph.

The first club to be automatically promoted to the Fourth Division of the Football League

Although the Alliance Premier League was formed in 1979/80 when non-league football in England and Wales was restructured into a 'pyramid' with graded 'feeder' leagues, it was not until the 1987/8 season that automatic promotion to the Football League was introduced. In the intervening period the champions of the Alliance Premier League (which subsequently became known first as 'The Gola League' and then 'The GM Vauxhall Conference') were nominated for membership each season, but none were actually admitted.

Scarborough, having narrowly missed relegation in 1985/6, powered through to take the 1986/7 GM Vauxhall Conference title and, in the process, became the first club to be automatically promoted to the Football League.

The Scottish Football League was founded in the 1890/1 season and, over its lifetime, has seen an incredible number of changes to its make-up. It began with one division of ten clubs, increased to twelve next season, then went back to ten clubs for one season until the Second Division was formed in 1893/4. During the First World War, the Second Division was suspended and was not reformed until 1921/2 although, in the meantime, numbers had altered both up and down. A Third Division was formed in 1923 but this was dropped in 1926. After more changes and suspension for the duration of the Second World War, the clubs were split into 'A' and 'B' Divisions and a 'C' Division was added from 1946–55. In 1956/7, the divisions were redesignated First and Second and, in 1975/6, the present Premier Division of ten clubs with First and Second Divisions of 14 clubs were adopted. As with the Scottish FA Cup, Rangers and Celtic have monopolized the competition for most of its lifetime.

The first person to score a goal in the Scottish League

Renton's Cameron scored the first Scottish League goal in the very first minute of his club's first League game against Celtic. Renton won the game, which was played on 16 August 1890, 4–1, and although their record was subsequently deleted from the final League table (see later item) Cameron's goal must stand as the first one scored.

The first person to score a hat-trick in the Scottish League

A week later, on 23 August 1890, Rangers' J MacPherson scored the first recorded hat-trick in the league against Cambuslang. Rangers won the game 6–2.

The first Scottish League club to be suspended

Renton FC (winners of the Scottish FA Cup in 1887/8) were one of the original members of the Scottish League but, after playing five games, were suspended by the Scottish FA for 'professionalism' in September 1890 and their record was deleted from the League table.

The first Scottish League champions

After both finished with 29 points from 18 games, Dumbarton FC and Rangers FC played-off for the first championship. As the play-off ended in a 2–2 draw, it was decided to declare both teams joint champions. Dumbarton just failed to pull off the first double going down 1–0 to Hearts in the Scottish Cup Final.

The first club to fail to be re-elected to the Scottish League

Cowlairs, who finished the first season with only six points from 18 games (four points had been deducted for fielding an ineligible player) became the first club to fail to be re-elected to the Scottish League.

The first player to score a penalty in the Scottish League

Renton FC were re-admitted to the League in 1891/2 and it fell to one of their players, Alex McColl, to score the first penalty which he did on 22 August 1891 in his side's 3–2 away victory over Leith Athletic.

The first double-figure victory in the Scottish League

On 15 August 1891 Clyde beat Vale of Leven 10–3 to achieve the first double-figure victory in the Scottish League.

The first club to concede 100 goals during a season in the Scottish League

Vale of Leven played 22 games in the 1891/2 season without winning any (they drew five), and conceded exactly 100 goals, an average of over four each game! Although other clubs have conceded over 100 goals since, this abysmal average has yet to be matched.

The first club to retain the Scottish League championship

Dumbarton, joint champions in the first year of the League, went on to win the 1891/2 championship by two clear points to retain the title and to become the first outright winners.

The first club to win the Scottish Second Division championship

Hibernian, who won the first Second Division championship with 29 points from 18 games, could rightly feel aggrieved that third-placed Clyde (who obtained only 24 points) were elected to the First Division instead of them. However, the following season (1894/5) they won the Second Division championship once again and were promoted themselves.

The first British club to be awarded the points without actually playing

Dundee Wanderers became the first club to be awarded both points when Renton failed to turn up for their Scottish League Second Division return game in the 1894/5 season.

THE SCOTTISH LEAGUE

The first club to go through a season in the Scottish League without drawing

Second Division club Partick failed to register a single draw from 18 games in their first season in the league (1893/4) and the following season, Clyde, a First Division club achieved the same feat.

The first club to win the Scottish League championship without dropping a point

In 1898/9 Rangers won all 18 of their League matches to become the first and only British club to win all of its league fixtures in a season. They lost 1–0 to Celtic in the Scottish FA Cup final and like Dumbarton in 1890/1 just missed the double.

The first player to score a hat-trick of penalties in a league match in Britain

St Mirren's David Lindsay became the first player to notch up a hat-trick of penalties and in doing so helped his club to beat Rangers 5–4 on 9 January 1904. A further penalty was scored in this Scottish League match which was the first ever game in which four penalties were scored.

The first Scottish club to achieve the 'double'.

It was not until the 1906/7 season that the first Scottish 'double' was achieved, although three clubs had come close previously. Ironically, it was one of these, Celtic, which notched up the first double by hammering Hearts 3–0 in the Cup final and winning the championship by seven clear points.

The first Scottish club to score 100 League goals in a season

No doubt assisted by an increase in 1906/7 in the number of fixtures played (up to 34), in 1907/8 Falkirk broke the 'one hundred barrier' with 102 goals. Despite this achievement, they only finished runners-up to Celtic who scored 86 goals.

The first British club to have all their first-team squad score in a season

This somewhat bizarre 'first' was chalked up by the Scottish First Division club Greenock Morton in the 1912/3 season. In these days of 'sweepers' and 'utility' players it becomes difficult to think in terms of fixed positions but it is not so long ago that a player was likely to retain one position throughout his career. There were, however, exceptions, and James Gordon of Rangers played in every position from goalkeeper to outside-left between 1910 and 1930—the first player to do so!

The first player to score a goal directly from a corner kick

Although corner-kicks were first introduced in

James Gordon, Rangers' most versatile player.
(Colorsport)

1872, it was not until the 1924/5 season that players could score directly from them. St Bernards' Billy Alston scored the first goal direct from a corner on 21 August 1924 against Albion Rovers (in the Scottish Second Division).

The first player to score over 60 goals during a season in British league football

The 1927/8 season provided an absolute feast of goals both north and south of the border. O McNally of Arthurlie scored eight against Armadale in a Scottish Second Division match on 1 October 1927 and both the English and Scottish League goalscoring records were broken later in the season. No fewer than seven English clubs and two Scottish clubs scored over one hundred goals.

Ayr United's Jimmy Smith scored 66 goals (still 13 goals more than anyone else has achieved) and reached 60 on 9 April 1928. A month later Dixie Dean of Everton scored his 60th goal on the last day of the season.

(Right) Bury once turned down Jimmy McGrory (after a trial), but he went on to become the most consistent goalscorer that British football has seen. (J Sinclair Ltd)

(Below) Paul Sturrock whose five-goal spree for Dundee United earned him a place amongst the Scottish League's Premier Division firstmakers. (ASP)

The first footballer to average more than a goal per game over a complete career in British first-class football

Jimmy McGrory of Clydebank and Celtic, twice the top Scottish League scorer with 49 in 1926/7 and 50 in 1935/6, scored a total of 410 goals in just 408 matches between 1922 and 1938 to achieve this exceptional feat.

The first six-figure league attendance in Europe

The New Year 'Old Firm' game between Rangers and Celtic at Ibrox (on 2 January 1939) was watched by an unbelievable 118 567 spectators. A very much on-form Rangers won the game 2–1 and went on to win the championship by 11 clear points from runners-up Celtic.

The first away club to score double figures in the Scottish League

It was not until 8 March 1947 that the first double-figure away victory was achieved in the Second Division of the Scottish League. Dundee defeated Alloa Athletic at their Recreation Ground home by a margin of 10–0 and went on to win the championship, scoring 113 goals in only 26 games.

The first Scottish club to win the 'Treble'

Although it took 16 seasons for the first Scottish 'double' to be achieved, Rangers notched up the first treble in only the third year after it became a possibility (ie after the commencement of the Scottish League Cup). In 1948/9, they beat Clyde 4–1 in the Scottish FA Cup, Raith Rovers 2–0 in the Scottish League Cup and then won the championship by one point from Dundee.

The first Scottish League match to be televised

The first Scottish League game to be televised was the First Division fixture at Shawfield Stadium on 3 September 1955. Clyde's visitors that day were Aberdeen FC.

The first floodlit Scottish League fixture

The first unofficial floodlit League match was played at Rangers' Ibrox Stadium in 1952, but this game, against St Mirren, was only partly played under floodlights without the permission of the Scottish Football League. The first official floodlit League match was again at Ibrox on 7 March 1956 when Rangers defeated Queen of the South FC 8–0.

The first substitute to appear in a Scottish League match

Queens Park's P Conn became the first substitute to be used in the Scottish League when he came on against Albion Rovers in a Second Division fixture on 24 September 1966. Way back on 20 January 1917 a Partick Thistle player, Morgan, is believed to have replaced Morrison in a League game against Rangers but, since there was at that time no such thing as a 'substitute', it would be incorrect to classify him as the first 'substitute'.

The first player to score a goal on a Sunday in the Scottish League

It was not until 1974 that the first Sunday League matches were played and Dundee's Duncan Lambie scored the first 'Sunday' goal in his side's 4–1 victory over Partick Thistle on 3 February 1984.

The first 'elite' premier league in Britain

The Scottish League's decision to restructure their members to form a 'Premier' division in 1975/6 could well be described as the formation of the first 'elite' British league. A whole host of 'firsts' thus resulted: The first player to score a goal was Bobby Ford of Dundee who put his club ahead in the second minute of the game against Aberdeen and on 11 August 1975, Rangers' Sandy Jardine became the first player to score both a penalty and a hat-trick in his club's 6–1 defeat of Airdrie. Alex MacDonald of Rangers became the first player to be sent off in the 'Old Firm' game against Celtic on 30 August 1975 and Rangers went on to become the first champions of the Premier Division, winning by six clear points from Celtic.

Other less significant firsts followed, Alex Macdonald again figuring in one when he became the first player-manager in the Premier Division, first appearing for Hearts against St Johnstone on 20 August 1983. Celtic's Frank McGarvey became the first player to score a century of Premier Division goals on 24 November 1984 and a week earlier Dundee United's Paul Sturrock had become the first player to score five goals in a single game. Morton, the team against which Sturrock had scored his five goals, went on to become the first team to concede a century of goals in a season in the Premier Division.

Clydebank became the first club to be promoted in consecutive seasons in 1975/6 and 1976/7 and Kilmarnock became the first club to be relegated the season after being promoted to the Premier Division.

The first Scottish club to install undersoil heating

Hibernian, who were the first Scottish club to wear a sponsor's name on their shirts (in the late 70s), installed undersoil heating at their Easter Road ground in June 1980. Their inventive flair undiminished, they went on to become the first Scottish League club to install an electric scoreboard on 24 September 1983.

Their neighbours, Hearts, became the first Scottish club to install video cameras at their ground on 27 October 1984 and they were first used for the game against Hibernian!

The first Scottish club to be relegated in consecutive seasons

St Johnstone, who were promoted to the Premier Division at the beginning of the 1983/4 season, finished second from bottom and were demoted that year back to the First Division. Finishing in the relegation zone again, they became the first club to 'achieve' the double relegation at the end of the 1984/5 season.

The first to end all firsts

Colin Harris, making his League debut for Dundee against Rangers at Dens Park on 25 February 1984, scored his first goal with his first touch in the first minute that he was on the field during his first game!

4 THE FA CUP

The Football Association Challenge Cup (to give it its full title) was first suggested by the FA secretary at a meeting held on 20 July 1871 and was embodied in a later meeting on 16 October 1871 with 12 clubs agreeing to enter the competition. These were Barnes, Chequers, Civil Service, Clapham Rovers, Crystal Palace (not the current club), Hampstead Heathens, Harrow School, Lausanne, Royal Engineers, Upton Park (not the current West Ham Utd club), Wanderers and Windsor Home Park. Before the draw for the first round was made, Lausanne, Harrow School and Windsor Home Park withdrew, but six other clubs, Great Marlow, Hitchin, Maidenhead, Reigate Priory, Donington School and Queens Park, all agreed to enter. The competition was organized from the outset on a straight knock-out basis with a single-legged final match and is the oldest of all cup competitions.

The first FA Cup goal

In the first-ever round of the FA Cup competition on 11 November 1871 four games were actually played. In addition, Reigate Priory and Chequers both scratched to give walkovers to Royal Engineers and Wanderers respectively. Hampstead Heathens were given a bye and Donington School and Queens Park, Glasgow were both allowed through to the second round because they were unable to agree a date for the tie.

Clapham Rover's Kenrick scored the first ever FA Cup goal against Upton Park in a game which his team won 3–0. Crystal Palace and Hitchin drew 0–0 and became the first teams to progress in the FA Cup after only drawing (they both went through to the second round).

The first FA Cup semi final

Both 1871/2 semi finals were played at Kennington Oval and the first of these, between Royal Engineers and Crystal Palace, was played on 17 February 1872 and ended in a 0–0 draw. The other semi final between Wanderers and Glasgow's Queens Park also ended with a similar scoreline on 5 March 1872. The Royal Engineers' player, H Renny-Tailyour, scored the first ever semi-final goal in his side's replay against Crystal Palace on 9 March 1872 and went on to score another in 3–0 victory. Queens Park could not afford to travel for their semi-final replay and Wanderers were given a walkover.

The first FA Cup Final

Playing at Kennington Oval on 16 March 1872, Wanderers faced Royal Engineers before a crowd of 2000. Lieutenant Cresswell of the Royal Engineers became the first player to retire injured from an FA Cup Final when he fractured his collar-

The victorious Spurs team with manager McWilliam, leaving Stamford Bridge after the 1920/21 FA Cup Final. (Photosource)

THE FA CUP

bone in a collision. This injury left his side disadvantaged against the strong Wanderers team. Matthew P Betts scored the first FA Cup Final goal to give Wanderers the first FA Cup win. The trophy, made by Martin Hall and Co for £20 was presented to the Wanderers on 11 April 1872 at the Pall Mall Restaurant.

The first FA Cup disciplinary action

The 1872/3 second-round tie between South Norwood and Windsor Home Park developed into something of a fiasco and both teams walked off the pitch. A replay was consequently ordered and South Norwood won this 1–0.

THE FA CUP

The first club to appear in two consecutive finals

Wanderers again reached the 1872/3 final on 29 March 1873, this time against Oxford University. It would have been difficult to imagine a worse day for a final from the Oxford University point of view, as this was the date fixed for the Oxford/Cambridge boat race. However, soccer was then a game for gentlemen and the final was played at the Lillie Bridge Amateur Athletic Ground in the morning so that both teams could watch the boat race! In the final, Kinnaird and Wollaston scored for Wanderers to give them their second FA Cup win. It was obviously not a good day for Oxford as Cambridge then won the boat race!

The first FA Cup tie to be decided on the toss of a coin.

In the first round of the 1873/4 competition, Sheffield played out two 0–0 draws against Shropshire Wanderers and then tossed a coin to decide which of the teams progressed to the next round. Sheffield won and went on to beat Pilgrims in the next round. Drawn against Clapham Rovers in the third round, the Sheffield and Clapham teams seem to have struck a happy compromise on travelling when they played the game at Peterborough—midway between Sheffield and Clapham.

The first beaten finalists to win the FA Cup the following year

Oxford University again reached the final in 1873/4, this time against the Royal Engineers, in a game played at Kennington Oval before a 2000 crowd. An unusual first which has rarely been repeated, occurred when Oxford University fielded William Rowson and the Royal Engineers fielded Herbert Rowson, his brother! Oxford reversed their fortunes in the final and, in winning 2–0, became the first losing finalists to win the cup the next year.

The first recorded hat-trick in the FA Cup competition

Whilst it is possible that a hat-trick may have been scored in a Royal Engineers 7–0 win in 1873, no details of the goalscorers have survived and the first recorded hat-tricks were all scored on 31 October 1874 in the first round of the 1874/5 competition. Oxford University's Parry scored three in their 6–0 victory over Brondesbury and, on the same day, two other hat-tricks were scored for Wanderers. Playing against Farningham, Wanderers registered the first double-figure FA Cup competition win with a 16–0 victory. Kingsford scored five, Wollaston scored four and three other players scored two goals.

The first FA Cup Final to be replayed

The 1874/5 final between Royal Engineeers and Old Etonians was drawn 1–1 and became the first final in which extra-time was played to try to obtain a result. Still ending 1–1, a replay was arranged for three days later and Royal Engineers won this 2–0.

The first club to win the FA Cup three times

Playing Old Etonians in the 1875/6 final, Wanderers could only draw the first final game 1–1 but in the replay a week later, they fielded the same team against a slightly weaker Old Etonian side. Wollaston scored their first goal to become the first player to score in two finals and Hughes added two more to become the first player to score more than one goal in a final. This win actually resulted in Wanderers winning the Cup outright, but they gave it back to the FA for future competitions.

The first player to score an own goal in an FA Cup Final

Lord Kinnaird who played in more FA Cup Finals than any other player (9 finals, 5 Winner's medals) is, in some reports, classed as the first player to score an own goal in a final because a Waddington shot struck him and went into the Wanderers' goal in their 1876/7 final against Oxford University. Other reports award the goal directly to Waddington, but in the sort of 'rush' attack which was prevalent at that time, there is little wonder that newspaper correspondents sometimes differed.

Lord Kinnaird achieved another unusual feat by becoming the first player to gain FA Cup winner's medals with different clubs playing for the 1876/7 and 1877/8 Wanderers teams and then for the 1878/9 Old Etonian team. In fact he seemed at one time to change about between Wanderers and Old Etonians depending on which team reached the final!

The first player to gain five FA Cup winner's medals

CHR Wollaston was the only player to appear in all five of the Wanderers Cup-winning teams which carried off the 1871/2, 1872/3, 1875/6, 1876/7 and 1877/8 trophies and consequently the first player to be awarded five winner's medals. Wanderers themselves achieved the distinction of becoming the first club both to appear in three consecutive FA Cup Finals and (with a 3–1 win over Royal Engineers in 1877/8) also the first club to win three consecutive FA Cup Finals.

The first FA Cup Final game involving a future Football League club

Blackburn Rovers' appearance in the 1881/2 FA Cup Final against Old Etonians marked the turning point away from its domination by the Public Schools and London 'club' teams. Although Old

THE FA CUP

Etonians won the game 1–0, the tie heralded the arrival of the teams which we know today and, indeed, Old Etonians' appearance in the 1882/3 final was the last one by that type of club.

The first club to 'train' before an FA Cup Final

As mentioned previously, the 1882/3 final provided the real change from the previous 'Old School' regime and the Northern club, Blackburn Olympic actually trained specifically for the final match. Quite how energetic this training was is not known but since Blackburn Olympic came back from being a goal behind at half-time to win 2–1, it cannot have done them any harm!

The first Scottish club to appear in an FA Cup Final

Although they had dabbled in the early FA Cup competitions, Queens Park did not launch a serious assault until the 1883/4 season. Then without doubt the best club in the world, they despatched Crewe Alexandra 10–0 in the first round, Manchester 15–0 in the second round, Oswestry 7–1 in the third round, Aston Villa 6–1 in the fourth round, Old Westminsters 1–0 in the quarter final and the holders, Blackburn Olympic 4–1 in the semi final. In the final, Queens Park failed to appeal to the referee against an 'offside' goal scored against them (referees at that time were merely available to adjudicate when a dispute arose) and consequently went down undeservedly, 2–1. Blackburn Rovers thus became the first future Football League club to win the FA Cup.

The first club to score an FA Cup goal before their opponents took the field

In the 1884/5 competition, the Welsh club Druids arrived to play a fourth-round tie against West Bromwich Albion with only ten men and refused to kick off. West Bromwich kicked off and, not surprisingly, scored within seconds. At this the Druids took the field and played out the rest of the match. The score is given variously as 2–0 (including the goal) or 1–0 (excluding the goal).

The first 'repeat' FA Cup Final

The 1885/6 final was again between the Scottish giants Queens Park and Blackburn Rovers and, unfortunately for Queens Park, once again ended in a win for Blackburn Rovers (2–1). This game was, additionally, the first FA Cup Final to attract a five-figure crowd with 12 500 packing into Kennington Oval.

The first player to score in three consecutive FA Cup Finals

The Blackburn Rovers player Jimmy Brown scored their first goal in the 1885/6 FA Cup Final replay, to become the first player to score in three consecutive finals. This replay, after a 0–0 draw at Kennington Oval, was the first FA Cup Final to be played outside of London, being staged at the Racecourse Ground, Derby. Considering the geographical location of the two participating clubs this was a fair compromise and the 12 000 attendance well justified the choice. This final, also the first between two future Football League clubs, is widely regarded at the first 'all-professional' FA Cup Final.

The first FA Cup tie to be abandoned

In the 1887/8 competition, the fifth-round tie at Perry Barr between Aston Villa, the holders, and Preston North End was abandoned in the second half when the crowd invaded the pitch. Preston North End were leading 3–1 at the time of the invasion and it was decided later that the result would stand. Preston reached the final but lost the game 2–1 to another Midland club, West Bromwich Albion, who claimed to be the first 'all-English' team to win the FA Cup.

The first club to achieve the 'Double'

The Football League came into existence in the 1888/9 season and the magnificent Preston North End team walked away with the first Football League championship without even losing a game.. Their performance in the FA Cup was, if anything, even better, and they became the first club to reach an FA Cup Final without ever conceding a goal. They won the final, against Wolverhampton Wanderers, 3–0 and became not only the first club to win the FA Cup without conceding a goal, but also the first club to achieve the 'double'.

The first player to score a hat-trick in an FA Cup Final

The 1889/90 FA Cup Final saw the highest score that any side has yet achieved in a final when Blackburn Rovers thrashed The Wednesday (Sheffield Wednesday) 6–1. William Townley scored the first ever FA Cup Final hat-trick in a game dominated by Blackburn Rovers. Wednesday were, at that time, members of the Football Alliance and became, therefore, the first non-League club to reach an FA Cup Final after the formation of the Football League.

H Campbell, a Scot playing for Blackburn Rovers, achieved the distinction that day of becoming the first person to gain winner's medals in both the FA Cup and the Scottish FA Cup, (he had won his Scottish FA Cup winner's medals with Renton in 1888).

The first occasion that goal nets were used in an FA Cup Final

The 1891/2 FA Cup Final between the two

THE FA CUP

Midland sides, West Bromwich Albion FC and Aston Villa FC, was the first final for which nets were used. West Bromwich Albion FC won 3–0.

The first club to win the FA Cup at a venue outside of London (excluding replays)

Although the 1885/6 final replay had been staged outside London, the first final match proper to be so staged was the 1892/3 final which was played at Fallowfield, Manchester. With a crowd of 45 000 (almost twice as many as any previous final), the move seems to have been a success. Wolverhampton Wanderers FC beat Everton FC 1–0, thus to become the first club to win the trophy at a non-London venue.

The first Second Division club to win the FA Cup

In the 1893/4 final a member of the Football League Second Division (which was only formed in the previous season) appeared in the FA Cup Final playing at Goodison Park, Liverpool. This team, Notts County (formed in 1862—the longest established club in the League), were not in the least overawed by an unimpressive Bolton Wanderers side. With Logan scoring the second Cup Final hat-trick they won the game 4–1, to become the first Second Division club to win the FA Cup.

In the same year Old Carthusians defeated Old Etonians in the first FA Amateur Cup Final and, in doing so, became the first club to have won both the FA Challenge Cup and the FA Amateur Cup.

The first Englishman to gain FA Cup and Scottish FA Cup winner's medals

J Welford, who played in the Aston Villa team which beat West Bromwich Albion FC 1–0 in the 1894/5 final, went on to play for Celtic FC in the 1898/9 Scottish FA Cup Final and became the first Englishman to compete the 'double' of winner's medals.

Villa themselves were the last team to win the original FA Challenge trophy because it was stolen in 1895 whilst on display in a Birmingham shop window and was never recovered. An identical trophy was made by Vaughtons Ltd of Birmingham and was used until 1910 when it was withdrawn and presented to Lord Kinnaird (who appeared in more FA Cup Finals than any other player—nine) to commemorate 21 years as President of the Football Association.

The first player to score in every round of an FA Cup

The 1900/1 FA Cup Final was remarkable for a number of notable firsts. Firstly, the attendance at Crystal Palace on 20 April 1901 was the first six-figure crowd at a football match staged in England.

The venue was changed from Kennington Oval in 1891/2 and, after two matches at northern grounds, moved to Crystal Palace in 1894/5. This move coincided with the vast upsurge in the game's popularity and crowds of 60–70 000 were usual at finals. No doubt the presence of a London club in the final for the first time since the formation of the Football League swelled the gate further and a massive crowd of 114 815 crammed into the Crystal Palace ground to see Tottenham Hotspur FC draw 2–2 with Sheffield United FC.

The replay was staged at Bolton's Burnden Park and ended in a 3–1 victory for Spurs whose manager, James Cameron, became the first 'player-manager' to appear in a final and he scored a goal in the process. Alexander Brown, Tottenham's centre-forward, scored in both the final and the replay and, having already scored in all the previous rounds, became the first player to score in every round of an FA Cup (his 15 goals tally is still the record for an FA Cup). Spurs did not, in fact, join the League until 1908 being members of the Southern League at the time of their 1901 victory and, thus, they became the first non-league club to win the FA Cup after the formation of the Football League.

The following year another Southern League club, Southampton, reached the final and Sheffield United were, once more, the opponents but, after drawing the first game, United managed to win the replay.

The first club this century to win the FA Cup without conceding a goal in any round

Bury FC who trounced Derby County FC 6–0 in 1903 to equal the highest final score, became the first club this century to emulate Preston North End's achievement of winning the Cup without conceding a goal.

The first player to score from a penalty in an FA Cup Final

Penalty kicks were first introduced in the 1891/2 season and it is perhaps a little surprising that the first penalty to be awarded in an FA Cup Final should not have occurred until the 1909/10 replay between Newcastle United and Barnsley. This, effectively, was a run of 22 games before a penalty was awarded!

After a 1–1 draw at Crystal Palace, the replay was staged at Goodison Park, Liverpool and Albert Shepherd of Newcastle United took and scored the first ever FA Cup Final penalty. He also scored his side's other goal in their 2–0 win.

The first winners of the present FA Challenge trophy

As mentioned previously, the second FA Trophy, which was made in 1895 to replace the first cup which had been stolen, was presented as a gift to Lord Kinnaird in 1911. The present trophy was made by Fattorini & Sons of Bradford and, appropriately, was first won by Bradford City FC who beat Newcastle United FC 1–0 in the 1910/11 FA Cup Final replay.

The first player to miss a penalty in an FA Cup Final

In the 1912/3 final, the first penalty to be awarded in an FA Cup Final first game fell to Aston Villa FC. Charlie Wallace took the kick and failed to score to become the first player to miss a penalty in an FA Cup Final. Despite this miss, Villa still beat Sunderland FC 1–0 to win the cup in the first final between the top two clubs in the First Division. Sunderland, however, won the League Championship with Aston Villa runners-up.

The first reigning monarch to attend an FA Cup Final

Liverpool FC's first FA Cup Final was the 1913/4 final in which they were defeated 1–0 by Burnley FC. His Majesty King George V attended the game at Crystal Palace along with 72 777 others, and became the first reigning monarch to attend an FA Cup Final.

The first Cup Finalists to be 'relegated' from that season's First Division.

The 1914/5 wartime final between Sheffield United FC and Chelsea FC was moved from the capital to Old Trafford, Manchester and was the last to be staged until the end of the War. Chelsea FC, who lost the game 3–0, finished second from bottom of the First Division and, but for the suspension of the Football League for the duration, would have been relegated in the 1915/6 season. As it happened, when the Football League restarted the First Division was increased in size by two extra clubs and Chelsea kept their First Division status. Tottenham Hotspur must have felt badly treated since they finished bottom in 1914/5 but were not re-elected because the Second Division's fifth-placed team, Arsenal, were preferred.

The first person to play for and later manage an FA Cup-winning side

Peter McWilliam, who played for the 1909/10 Newcastle United Cup-winning team, went on to manage the Spurs team which stormed back into the First Division in 1919/20 after winning the Second Division Championship by six clear points and then reached the 1920/1 FA Cup Final. Their 1–0 victory over Wolverhampton Wanderers FC made him the first man to gain an FA Cup winner's

medal and subsequently to manage a winning team.

The first bespectacled player to appear in an FA Cup Final

Preston North End's goalkeeper, JF Mitchell, became the first bespectacled player to appear in a final when he played against Huddersfield Town in the 1921/2 final. His team lost 1–0.

The first Wembley FA Cup Final

On 28 April 1923 a huge crowd, estimated to be in excess of 200 000 (officially 126 047) attended the first Wembley Final betweeen Bolton Wanderers FC and the Second Division runners-up, West Ham United FC. The start was delayed until police had cleared thousands of supporters from the pitch. David Jack of Bolton Wanderers scored the first 'Wembley' goal and JR Smith scored the other in Bolton's 2–0 victory. His Majesty King George V was also present at this 'White Horse Final' to witness the amazing scenes and became the first monarch to attend a game at Wembley.

The first all-ticket FA Cup Final

Following the incredible scenes of the previous year, the 1923/4 final (and all subsequent finals) was made, understandably, all-ticket.

The first player to score a goal directly from a corner in an FA Cup tie

Whilst corners were first introduced by the Football Association in 1872, it was not until 1924 that the rules were changed to allow goals to be scored directly from corners. On 7 March 1925 Cardiff's William Davies scored his side's winner directly from a corner with the very last kick of the match to become the first player to score thus in the FA Cup.

The first FA Cup Final to be broadcast by radio

The 1925/6 final in which Bolton Wanderers FC beat Manchester City FC 1–0, was broadcast to listeners in public halls in both Bolton and Manchester. As such, this was the first game to be heard over the radio in this manner, although the broadcast could not be described as a public broadcast in the normal sense of the word.

The first FA Cup Final to be publicly broadcast by radio

The 1926/7 final between Cardiff City and Arsenal was the first game to be publicly broadcast live by radio throughout the country. Cardiff City, in winning the game 1–0, became the first non-English club to win the FA Cup.

THE FA CUP

The first club to finish runners-up in both the Football League and the FA Cup in the same season

Huddersfield Town FC, who had won three consecutive League Championships from 1923 to 1926, finished runners-up in 1926/7 and then did so again in 1927/8. That year they went down 3–1 to Blackburn Rovers FC in the FA Cup Final and became the first 'double runners-up'.

The first player to be sent off in an FA Cup semi final

Hull City were languishing near the foot of the Second Division when they met Arsenal in their first FA Cup semi-final game, which they drew 2–2. In the replay they were reduced to ten men when Arthur Childs became the first player to be sent off in an FA Cup semi final and they went down 1–0 despite putting up a brave fight.

The first person to manage two different FA Cup-winning clubs

Herbert Chapman, who had managed the victorious Huddersfield Town team which won the 1921/2 final against Preston North End, went on to manage the magnificent Arsenal team. Ironically, they met his former club in the 1929/30 final and their 2–0 victory ensured that he became the first person to manage two different FA Cup-winning clubs.

The first club to be promoted from the Second Division in the season that they won the FA Cup

In the 1930/1 'Midland' final between West Bromwich Albion and Birmingham, West

THE FA CUP

Millwall, the first Third Division FA Cup semi-finalists. (Colorsport)

Bromwich became the first Second Division club to win the FA Cup at Wembley when they emerged 2–1 victors. This capped a fine season in which they gained promotion from the Second Division exactly one week after the final, when they beat Charlton Athletic 3–2 to finish runners-up to Everton.

The first club to score first and then lose an FA Cup Final at Wembley

In the 1931/2 final, the Arsenal left-winger, John, opened the scoring for his team against Newcastle United, who came back to win with two goals from Allen and, in doing so, became the first club to come from behind and win a Wembley FA Cup Final.

The first FA Cup Final for which player's shirts were numbered

In the 1932/3 final, both Everton and Manchester City's shirts were numbered in an experiment which preceded the official introduction of numbering by seven years. The unusual numbering arrangement was: Everton, numbers 1–11 and Manchester City, numbers 12–22. Everton, fielding the legendary 'Dixie' Dean, won 3–0.

The first Third Division club to reach the semi final of the FA Cup

After sensationally disposing of that year's League Champions (Manchester City FC) in the quarter finals of the 1936/7 FA Cup, Millwall FC went on to become the first Third Division club to reach the semi finals. Their opponents were Sunderland FC who struggled to beat them 2–1.

37

THE FA CUP

The first FA Cup Final to be televised

In 1936/7 Sunderland FC, having beaten Millwall in the semi final, met Preston North End FC in the first final to be partially televised. Sunderland won the game 3–1.

The first FA Cup Final to be televised live

Preston North End FC returned to Wembley in the 1937/8 final to face Huddersfield Town, and in doing so quite a number of firsts were recorded. After the partial TV coverage of the previous final, the whole of the match was televised live (with the exception of 1946 and 1952, all subsequent finals have also been televised live), although the TV audience of about 10 000 was far surpassed by the 93 947 attending the game.

Level at full-time, with a 0–0 scoreline, the game became the first Wembley final to go into extra-time and, when George Mutch scored Preston's winner from the penalty spot he scored the first Wembley Cup Final penalty and the first penalty goal win.

Huddersfield's Joe Hulme who had played in four previous finals with Arsenal, became the first player to appear in five Wembley finals.

(Right) J Hulme, pictured in his Arsenal days, became the first person to appear in five Wembley finals in 1938, after transferring to Huddersfield Town. (Pattrieoux)

(Below) George Mutch scores Preston's extra-time penalty goal in the 1937/8 FA Cup Final. (Photosource)

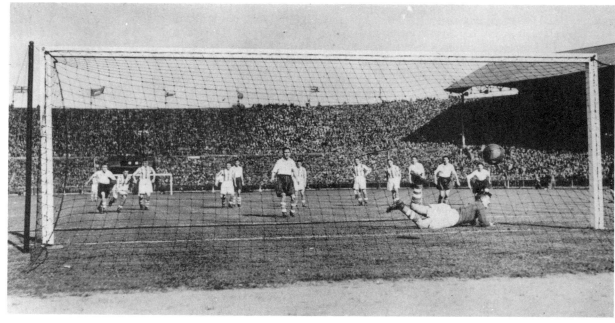

THE FA CUP

The first player to score for both sides in an FA Cup Final

In the 1945/6 FA Cup Final between Derby County FC and Charlton Athletic FC, the score at full-time stood at 1–1. One player, Bert Turner of Charlton Athletic, had scored both goals and had become the first person to score for both sides in an FA Cup Final. His side collapsed in extra-time and lost the game 4–1, a fitting end to an unusual final which had also seen the first ever match ball 'burst'!

The first club to win the FA Cup after playing all of its matches away from home

It is something of an 'old chestnut' that, as a result of bomb damage, Manchester United's ground, Old Trafford, was not used by them during the seasons immediately after the Second World War, and their 1947/8 cup run was all 'away' from home. What cannot be denied is the way in which Matt Busby's team performed against Blackpool in what has been described as Wembley's finest footballing match. Despite going behind in the 13th minute to the first FA Cup Final goal by a full-back, (an Eddie Shimwell penalty), United won the game 4–2 with a scintillating display.

The first club this century to retain the FA Cup

The 1950/1 final between Newcastle United FC and Blackpool was a close-fought thing with Blackpool trailing 1–0 but looking dangerous, when Jackie Milburn unleashed a tremendous left-foot shot which rocketed into the Blackpool net. This goal, claimed by many to have been the best ever scored at Wembley, gave Newcastle the Cup. The following year, this time playing Arsenal, Newcastle became the first club this century to retain the Cup, although their 1–0 victory is best remembered for the grim defence which Arsenal (down to eight fit men) put up.

The first player to score a hat-trick in an FA Cup Final at Wembley

The 1952/3 final between Blackpool FC and Bolton Wanderers FC is usually described as the 'Stanley Matthews Final'. Blackpool were trailing 3–1 with 22 minutes to play when Matthews, moving into top gear, tore down the wing and crossed for Stan Mortensen to score his second goal. Mortensen then scored his third with a cracking free-kick to become the first person to score a Wembley FA Cup Final hat-trick, and Matthews made the winner in injury time.

The first FA Cup tie to be played under floodlights

A 1955/6 qualifying-round replay between Kidderminster Harriers FC and Brierley Hill Alliance FC on 14 September 1955 was,

Newcastle United's free-scoring forward, Jackie Milburn, pictured on a typical goalward run. (D C Thomson Ltd)

surprisingly, the first FA Cup tie to be played under floodlights. This may seem relatively recent but it is worth recording that even Manchester United's first official floodlit match did not take place until March 1957!

The first floodlit FA Cup tie between Football League clubs

Two months after the first floodlit FA Cup tie at Kidderminster, Carlisle United met Darlington in a floodlit FA Cup first round second replay at St James' Park, Newcastle on 28 November 1955. This, in itself, was not such a novel event at Newcastle where the first official floodlit match had been played in February 1953.

The first club to appear in ten FA Cup Finals

Appearing in their third final in five years, Newcastle United faced Manchester City in the 1954/5 final and once more, Jackie Milburn, with a header in only the first minute, set them on the road to victory. Their 3–1 victory was their third in five years and their sixth out of ten appearances.

THE FA CUP

The first player to score in consecutive FA Cup Finals at Wembley

Bobby Johnstone of Manchester City, who scored his side's consolation goal in the 1954/5 final against Newcastle United, scored again in the following year's final against Birmingham City which this time they won 3–1. This was the final in which the City goalkeeper, Bert Trautmann, played the last 12 minutes of the game with a broken neck!

The first player to be sent off in three English domestic competitions

This unenviable distinction fell to Ambrose Fogerty who was first dismissed whilst playing for Sunderland against Everton in an FA Cup tie in January 1958; then, whilst playing for Hartlepool United against Barnsley in a Football League fixture in October 1965 and, finally for Hartlepool United against Bradford Park Avenue in the League Cup in August 1966.

The first club to win the FA Cup at Wembley after being reduced to ten players through injury

In the 1958/9 final, Nottingham Forest, reduced to only ten men by injury, still managed to beat lowly Luton Town 2–1 to become the first team reduced by injury to win the FA Cup.

Spurs' Dave Mackay challenges Liverpool's Tony Hateley for a high ball. (ASP)

The first club this century to achieve the 'double'

Tottenham Hotspur started the 1960/1 season in tremendous form and had already sewn up the Football League title before they faced Leicester City in the FA Cup Final. With a defence ably marshalled by Danny Blanchflower, Spurs emerged convincing winners with goals by Smith and Dyson to become the first club to achieve the double since Aston Villa did so in 1896/7. Dave Mackay, the Spurs midfield dynamo, who had already won a Scottish championship and Cup winner's medal with Heart of Midlothian became the first player to win all four medals when, in 1960/1 he added the two English competitions to his tally.

The first Fourth Division club to reach the quarter finals of the FA Cup

Oxford United, who were not admitted to the Football League until 1962 (when they replaced Accrington Stanley) were the first Fourth Division club to reach the quarter finals of the FA Cup, when in 1963/4 they went down 2–1 to Preston North End.

The first 'all London' FA Cup Final since the formation of the Football League

Considering that there are at least 11 Football League sides which could be classified as 'London' clubs, it is quite surprising that it was not until the 1966/7 final (in which Tottenham Hotspur met Chelsea) that two of them played one another in an FA Cup Final. Spurs won the game 2–1.

The first substitute to appear in an FA Cup Final

West Bromwich Albion's Derek Clarke became the first substitute to be used in an FA Cup Final when, in the 1967/8 final, he replaced John Kaye. West Bromwich won the game, against Everton, when Jeff Astle scored the only goal of the match in extra-time.

The first FA Cup Final at Wembley to go to a replay

It seems incredible that there should have been 41 FA Cup Finals at Wembley before one ended in a draw after extra-time. Nevertheless, it was not until the 1969/70 final (the 42nd) between Chelsea and Leeds United that a replay became necessary when there was a 2–2 draw after extra-time. Chelsea won the replay at Old Trafford 2–1, again after extra-time.

The first substitute to score in an FA Cup Final

In Arsenal's double-winning year, 1970/1, their substitute, Eddie Kelly, who came on in place of

THE FA CUP

Storey, scored the first final goal to be scored by a substitute. Arsenal won the game 2–1 after extra-time.

The first FA Cup tie to be played on a Sunday

On Sunday 6 January 1974, Cambridge United and Oldham Athletic played out a 2–2 draw in the first Sunday FA Cup tie at the Abbey Stadium.

The first player, this century, to gain winner's medals with different clubs in consecutive FA Cup Finals

Brian Talbot, a member of Ipswich Town's 1977/8 Cup-winning side, transferred to Arsenal, the beaten finalists, the next season and became the first player this century to gain consecutive winner's medals with different clubs when Arsenal beat Manchester United 3–2 in the 1978/9 final. The following year, in the first match in Britain to have receipts in excess of £1 million, he appeared again for an Arsenal side which became the first club this century to appear in three consecutive finals. West Ham United won the game 1–0.

The first FA Cup Final to be replayed at Wembley

As the 92 000 gate bears testimony, the decision to replay the 1980/1 FA Cup Final at Wembley was a very popular move. Tottenham Hotspur won the game against Manchester City 3–2 after drawing the first game 1–1.

The first woman to officiate at an FA Cup tie

Mrs Liz Forsdick, who was a lines-woman at an FA Cup third qualifying-round tie between Burgess Hill Town and Carshalton, achieved this distinction on 17 October 1981.

The first FA Cup tie to be played on artificial turf

Needless to say, this took place at Queen's Park Rangers' ground, Loftus Road, when on 2 January 1982 QPR drew 0–0 with Middlesbrough.

The first player to appear in a major cup final in both Scotland and England during the same season

This occurred when Brighton's Gordon Smith, on loan to Rangers, played against Celtic in the 1982/3 Scottish League Cup Final then, having been recalled by his club, scored a goal in the drawn 1982/3 English FA Cup Final against Manchester United. United won the replay 4–0.

The first player to be sent off in an FA Cup Final

It seems incredible that it was not until the 116th FA Cup Final game (including replays) that a player was sent off. Kevin Moran of Manchester United must count himself unlucky to have earned this notoriety with a late tackle on Everton's Peter Reid. There can be no doubt that far worse fouls were perpetrated in several of the preceding 115 games but the referee, Mr Peter Willis, was certainly justified in his decision. As often happens, the sending-off had a positive effect on Manchester United, and they went on to win the match 1–0.

The loan system enabled Gordon Smith of Brighton to play for Rangers in the 1982/3 Scottish League Cup Final. (ASP)

Manchester United's Kevin Moran supported by Mark Hughes and Bryan Robson, protesting his innocence to Mr Peter Willis, after being ordered off for a late tackle on Everton's Peter Reid. (Eddie Fuller)

THE FA CUP

The first goalkeeper to save a penalty in an FA Cup Final at Wembley

Wimbledon's Dave Beasant dived to his left and saved John Aldridge's penalty-kick on 14 May 1988. His save enabled Wimbledon, a non-league outfit only a few years earlier, to pull off one of the biggest shocks of all time when they defeated Liverpool 1–0. In addition Beasant achieved the distinction of becoming the first goalkeeper to captain an FA Cup-winning side at Wembley.

Dave Beasant and Wimbledon's moment of triumph. (Allsport/David Cannon)

The Scottish FA Cup, played on a straight knockout basis, is one of the oldest competitions in Football with over one hundred finals having been staged. Although Scotland's oldest club, Queens Park FC, dominated the early competitions, the 'Old Firm' of Celtic and Rangers then took over their monopoly.

The cup's origins went back to 13 March 1873 when eight clubs attended a meeting called by Queens Park FC to form the Scottish Football Association and to institute the Scottish FA Cup. Sixteen clubs (15 of whom subscribed towards the purchase of the cup itself) entered the first Scottish FA Cup competition.

The first ever Scottish FA Cup tie

When Renton FC defeated Kilmarnock FC (who fielded only ten men) 3–0 at Crosshill, Glasgow on 18 October 1873, they became the first club to win a Scottish FA Cup tie. The two clubs naturally became the first teams to play a Scottish FA Cup tie.

The first Scottish FA Cup Final

This was played at the first Hampden Park on 21 March 1874. It provided a good deal of controversy for the 2–3000 spectators who had paid 6d (2.5p) per head to watch the unbeaten Queens Park FC (the first Scottish club to be founded—9 July 1867) play Clydesdale FC (a team containing a number of their ex-players). Early in the first half, Fred Anderson of Clydesdale took a pass from James Lang—who is reputed to have become the first 'Anglo-Scot' when he joined the Wednesday (later Sheffield Wednesday) in 1876—and his shot beat the Queens Park goalkeeper, striking the knee of a spectator standing behind the goalposts. This 'goal' would have been the first conceded by the Queens Park club (despite their having been founded seven years earlier!) had the referee not prompted them to claim 'no goal', just as they were about to kick-off. As it was, the appeal was upheld and it thus became the first disallowed goal in a Scottish FA Cup Final.

The first goal actually scored was by William McKinnon of Queens Park FC 20 minutes before time, and they went on to become the first winners by a 2–0 margin. In the process, they became, additionally, the first club to win the Cup without conceding a single goal.

The first club to retain the Scottish FA Cup

Queens Park FC, still undefeated, went on to retain the Cup on 10 April 1875 by beating Renton FC 3–0 in the second final. A total of 49 clubs entered the

competition that year—ample proof of the game's phenomenal growth.

The first club to win three successive Scottish FA Cup Finals

Queens Park's absolute domination of the game culminated in their third consecutive appearance in the third Scottish FA Cup Final against Third Lanark FC on 11 March 1876. (A notable football third?). The first game, which ended in a 1–1 draw, led to the first Scottish FA Cup Final replay and Queens' 2–0 victory in that game enabled them to become the first club to achieve a hat-trick of wins.

The first Scottish FA Cup Final to go to a second replay

In 1876/7 Vale of Leven FC achieved the distinction of becoming the first club to knock the holders Queens Park FC out of the cup and went on to meet Rangers FC in the final. After drawing the first game 1–1, the replay ended in a 0–0 draw and the first 'double replay' was played on Friday 13 April 1877. Vale of Leven FC took this game 3–2 to become the first non-Glasgow team to gain the trophy despite their player, McDougall, achieving the 'distinction' of becoming the first player to concede an own goal in a final.

The first person to referee a Scottish FA Cup Final, having appeared as a player in a previous final

Robert Gardner, the Scottish Football Association President, who had played in goal for Clydesdale FC in the very first final, achieved this unusual distinction on 30 March 1878 when he refereed the Vale of Leven FC v Third Lanark FC final. Vale of Leven won by the only goal of the match, an own goal by Hunter of Third Lanark—the first occasion that an own goal alone decided the fate of the Cup.

The first floodlit match in Scotland

On the evening of Friday 28 October 1878, Vale of Leven FC played a floodlit friendly match at Third Lanark's ground—the first floodlit match in Scotland. A single beam, mounted on a platform, was directed at the ball to spotlight the play. The game could not have been too demanding as, the next day, Vale of Leven thrashed Renton Thistle 11–0 in a second-round Scottish FA Cup tie!

The first club to fail to turn up for a Scottish FA Cup Final

Rangers FC failed to turn up for the Cup Final replay on 26 April 1879 and Vale of Leven FC became the first club to win the Cup by default.

THE SCOTTISH FA CUP

Rangers, aggrieved by a disallowed goal in the first game, literally refused to play the replay!

The first occasion that gates were closed at a match

In 1881, despite the fact that the first final between Queens Park FC and Dumbarton FC had ended with a 2–1 scoreline, a replay was ordered after an appeal by Dumbarton. This was adjudged to have been necessary because of encroachment by the 20 000 crowd onto the pitch when the winning goal was scored and became the first result made void by crowd intervention. The replay on 9 April 1881 was the first occasion that the gates were closed at a final, as the 10 000 crowd testifies. Queens Park won the replay 3–1.

The first 'repeat' Scottish FA Cup Final

After beating Dumbarton FC in the 1881 final, Queens Park FC repeated their victory the following year when their opponents were, once again, Dumbarton. The 1882 final ended 2–2 and Queens Park won the replay 4–1.

The first club to be in both the Scottish FA Cup Final and the English FA Cup Final in the same year

In 1884 Queens Park FC reached both finals—against Vale of Leven FC in the Scottish FA Cup Final and against Blackburn Rovers FC in the English FA Cup Final. The Scottish final never took place because Vale of Leven did not turn up and Queens Park were awarded the game by default.

In the English final, a different interpretation of the offside laws resulted in Queens Park losing, because they failed to appeal to the referee against an offside goal scored against them (referees at that time were merely available to adjudicate when a dispute arose). Smarting at the injustice of the matter Queens went back to Scotland but returned to appear in the 1885 English final (again unsuccessfully).

The first club to score six goals in a Scottish FA Cup Final

In the 1888 final, Renton FC, appearing in their third final in four years, emphatically defeated the Lanarkshire village side Cambuslang FC 6–1 to become the first team to score six goals in a Scottish FA Cup Final. This score has only been equalled once and this was the first time that three players each scored more than one goal for their team in a Scottish FA Cup Final. On 19 May 1888 Renton went on to challenge the English FA Cup winners, West Bromwich Albion FC, to a 'World Championship Decider' which they won 4–1 and claimed to be the first 'Champions of the World'.

The first club to appear in ten Scottish FA Cup Finals

Queens Park FC achieved this in the 1892 final against Celtic FC (if the 1884 'walkover' is counted). In so doing they also became the first non-League club to appear in a Scottish FA Cup Final after the formation of the League. Celtic FC won the replayed final after the first game was disrupted by the crowd, McMahon scoring the first Scottish FA Cup Final hat-trick in their 5–1 victory.

The first club to win ten Scottish FA Cup Finals

Queens Park FC won their tenth final in 1893 when they, once again, played Celtic FC. The pitch was declared 'unsuitable for a final' and a friendly was played so as not to disappoint the 25 000 crowd. Celtic won this game 1–0 and the crowd, who were not informed that a friendly had been played, celebrated a Celtic 'victory'. Queens Park won the actual final 2–1 before a crowd of 22 000 and, in so doing, became the first non-League club to win the Scottish FA Cup after the formation of the League. This was also the first 'repeat' final when the losing club of the previous year played and beat the Cup-holders.

The first 'Old Firm' Scottish FA Cup Final

The 1894 Final played on 17 February was the first of many between Rangers FC and Celtic FC. A 17 000 crowd at the second Hampden Park saw Rangers win the game 3–1.

The first Second Division club to appear in a Scottish FA Cup Final

Renton FC, who had appeared in four previous finals, became the first Second Division club to appear in a Scottish FA Cup Final, when, in 1895, they lost 2–1 to the Edinburgh side St Bernards FC.

The first Scottish FA Cup Final to be played outside of Glasgow

The 1896 final between the two Edinburgh sides Heart of Midlothian FC and The Hibernians FC was, understandably, played in Edinburgh. The neutral ground of Logie Green (the home of the previous year's winners, St Bernards FC) was the venue when 17 034 spectators saw Hearts win 3–1.

The first beaten Scottish FA Cup Finalists to fail to gain re-election in the same year

Surprisingly, Rangers' opponents in the 1897 Final were Dumbarton FC—the bottom club in the Second Division, who failed to gain re-election after losing the final 5–1.

THE SCOTTISH FA CUP

The first British club, this century, to appear in a major Cup final at their own ground

The 1902 Scottish FA Cup Final was scheduled to be played at Ibrox Park but was postponed and then switched to Celtic Park (despite the presence of Celtic in the final) following the stand-collapse earlier in the month during the Scotland v England international at Ibrox. A gloomy crowd of 16 000 (no doubt affected by the loss of life at Ibrox) saw the home club lose 1–0 to The Hibernians.

The first club to win the Scottish FA Cup at the present Hampden Park

The third 'Old Firm' Scottish FA Cup Final on 16 April 1904 was also the first to be played at the present Hampden Park. The crowd of 65 000 (encouraged by a reduced admission charge) saw Rangers lose 3–2 despite going into an early two-goal lead.

The first Scottish club to win the 'Double'

Although Celtic came very close to achieving this feat in 1893, they lost the replayed final 2–1 to Queens Park and had to wait until the 1907 Final against Hearts before they actually pulled it off. William Orr became the first player to score a penalty in a Scottish FA Cup Final when, in the 55th minute, he converted a highly dubious award to score Celtic's second goal. The final result was 3–0.

The first time that the Scottish FA Cup was withheld

The notorious fourth 'Old Firm' Scottish FA Cup Final was first played on 10 April 1909 and ended quietly in a 2–2 draw. The replay also ended in a 1–1 draw and the 60 000 crowd roared for extra-time to be played, suspecting that a draw had been contrived to obtain more gate money. Since the Scottish FA Cup rules, at that time, would not allow extra-time to be played, the players left the field and a full-blown riot ensued. Pay-boxes were set on fire, goal posts broken, the pitch cut up and one hundred people (mostly policemen and firemen) were injured. Afterwards, when the two clubs petitioned that the final tie be abandoned, the Scottish Football Assocation concurred and withheld the Cup for 1909.

The first player, this century, to gain seven Scottish FA Cup winner's medals

After appearing for Celtic FC on seven occasions between 1904 and 1914, and winning six winner's medals (no medals being awarded in 1909), Jimmy McMenemy moved to Partick Thistle as their team coach. Despite this, he went on to win his seventh

winner's medal when he appeared in the 1921 final, specifically to 'calm the nerves of the younger players'. Partick Thistle beat Rangers 1–0.

The first player to score from a direct free kick in a Scottish FA Cup Final

In the 1922 final between Greenock Morton FC and Rangers FC, Jimmy Gourlay's 30 yd (27 m) free kick sneaked in under the crossbar to become the first goal scored from a direct free kick in a Scottish FA Cup Final. Greenock Morton won the match 1–0.

The first match at Hampden Park to be attended by Royalty

In February 1923, an astounding crowd of 50 000 were at Hampden Park to see HRH Prince Albert the Duke of York (later King George VI) kick-off the second round Scottish FA Cup tie between Queens Park FC and Bathgate FC. Sporting a bowler hat and carrying a rolled-up umbrella the Duke thus became the first member of the Royal Family to attend a match at Hampden Park.

The first Scottish FA Cup Final to be broadcast

The 1927 final at Hampden Park between Celtic FC and Second Division East Fife FC was the first to be broadcast live by radio and, indeed, as this final was played a week earlier than the English FA Final, it also became the first final in Britain to be given a live radio broadcast. Celtic won the game 3–1.

The first Scottish FA Cup Final to attract a six-figure attendance

Another 'Old Firm' meeting at Hampden Park on 14 April 1928 saw the first 100 000 attendance at a Scottish FA Cup Final. In front of a crowd of 118 115, Rangers notched their first victory for 25 years when they won 4–0.

The first player to miss a penalty in a Scottish FA Cup Final

Rangers' Tully Craig whose 16th minute penalty kick was brilliantly saved by Clemie (the Kilmarnock goalkeeper), was the first player to fail to score from a penalty in a Scottish FA Cup Final. This happened in the 1929 final which Kilmarnock won 2–0 and in which Jock Buchanan of Rangers achieved the unenviable distinction (in the 88th minute) of becoming the first player to be sent off in a final.

The first foreigner to gain a Scottish FA Cup winner's medal

Joe Kennaway, a Canadian goalkeeper playing for Celtic FC became the first foreign player to win a cup-winners medal when he kept a 'clean sheet'

THE SCOTTISH FA CUP

against Motherwell FC in 1933. He also won a second medal in 1937.

The first all-ticket Scottish FA Cup tie

Brockville Park, the home of Falkirk FC was the venue for the first all-ticket Scottish FA Cup quarter-final tie on 19 March 1938, when Falkirk were drawn at home to Rangers. Rangers won the match 2–1.

The first all-ticket Scottish FA Cup Final

After the huge 1937 Scottish Cup Final crowd of 146 433 (with 20 000 more locked out), the Scottish Football Association decided to make all future finals all-ticket. The first such final was played on 23 April 1938 when East Fife FC held

(Right) Scottish soccer supremo, the late Jock Stein, pictured in May 1984. (ASP)

(Below) Eric Black, one of the stars in Aberdeen's Scottish FA Cup and European Cup Winners Cup double, 1983. (ASP)

Kilmarnock FC to a 1–1 draw and became the first Second Division club to reach a Cup Final replay. The following Wednesday, they went one better and became the first Second Division club to win the Scottish FA Cup when they won the replay 4–2. Remarkably, the East Fife FC were so depleted by injuries that they had to sign two players — Danny McKerrell a Falkirk FC reserve and John Harvey, a Hearts reserve (both of whom had not played in that season's competition) — so that they could field a full side! The two men became the first players to gain winner's medals in their first games for their new side.

The first foreigner to score a goal in a Scottish FA Cup Final

Dougie Wallace, a South African, who scored the first goal for Clyde FC in their 4–0 win over Motherwell FC in the 1939 final at Hampden Park, became, in so doing, the first foreigner to score in a Scottish FA Cup Final.

The first club to achieve the Scottish treble

On 23 April 1949, League champions Rangers FC defeated Clyde FC 4–1 in the Scottish FA Cup Final to become the first club to achieve the treble, having already beaten Raith Rovers 2–0 in the Scottish League Cup Final.

The first Scottish FA Cup Final to be televised live

Surprisingly, since English FA Cup Finals had been televised live from 1938 onwards, the first Scottish FA Cup Final to be televised live was not until 23 April 1955. The game, between Clyde FC and Celtic FC, ended in a 1–1 draw after Clyde's Archie Robertson became the first player to score direct from a corner in a Scottish FA Cup Final with his 88th-minute equalizer.

The first club to win a European competition in the same year as it won the Scottish FA Cup

Jock Stein's 1966/7 Celtic FC team made a clean sweep of every competition that it entered. Firstly they won the 1966/7 Scottish League Cup by beating Rangers FC 1–0, then they beat Aberdeen 2–0 in the Scottish FA Cup, and went on to win the League Championship and, on 25 May 1967, the European Cup.

The first substitutes to be used in a Scottish FA Cup Final

The poorly attended 1968 final between Dunfermline Athletic FC and Heart of Midlothian FC was the first occasion that substitutes were used in a final. Dunfermline's Thomson replaced Edwards and Hearts' Maller (who achieved the regrettable record of also becoming the first

substitute in a Scottish FA Cup Final to be booked), replaced Traynor. Dunfermline won the match 3–1.

The first subtitute to score a goal in a Scottish FA Cup Final

When Rangers' substitute D Johnstone scored their 86th-minute equalizer in the 1970/1 'Old Firm' final he became the first substitute to score in a Scottish FA Cup Final. He also came on as substitute in the replay but could not then notch up another goal to prevent Celtic from winning 2–1.

The first Scottish FA Cup Final at Hampden Park to be attended by a member of the Royal Family

Princess Alexandra attended the Scottish Football Association's 'Centenary' Final between Rangers FC and Celtic FC on 5 May 1973 and became the first member of the Royal Family to see a match at Hampden Park since King George VI (then Duke of York) in 1923. Her attendance at the game (which Rangers won 3–2) was the first ever by Royalty at a Scottish FA Cup Final.

The first player to score a goal on a Sunday in the Scottish FA Cup

The introduction of Sunday Scottish FA Cup ties inevitably resulted in a number of inconsequential firsts, on which we do not propose to expand. It is significant, however, that John 'Dixie' Deans, Celtic's hat-trick hero of the 1972 final, should have scored the first 'Sunday Cup goal', which he did against Clydebank on 27 January 1974. Celtic won the tie 6–1 and went on to win the Cup by beating Dundee United FC 3–0.

The first Scottish clubs to play League and Cup matches over one weekend

The other 'Sunday' first that merits recording is the unusual one achieved when Morton and Raith Rovers played their respective League fixtures on Saturday 2 February 1974 and, the next day, played one another in a Scottish FA Cup third-round replay. This replay, staged at the neutral ground of Tynecastle Park, Edinburgh, attracted a very reasonable attendance and Morton won 1–0 with a 44th-minute goal.

The first 'repeat' final this century

In the 1981/2 final Aberdeen FC beat Rangers FC 4–1 thanks to three extra-time goals and, in 1982/3, facing them once more in the final, again won 1–0 thanks to an extra-time goal by Black. Aberdeen also achieved another significant first that year when they won the European Cup-Winners Cup and became the first Scottish club to win that trophy and the Scottish FA Cup in the same year.

6 THE FOOTBALL LEAGUE CUP

The most recently-established of all the major British domestic competitions (1960/61), this also became the first major competition to change its name as a result of sponsorship when, in 1981/2, the National Dairy Council took up a five-year sponsorship. As a consequence, the competition was then retitled 'The Milk Cup'. At the commencement of the 1986/7 season the pools firm, Littlewoods, took over the sponsorship of the competition.

The League Cup was organized from the outset on a straight knockout basis with a two-legged semi final and final and remained that way until 1966/7 when a single-game Wembley final was introduced. Since 1975/6 the first round has been played on aggregate over two games.

Although Liverpool and Aston Villa have both appeared in a number of finals (with Liverpool achieving the greatest number of wins) no clubs have monopolized the competition throughout the 25 seasons of its existence and there have been over a dozen different winners to date.

The first player to score a goal in the Football League Cup competition

In the 9th minute of the very first game of the competition, at the Eastville Stadium, Bristol (on the evening of 26 September 1960) Maurice Cook scored the first ever League Cup goal to put Fulham FC into the lead against Bristol Rangers FC. Despite this early setback, Bristol Rovers struck back to win the game 2–1 before a crowd of 20 022. A second tie on the same night resulted in a 3–1 win for West Ham United FC against Charlton Athletic FC.

The first player to score an own goal in the Football League Cup competition

Peterborough United's full-back Walker conceded the first own goal in the Football League Cup on 11 October 1960 when his team lost 4–1 away to Preston North End FC.

The first player to score a hat-trick in the Football League Cup competition

Inside-right Walsh of Leicester City FC became the first player to score a hat-trick in the Football League Cup competition (at Filbert Street, on 12 October 1960) before a crowd of 7070, when Leicester City FC beat Mansfield Town FC 4–0 in the first round of the competition. On the same night Bradford's winger Hooley scored the first

Terry Venables, the first and only player to represent England at all five levels (schoolboy, youth, amateur, under 23 and full). (ASP)

penalty goal in the competition when his side drew 2–2 at Lincoln City FC.

The first English domestic final to be held over to the next season

The first League Cup Final was not staged until 22 August and 5 September 1961, the first major competition to be held over until the next season.

The first club to win the Football League Cup

When Aston Villa FC defeated Rotherham United FC 3–0 at Villa Park on 5 September 1961, after losing the first leg at Millmoor 2–0, they became

THE FOOTBALL LEAGUE CUP

the first League Cup winners. In addition they also became the first club to have won all three major competitions (The FA Cup, The League Championship and The League Cup).

The first goal to be scored in a League Cup Final was scored by the Rotherham player Barry Webster during the first-leg match. Interestingly, 87 clubs entered the competition in the first season—a number not surpassed until 90 clubs entered the 1966/7 competition.

The first Fourth Division club to appear in the final of a major domestic competition in England

Rochdale FC, who lost both the home and the away legs of the 1962 League Cup Final 2–0 to Norwich City FC, were the first Fourth Division club ever to appear in a major English domestic final.

The first club to appear in two League Cup Finals

In the 1963 all-Birmingham final, Aston Villa FC became the first club to appear in two finals. They lost 3–1 at Birmingham City FC in the first leg and drew 0–0 in the second leg.

The first London club to win the Football League Cup

Chelsea FC became the first London club to win the League Cup when, in 1965, they beat Leicester City FC 3–2 at Stamford Bridge in the first leg and drew 0–0 in the second leg. Terry Venables became the first player to score a penalty in a League Cup Final when he scored Chelsea's second goal in the first leg.

The first player to score in every round of the Football League Cup competition

Tony Brown of West Bromwich Albion FC scored in every round of the 1965/6 League Cup competition and, in all, netted 11 goals including a semi-final hat-trick against Peterborough United FC. In the final, West Bromwich Albion FC beat West Ham United FC 5–3 on aggregate to win the competition for that season.

The first substitutes to be used in the Football League Cup competition

On 23 August 1966 Shires and Webb of Colchester United FC and Reading FC respectively came on for their clubs in first-round games at Queens Park Rangers FC and Watford FC. The following day

Tony Brown of West Bromwich Albion, pictured somewhat later in his career (1978), scored in every round of the 1965/6 League Cup. (ASP)

THE FOOTBALL LEAGUE CUP

Oxford United's Buck came on for Evanson and became the first substitute to score a goal in a League Cup match.

The first Third Division club to win the Football League Cup

It is often said that 1966/7 was the season in which the League Cup came of age and, indeed, the 1967 League Cup Final was notable for a succession of firsts. It was the first single-legged League Cup Final and also the first League Cup Final to be played at Wembley. Queens Park Rangers FC were the first Third Division club to play in a Wembley final and, additionally, were the first Third Division club to win the League Cup. Needless to say West Bromwich Albion FC, their opponents, who lost 3–2, were the first club from Division One to lose a League Cup Final at Wembley. The one bright spot for West Bromwich was that Clark (who scored both of their goals) became the first player to score in consecutive finals.

Everton's Kenyon pictured in action in November 1983. (ASP)

The first Football League Cup competition in which all 92 clubs took part

In 1967/8, when both Everton FC and Liverpool FC, the last two clubs to refuse to take part, re-entered the competition, all 92 clubs participated for the very first time. This decision was no doubt prompted by the Wembley final, coupled with the UEFA Cup nomination for the winners (instituted for the first time from 1967).

The first Football League Cup Final at Wembley to go into extra time

The 1970 final between Manchester City FC and West Bromwich Albion FC was tied 1–1 at full time after Doyle had equalized for City and Glyn Pardoe scored in extra time to give Manchester City a 2–1 win. In doing so Manchester City became the first club to win all three major competitions in successive years. (League Champions 1967/8; FA Cup Winners 1969 and League Cup Winners 1970).

The first Football League Cup competition into which all 92 clubs' entries were compulsory

Entry became compulsory for the 1971 competition although all clubs had entered voluntarily since 1967/8.

The first club to win the Football League Cup twice

Tottenham Hotspur FC beat Norwich City FC 1–0 on 3 March 1973 to become the first club to win the Football League Cup twice. Their previous win was in 1971 when they beat Aston Villa FC 2–0.

The first Football League Cup Final to be replayed

The 1977 final between Aston Villa FC and Everton FC was not only the first final to require a replay, but, in fact, also the first final to require two replays. The match at Wembley ended 0–0 and the first replay at Hillsborough ended 1–1 after being 0–0 at full-time. Even the second replay at Old Trafford went into extra-time before Villa won 3–2, and in doing so, they became the first club to win the Cup three times. Everton's Kenyon conceded an own goal in the first replay, the first one in a League Cup Final.

The first club to win both the Football League Championship and the Football League Cup in the same season

In the 1977/8 season Nottingham Forest FC became the first club to achieve the 'New Double' of League Champions and League Cup winners. Playing the European Champions, Liverpool FC, Forest drew

THE FOOTBALL LEAGUE CUP

0–0 at Wembley and took the replay at Old Trafford 1–0 to achieve this distinction. Another unusual first occurred for Forest that day, when Chris Woods (who replaced the injured Peter Shilton) became the first player to appear in a Wembley final before making his Football League debut.

The first club to retain the Football League Cup

Nottingham Forest FC became the first club to retain the League Cup in 1979 when they beat Southampton FC 3–2, with two goals from Garry Birtles and a third from Tony Woodcock.

The first club to appear in three consecutive Wembley finals

In 1980, Andy Gray of Wolverhampton Wanderers FC scored the only goal of that year's League Cup Final to ensure that Nottingham Forest FC only achieved the distinction of becoming the first club to appear in three consecutive finals and failed in their bid to become the first team to win the Cup on three occasions.

The first club to win three consecutive Football League Cup Finals

What Nottingham Forest FC failed so narrowly to achieve in 1980, Liverpool FC went on to achieve in 1983. They won the competition for the first time in 1981 by beating West Ham United FC 2–1 in the replay at Villa Park after drawing the first game 1–1, then the following year beat Tottenham Hotspur FC 3–1. During 1982 the National Dairy Council's sponsorship began in mid-season, the name of the competition changing to the Milk Cup, and although Liverpool became the first club to win the Milk Cup, they were also, that year, presented with the Football League Cup Trophy. Spurs themselves achieved two notable firsts that year when they became the first club to appear in both domestic finals in the same season and, also, became the first club to reach the League Cup Final without conceding a single goal in any of their seven matches en route. In 1983 Manchester United FC made a real fight of it before going down 2–1 in extra time, enabling Liverpool FC to achieve the hat-trick of consecutive wins, and Bob Paisley, himself, climbed the steps at Wembley to be presented with the trophy—the first manager ever to do so! In 1984 Liverpool beat Everton 1–0 in a replay, after drawing the final 0–0 and became the outright winners of the Milk Cup Trophy and the first club to win four consecutive League/Milk Cup Finals.

Bob Paisley, the first manager to be presented with the Milk Cup, pictured at the 1983 PFA awards evening, flanked by Kenny Dalglish and Ian Rush. (Allsport)

THE FOOTBALL LEAGUE CUP

Asa Hartford during his Manchester City days in March 1979. (ASP)

came on as substitute when Arsenal lost 3–1 to Swindon Town FC.

The first winners of the League/Milk Cup to be relegated in the same season

The 1985 final later proved to be one where a number of firsts were achieved. The unusual feat of Asa Hartford has already been covered, but the winners (Norwich City FC) went on to become the first winners to be relegated in the year of their triumph. (They were, incidentally, the first club other than Liverpool to win the Milk Cup.) Additionally, the losing team, Sunderland, were also relegated, thus providing the first occasion when both finalists were relegated in the same season—a first that, doubtlessly, both clubs would have been happy to avoid!

George Graham—whose substitution of George Armstrong in the 1969 League Cup Final earned him a unique first. (Allsport)

The first double-figure score in the Football League Cup competition

Although aggregate double-figure scores had been achieved on several occasions, it was not until 25 October 1983 that a single game's score went into double figures. West Ham United FC beat Bury FC 10–0 at Upton Park to progress to the third round with Cottee scoring four of his side's goals.

The first footballer to appear in three Football League Cup Finals with different clubs

George Graham who subsequently became the manager of Arsenal FC appeared in his first League Cup Final in 1963 for Aston Villa FC. In 1965 he was in the Chelsea FC team and in 1969

7 THE SCOTTISH LEAGUE CUP

During the Second World War, a new competition, 'The Scottish Southern League Cup' was instituted and, such was its success, that in the 1946/7 season the 'Scottish League Cup' replaced it. Originally this was organized on the basis of eight or nine groups of either four or five clubs each playing one another twice, with the winners going through to a two-legged quarter final and, thereafter, a straight knockout. In 1977 a straight two-legged knockout system of three rounds replaced the group part of the competition but this proved so unpopular that it was changed back to a group system in 1981. In 1984/5 it reverted to a straight knockout without replays. The semi finals have been two-legged since 1980. Celtic had an incredible run of 14 consecutive appearances in the final (every year from 1964/5–1977/8) but Rangers have registered more wins.

The first Scottish League Cup competition hat-trick

The first 14 ties were played on 21 September 1946 and a flurry of 57 goals were scored. Two players scored hat-tricks that day: Beattie of Ayr United FC scored three of his side's goals in their 5–4 defeat at Albion Rovers FC and Hamilton of Aberdeen FC went one better when scoring all four goals in Aberdeen's 4–3 home victory over Falkirk FC. Hamilton scored a total of 11 goals for Aberdeen in the first year's competition.

The first winners of the Scottish League Cup

Before a huge crowd of 82 700, Rangers FC played Aberdeen FC in the first final at Hampden Park (a re-run of the 1945/6 Southern League Cup Final). Duncanson of Rangers scored the first goal in a Scottish League Cup Final and went on to score a further one of Ranger's four goals. Aberdeen failed to score and Rangers ran out worthy winners of the first final.

The first Second Division club to win the Scottish League Cup

The 1947/8 Scottish League Cup competition began in early August 1947 and the final was played at Hampden Park on 25 October 1947, between East Fife FC (the first Second Division club to appear in the final) and First Division Falkirk FC. This ended in a 0–0 draw and was the first Scottish League Cup Final to go to a replay. A

Archie Gemmill on the ball for Derby County in 1972. (ASP)

week later, East Fife won the replay 4–1 and, in so doing became the first Second Division club to win the Cup, a feat that has yet to be repeated. East Fife's Davie Duncan became the first player to score a hat-trick in a Scottish League Cup Final notching up three of his club's goals. Aikman scored the only goal for Falkirk.

The first double-figure score in the Scottish League Cup

The first double-figure score in the Scottish League Cup was Ayr United's 11–1 Division B victory over Dumbarton on 13 August 1952 in which both Japp and Fraser scored hat-tricks (Fraser scored 5). The return match two weeks later ended 1–1!

THE SCOTTISH LEAGUE CUP

The first double-figure away score in the Scottish League Cup

When Third Lanark FC (who dropped out of the Scottish League at the end of the 1966/7 season) scored ten goals in the Cup at Alloa on 8 August 1953, they became only the second club to hit double-figures and the first to do so away from home. The return match ended 3–1 in their favour.

The first club to retain the Scottish League Cup

Dundee FC, who defeated Rangers FC in the 1951/2 final retained the Cup in the following year when they beat Kilmarnock 2–0. Their centre-forward Flavell scored both goals in the 1952/3 final and became the first player to score in consecutive Scottish League Cup Finals.

The first club to win three Scottish League Cup Finals

When East Fife FC beat Partick Thistle FC 3–2 in the 1953/4 final on 24 October 1953, they achieved the distinction of becoming the first club to win the Cup three times.

The first player to score a penalty in a Scottish League Cup Final

Motherwell's Redpath scored the first penalty in the ninth final on 23 October 1954. His first-half spot kick was small consolation as Heart of Midlothian won the match 4–2.

The first player to score an own goal in a Scottish League Cup Final

St Mirren's Mallan achieved the unenviable distinction of scoring the first own goal in a final during the 1955/6 match which Aberdeen FC won 2–1.

The first 'Old Firm' Scottish League Cup Final

Surprisingly it was not until the 12th final that the 'Old Firm' met, on 19 October 1957. Celtic, appearing in their second consecutive final, recorded their second consecutive win in the most one-sided final ever. The winning score of 7–1 was the highest that there has ever been at an 'Old Firm' final or any other major British final to date.

The first six-figure attendance at a Scottish League Cup Final

On 26 October 1963, when Rangers FC beat Morton FC 5–0 in the 1963/4 final, the attendance was 105 907. This was the first ever six-figure crowd at a final match although the 1946/7 semi final between Rangers and Hibernian (at Hampden Park) attracted a crowd of 125 154! Forrest scored four of Rangers' goals, the most ever scored by one player in a final.

The first club to score three consecutive Scottish League Cup wins.

In 1965/6 Celtic began their record-breaking run of victories by beating Rangers 2–1 and, the following year, beating them again 1–0. The hat-trick of victories came in their European Cup-winning year on 28 October 1967, when they beat Dundee 5–3. The victories continued in 1968/9, and in 1969/70 they made it five in a row by beating St Johnstone 1–0.

The first substitute to appear in a cup tie in Scotland

Archie Gemmill became the first-ever substitute in a cup tie in Scotland when, on 13 August 1966, he appeared for St Mirren FC at Clyde FC in a Scottish League Cup match. Clyde won 1–0. Later the same day, Motherwell's substitute, Gus Moffatt, became the first substitute to score in a Scottish League Cup match when he did so against Dunfermline who won the tie 2–1.

The first substitutes to appear in a Scottish League Cup Final

Celtic's Chalmers and Rangers' Wilson became the first substitutes to be used in a League Cup Final when they both came on in the 1966/7 final.

The first player to score in three consecutive Scottish League Cup Finals

Celtic's Lennox scored the only goal in the 1966/7 'Old Firm' final, then, having scored a further goal in the 1967/8 final, made it three scoring finals in a row with a hat-trick against Hibernian in the 1968/9 final.

The first club to appear in ten consecutive Scottish League Cup Finals

Celtic began a quite remarkable run of final appearances on 24 October 1964 (when they lost 2–1 to Rangers in the 1964/5 final) which reached ten in a row on 15 December 1973 (when they lost 1–0 to Dundee). They went on to make a further four appearances to achieve a phenomenal total of 14 consecutive finals.

The first substitute to score in a Scottish League Cup Final

The 1974/5 Scottish League Cup Final became the highest-scoring final ever, with a total of nine goals being scored. Celtic's Murray, who came on as substitute for Duncan, scored their sixth goal, and, in so doing, became the first substitute to score in a final.

THE SCOTTISH LEAGUE CUP

The first player to be sent off in a Scottish League Cup Final

Doug Rougvie of Aberdeen achieved the unenviable distinction of becoming the first player to be sent off in a Scottish League Cup Final, against Rangers on 31 March 1979. His departure placed further pressure on Aberdeen (who had conceded an own goal by McMaster) and they lost the game 2–1.

The first Scottish League Cup Final to be played at the ground of one of the finalists

In 1980 when the two Dundee sides reached the final of the Scottish League Cup, it was decided to stage the match at Dundee's Dens Park. Thus, Dundee became the first club ever to stage a Scottish League Cup Final at its own ground, although Dundee United's own ground was a mere stone's throw away. The 'home' advantage proved unimportant and United won 3–0.

The first Scottish League Cup Final to be played on a Sunday

The ninth 'Old Firm' Scottish League Cup Final was played on Sunday 25 March 1984, the same day that the 1984 Milk Cup Final was played at Wembley, breaking the long tradition of Saturday finals. Rangers won the match 3–2 after extra time.

(Right) Doug Rougvie in 1982, displaying his aggressive, thrusting style. (ASP)

8 THE EUROPEAN CUP

Although the European Champion Clubs Cup (to give it its full title) was not established until the 1955/6 season, the original idea for the competition had its origins back in the 1920s.

In 1927, the Mitropa Cup was started between clubs from the old Austro-Hungarian nations. It was the brain-child of the Austrian Hugo Meisl and the name was a corruption of Mittel-Europa (Central Europe). The first Mitropa Cup was played in 1927/8 between the league champions and runners-up of Austria, Hungary, Czechoslovakia and Yugoslavia. Sparta beat Rapid 7–4 (on aggregate) in the first final, confirming that their success in the early 1920s in three small international club tournaments (when they won the European Cup, an elegant statuette of a Goddess) was well deserved. Italy, Switzerland and Rumania later participated but, by 1939, only eight clubs took part in the tournament and Ujpest won the all-Hungarian final as the Second World War put an end to further competition.

In 1949, the Latin Cup began with clubs from France, Spain, Portugal and Italy competing in the first tournament. FC Torino who were, without doubt, the best team in Europe were nominated to represent Italy but, on 4 May 1949, they became the first football club to be involved in an aeroplane crash when returning to Italy after playing a friendly against Benfica. Their plane crashed into the Basilica of Superga, killing the whole team (which included most of the Italian national side) and, in the wave of emotion which followed the crash, they became the first team to be awarded the Italian League championship by consensus. Although they could only raise a makeshift team, Torino progressed to the first Latin Cup final but were beaten 3–1 by the Sporting Club Lisbon.

Gabriel Hanot, the football editor of France's *L'Équipe* periodical who had, in 1934, proposed a 'European Football League', published his blueprint for a European Cup competition after Wolverhampton Wanderers FC had stirred European interest by defeating Honved, the crack Hungarian team, 3–2 in December 1954. Reaction from individual clubs was enthusiastic but both FIFA and UEFA did not want to become involved in organizing club tournaments and a committee comprised of individual club representatives met in Paris to progress the idea further. In June 1955 UEFA bowed to the inevitable and took over the organization of the competition which began in the autumn of 1955.

(Above) The 1954/5 Championship-winning side, Chelsea, which was 'advised' against honouring its commitment to enter the first-ever European Cup. (*Book of Football Champions*)

(Left) Watched by Walley Barnes and Alex Forbes, Arsenal's Jack Kelsey punches away during a raid by the Moscow Dynamos in the early 1950s. The first appearance in Russia by a Football League club. (*Book of Football Champions*)

The first club to withdraw from the European Cup competition.

The English representatives, Chelsea, although enthusiastic supporters of the concept of a European Cup, pulled out of the first competition in 1955/6 after being 'advised' against jeopardizing their domestic arrangements by a congestion of fixtures, by the Football League. Their place was taken by Gwardia Warsaw of Poland as the draw for the first round had already been made.

The first European Cup match

The very first European Cup fixture was played on 4 September 1955 in Portugal, when Sporting Club Lisbon (the first winners of the Latin Cup) met Partizan Belgrade before 30 000 spectators. The match ended in a 3–3 draw with Partizan's Milos Milutinovic grabbing two of his side's goals. In the return match at Belgrade he scored a hat-trick to dash Lisbon's hopes with a 5–2 defeat.

The first player to score a hat-trick in the European Cup competition

Palotas of the Hungarian club Voros Lobogo (Red Banner), rather better known by their previous title of MTK, scored the first European Cup hat-trick in the second European Cup game on 7 September 1955. Their opponents in Budapest were RSC Anderlecht who went down 6–3 on the night and 10–4 on aggregate.

The first British club to participate in the European Cup

Following Chelsea's withdrawal from the 1955/6 competition, the Scottish club, Hibernian was left to fly the flag for Britain. After wins over the German side Rot-Weiss Essen and the Swedes Djurgaarden, Hibernian went out to the French club Stade de Reims in the semi final.

The first European Cup Final

Played in Paris on 13 June 1956, the first final was between Stade de Reims and Real Madrid. Reims could hardly have hoped for a better start when, early in the game, Leblond headed the first European Cup Final goal after a mistimed clearance by Lesmes, the Real Madrid keeper, and minutes later were handed another goal by Lesmes who fumbled a shot. However, with goals from Di Stefano, Marquitos and Rial (2), Real Madrid stormed back to win the first championship 4–3.

The first footballer to appear in the final of the European Cup with different clubs

Before the 1955/6 final match, the Reims player Raymond Kopa had already played for his opponents Real Madrid in their 4–2 victory over Vasco da Gama in a friendly match and it was rumoured that he would soon sign for Real. His transfer duly took place and he then went on to appear for Real in the next year's final against Fiorentina. After three seasons with Real, he and his family became so homesick that he returned to his former club.

France's Raymond Kopa, whose brilliance on the soccer field earned him the nicknames 'Little Napoleon' and the 'French Stanley Matthews', pictured en route to Real Madrid. (D C Thomson Ltd)

THE EUROPEAN CUP

The first Football League club to compete in the European Cup tournament

The first Football League club actually to compete in the European Cup, Manchester United, took the 1956/7 preliminary round by storm when, after beating Anderlecht 2–0 in the away-leg, they recorded the first double-figure score with a 10–0 win in the home-leg. Both Viollet and Taylor scored hat-tricks in the game, which was played at Maine Road (the first time that two hat-tricks had been scored by one team in a single European Cup game). They went on to reach the semi final which they lost 5–3 on aggregate to Real Madrid.

The first club to play a European Cup Final on its own ground

The 1956/7 final between Real Madrid and Fiorentina was played in front of a crowd of 124 000 (the first six-figure final crowd) at Real's Charmartin Stadium in Madrid. Di Stefano scored Real's first goal from the penalty spot and became the first European Cup Final penalty-scorer and the first person to score in consecutive finals. Real Madrid won the game 2–0 and became the first club to retain the Cup.

Disaster! Firemen and BEA staff sift through the remains of Manchester United's Elizabethan aeroplane, which crashed after taking off from Munich in 1958. (Photosource)

The first European Cup Final to go to extra-time

The 1957/8 European Cup, holding for English fans the tragedy of the Munich air crash and its annihilation of the 'Busby Babes', culminated in the third consecutive final involving Real Madrid. Facing another Italian side, AC Milan, goals for Real by Di Stefano (the first player to score in three consecutive finals) and Rial enabled them to level the scores at full-time, 2–2. Gento scored the winner in extra-time and Real Madrid became the first club to win three consecutive finals.

The first club to be beaten in two European Cup Finals

Because of the Munich air crash, Manchester United were invited by UEFA to compete in the 1958/9 European Cup, despite failing to win the League Championship, but, once again, the Football League stepped in to frustrate a member club and to slight UEFA's generosity. Ruling that only the League champions could compete, they left Wolverhampton Wanderers FC as the only English representatives and Wolves went out in the first round to Schalke 04.

Meanwhile, for the fourth consecutive time, Real Madrid reached the final and their opponents were, once again, the French club Stade de Reims. Real won 2–0 and Reims became the first club to be

runners-up twice. Di Stefano scored to become the first player to score in four consecutive finals.

The first player to score a hat-trick in a European Cup Final

The 1959/60 final was the first to be played in Britain and was staged at Hampden Park, Glasgow, between Real Madrid and Eintracht Frankfurt. A record crowd of 127 621 turned up mostly to support Real Madrid, since the Frankfurt team had eliminated Rangers in the semi finals. Di Stefano scored Real's first goal to become the first player to score in five consecutive finals and scored a further goal before his team-mate, Ferenc Puskas, scored four goals to achieve the first European Cup Final hat-trick. Fittingly, Di Stefano scored another goal to gain his own hat-trick and to crown a marvellous display by Real Madrid with the first brace of hat-tricks in a final.

The first club to eliminate Real Madrid from the European Cup

Real Madrid's phenomenal run in the European Cup ended in the 1960/61 competition at the hands of their Spanish rivals Barcelona. After drawing the home leg 2–2 before a crowd of 100 000, Real Madrid lost the away leg in Barcelona 2–1. The crowd of 112 000 ensured that it was the first double six-figure attendance in the European Cup. Benfica beat Barcelona 3–2 in the final to become the first club, other than Real Madrid, to win the European Cup.

The first city to provide the finalists for Europe's top two competitions in the same year

In the 1961/2 season Real Madrid met Benfica in the European Cup Final (the first final they were to lose) whilst their neighbours, Atletico Madrid, met and defeated Fiorentina of Italy in the European Cup-Winners Cup Final.

The first British player to participate in the European Cup with three different clubs

Gordon Smith played for Hibernian FC in 1955/6, for Heart of Midlothian FC in 1960/61 and then for Dundee FC in 1962/3.

The first European Cup Final to be played at Wembley

The 1962/3 final at Wembley between Benfica, the holders and AC Milan attracted a disappointingly small crowd of only 45 000. Despite taking an early lead through Eusebio, Benfica lost 2–1 and AC Milan became the first Italian club to win the cup. In 1968 AC Milan won the European Cup-Winners Cup and became the first club to have won both trophies.

The first club to win the European Cup without being beaten in any round

In 1963/4 Inter-Milan of Italy beat Real Madrid 3–1 in the final, having previously played eight matches in the competition without losing one. Altogether, they won six and drew three games to become the first club to take the trophy without loss. Milan became the first city to have two of its clubs win the European Cup, Inter's neighbours AC Milan having won the Cup the year before.

The first British club to participate in the three major European competitions

Manchester United FC became the first British club to participate in all three competitions when they took part in the Fairs Cup (UEFA Cup) in 1964/5 having already competed in the 1963/4 European Cup-Winners Cup and the 1956/7 European Cup.

The first city to host the European Cup twice

Brussels in Belgium first hosted the 1957/8 final in which Real Madrid beat AC Milan 3–2 and, in 1965/6, became the first country to host the final twice when the winners were, once again, Real Madrid (who beat Partizan Belgrade 2–1). In 1985, when Brussels hosted the final for the fourth time, the infamous crowd violence, which resulted in the loss of 38 lives, erupted. The resulting ban on English clubs was the first blanket exclusion of a footballing nation because of the behaviour of its supporters.

The first British club to win the European Cup

Jock Stein's all-conquering Celtic FC swept everything before them in the 1966/7 season by winning all three of the Scottish domestic competitions and then they went on to become the first British club to appear in a European Cup Final. Their opponents, Inter-Milan, had won two of the previous three finals but Celtic were not impressed and they powered back from 1–0 down to win the Cup with Tommy Gemmell becoming the first British final scorer. This was the first occasion that a non-Latin country had won the Cup and proved to be the watershed for the northern clubs who won 15 of the next 16 finals.

Glasgow, represented by Rangers in the Cup-Winners Cup Final and Celtic in the European Cup Final, became the first British city to provide two major European competitions' finalists in the same year.

The first English club to win the European Cup

The 1967/8 final was staged at Wembley between

Trevor Francis scores the only goal of the 1979 European Cup Final to give Nottingham Forest victory over Malmo. (Colorsport)

the first English club to reach the final, Manchester United FC, and Benfica. Wembley became the first stadium to be used as a final venue three times and, before a packed house, Manchester United FC powered to a 4–1 extra-time win, to become the first English club to take the Cup. After the Munich tragedy of ten years earlier, it was fitting that the 'Red Devils' should become the first English winners of the Cup and with two of the aircrash survivors playing (Foulkes and Charlton) it proved a very emotional occasion.

The first British city to be represented by two clubs in the same European Cup competition

In the 1968/9 competition both Manchester United, the holders and Manchester City, the League champions represented England. This was the first time that two English clubs had participated in the same year and the first time that two clubs from the same city had participated. City went out in the first round to Fenerbahce and United lost to AC Milan in the semi finals.

The first club to have appeared in the final of all three major European competitions

Barcelona of Spain first appeared in the Fairs Cup Final (UEFA Cup) in 1958, in the European Cup Final in 1961 and, in 1969, became the first club to have appeared in all three major finals when they lost 3–2 to Slovan Bratislava of Czechoslovakia in the European Cup-Winners Cup Final.

The first player to gain winners' medals in the European Cup and the European Cup-Winner's Cup with different clubs

The Swedish player, Kurre Hamrin, won a European Cup-Winners Cup medal with Fiorentina in 1961 and, after moving to AC Milan, went on to win a European Cup medal in 1969.

The first player to be the leading scorer in two consecutive European Cup competitions

Bayern Munich's Müller was top scorer in the 1972/3 competition with 12 goals from only six matches (Bayern Munich only reached the quarter finals) and, the following year, made it two in a row when he was again top scorer with nine goals.

THE EUROPEAN CUP

The first European Cup Final to be replayed

The 1973/4 final at Brussels between Bayern Munich and Atletico Madrid was tied 1–1 with a goal by Bayern Munich in the last minute of extra-time. The replay two days later (also in Brussels) ended in a clear-cut 4–0 victory for Bayern Munich.

The first British club to win the European Cup twice

Liverpool became the second English club to win the European Cup (Leeds United FC had lost the 1974/5 final to Bayern Munich to become the first British club to lose in a European Cup final) when they beat Borussia Moenchengladbach 3–1 in the 1976/7 final and began a six year English domination of the event. The following year they became the first British club to retain the Cup when they beat FC Bruges 1–0 at Wembley.

The first country to have three of its clubs win the European Cup

In 1978/9 Nottingham Forest FC won the European Cup by beating Malmö FF 1–0 and became the third different English club to win the competition. The strength-in-depth that is the hallmark of the English League was further demonstrated in 1981/2, when a fourth English club, Aston Villa FC, took the championship.

The first meeting between two English clubs in the European Cup

In the first round of the 1978/9 competition, Liverpool FC, the holders, met Nottingham Forest FC, the League champions, in the first 'all-English' tie. Forest won 2–0 on aggregate.

The first British players to appear in the final of the European Cup with different clubs

In the 1979/80 final between Nottingham Forest FC and SV Hamburg, two players, Frank Gray of Nottingham Forest (who had previously appeared for Leeds United FC in the 1974/5 final) and Kevin Keegan of SV Hamburg (who had been in the victorious 1976/7 Liverpool FC team) achieved jointly the distinction of becoming the first British players to appear for different clubs in a European Cup Final.

The first crowd disaster at a European Cup Final

The 1984/5 final between Juventus of Italy and Liverpool FC proved to be the most horrific and distasteful experience that European soccer has ever had. A combination of poor policing, and violent melees between rival groups of 'supporters', culminated in 38 deaths when Italian fans panicked in the face of an onslaught from British spectators. The match itself was played despite the tragedy although both sides, sickened by the carnage, appeared to have no heart for the game.

Immediate bans on all English clubs by UEFA and FIFA were an inevitable, if somewhat hasty, reaction to the disaster. Only time will tell if English clubs are ever to be fully rehabilitated back into European competition, and the appalling behaviour of many of the Juventus fans does not auger well for the future.

Liverpool's retention of the European Cup in 1978 being celebrated at Wembley. (Photosource)

9 THE FAIRS CUP & UEFA CUP

Originally known by the unwieldly title of 'The International Inter-City Industrial Fairs Cup' this tournament can well claim to be the first of the major European competitions having commenced in 1955. Inter-city matches had been popular on the Continent since the turn of the century and Ernst B Thommen, the Swiss Vice-President of FIFA, had proposed the tournament in 1950 after he had arranged a successful match between Basle (his home city) and Belgrade. Without a European football union (UEFA was not created until 1954), progress was difficult and it was not until June 1954 that a Fairs Cup committee was set up. In April 1955, representatives of 12 cities in ten countries met to set the framework of the tournament and representative city sides initially competed against one another, ostensibly arranging fixtures to coincide with industrial trade fairs, where feasible.

The first tournament dragged on over three years and the cup almost died at birth due to the prolonged timing, plus a combination of composite and club teams and the unattractiveness of a two-legged final. However, continue it did, and, by the 1960/1 season, the tournament had become an annual event with 16 entrants, mainly club teams, competing. Within four years the entry had risen to a massive 48 teams and the competition was well and truly established. The name was changed, first to 'The Inter-Cities Fairs Cup', then 'The European Fairs Cup', then 'The Fairs Cup' (for ease of reference we will refer to the Fairs Cup for all entries before 1971/2).

For the 1971/2 season the competition was redesignated 'The UEFA Cup' and a new trophy was provided by UEFA although the competition itself continued in precisely the same format as before.

The first ever European competition tie

The very first game in the International Inter-City Industrial Fairs Cup competition (and also the first European competition proper) was appropriately staged at the St Jacob's stadium in Basle, Switzerland. As the competition was the brainchild of Ernst Thommen of Basle it was a fitting start to the tournament, and even the Lord Mayor of London (somewhat unenthusiastically) was present on 4 June 1955 to see London beat Basle 5–0.

The first player to score a goal in the competition was Holton (for London) who went on to score the first hat-trick of the competition in the same game.

The first all-floodlit match at Wembley

With 11 London League clubs to consider, Joe Mears (the selector) had immense difficulty in fielding a settled team and the problems of arranging training and practices in such a complicated situation soon began to tell.

Despite the difficulties of managing a 'composite' team, London's success continued on 26 October 1955 when they beat Frankfurt 3–2 in their second Fairs Cup tie in the first all-floodlit match to be staged at Wembley.

The first Fairs Cup Final

The first leg of the first Fairs Cup Final was played at Stamford Bridge, London on 5 March 1958, two years and nine months after the tournament began. The composite London team (the first British team to reach a European final) met CF Barcelona (who were extremely fortunate to beat Birmingham City FC in the semi-final play-off) and the game ended 2–2. Jimmy Greaves scored the first goal for London but by half-time Barcelona had taken a 2–1 lead. Jimmy Langley scored the first penalty goal to level the score at 2–2 but, in the second leg of the final at Gran Estadio, the much weakened London team was thrashed 6–0 and Bracelona became the first winners of the trophy 8–2 on aggregate.

The first British club to reach the final of a major European competition

Although the representative London side had reached the first Fairs Cup Final in 1958, the first British club side to do so were Birmingham City FC who met the holders Barcelona in the second final in 1960. After drawing 0–0 at Birmingham, Barcelona won the second leg in Barcelona 4–1 to become the first club to retain the Fairs Cup. Martinez who had scored in both legs of the first final scored his club's first goal to become the first player to score in consecutive finals.

Birmingham City FC appeared in and lost the next Fairs Cup Final in 1961 to AS Roma to become the first team to lose consecutive finals. Their full back Farmer conceded the first final own goal in the second leg in Rome.

The first double-figure score in the Fairs Cup competition

In the first round of the 1961/2 competition, MTK Budapest (who went on to lose 10–3 on aggregate to Valencia in the semi finals) thrashed Strasbourg 10–2 in Budapest after winning the first leg 3–1.

John Wark during his Ipswich Town days, with whom he scored a record-breaking 14 goals in the 1980/1 UEFA Cup competition. These goals helped Ipswich to win this competition beating AZ'67 of Amsterdam in the final. (ASP)

The first occasion that two clubs from the same country contested the final of a major European competition

The two Spanish clubs Barcelona and Valencia became the first clubs from the same country to contest a European final when they met in the Fairs

THE FAIRS CUP & UEFA CUP

Cup in 1961/2. Valencia won the first leg at home 6–2 and their striker Guillot scored the first Fairs Cup Final hat-trick. The second leg ended in a 1–1 draw and Valencia took the Cup 7–3 on aggregate. Barcelona themselves became the first team to appear in three Fairs Cup Finals and in 1970/1 they were invited to play the final winners of the trophy (before the UEFA Cup commenced) Leeds United FC, for the privilege of retaining the original Cup. They won and the Cup became permanently theirs.

The first club to appear in three consecutive Fairs Cup Finals

Having won the trophy in 1961/2, Valencia met Dynamo Zagreb in the 1962/3 final and easily retained the trophy 4–1 on aggregate, winning both legs. In 1963/4, in the first single-legged final, they chalked up the first hat-trick of consecutive appearances in Fairs Cup Finals against another Spanish club, Real Zaragoza, but in losing 2–1 were unable to retain the trophy.

The first Eastern European club to win a major European competition

Dynamo Zagreb the beaten finalists in the 1962/3 Fairs Cup Final were the first Eastern European club to reach a European final but, in 1964/5, in the same competition, the Hungarian club Ferencvaros, beat the ultra-defensive Juventus team 1–0 to become the first Eastern European winners of a European trophy.

The first club to win a Fairs Cup tie on the toss of a coin

Racing Strasbourg, after playing three drawn third-round matches against Barcelona in the 1964/5 Fairs Cup competition, went through to the quarter finals on the toss of a coin.

The first British club to win the Fairs Cup

After losing 2–0 on aggregate to Dynamo Zagreb in the 1966/7 final, Leeds United FC became the first British club to win the competition when they beat Ferencvaros 1–0 on aggregate the following year. This victory marked a six-year domination of the tournament by English clubs and was doubly unique in that Leeds United FC also became the first British club to win a European trophy without suffering a single defeat (won 7, drew 4).

The first club to win a Fairs Cup tie on the 'away goals' rule

In the 1966/7 competition, the eventual winners, Dynamo Zagreb, having drawn 4–4 on aggregate with Dunfermline Athletic FC became the first club to proceed to the next round by virtue of scoring more away goals. This was a decided improvement on the previous 'toss-of-a-coin' method which was still used in the event of a continued tie without away goal differences.

The first British club to win a European trophy on more than one occasion

Leeds United FC, the winners of the Fairs Cup in 1967/8, won the trophy for a second time in 1970/1 (the last time that the competition was called 'the Fairs Cup') to become the first English (and British) club to win a European trophy for the second time. Their victory in 1970/1 over the Italian club, Juventus, was achieved by virtue of the fact that Leeds United FC had scored more goals in the away-leg of the competition than their opponents. Thus, despite a 3–3 final scoreline, Leeds United FC became the first team to win a European trophy on the 'away-goals' rule.

The first club to be eliminated from a European competition on penalty kicks

Spartak Trnava eliminated Olympic Marseilles by scoring more penalties in the 'penalty shoot out' in the first round of the 1970/1 'Fairs Cup' competition. Previously, ties which were level had been decided on the toss of a coin.

The first European final to be contested by two English clubs

The first final of the UEFA Cup competition in 1971/2 was between Wolverhampton Wanderers FC and Tottenham Hotspur FC. Spurs took the first leg at Molyneux 2–1 and drew the second leg at White Hart Lane 1–1 to win the title.

The first European final where the two clubs had met in a previous final

'Repeat' finals are a rare event and, in the context of European competitions which are open to a potentially huge number of different clubs, it was not until 1976/7 that two teams met one another a second time. In 1972/3 Liverpool FC beat Borussia Moenchengladbach in the final of the UEFA Cup and in 1976/7 the two clubs met again in the final of the European Cup—Liverpool FC winning that trophy also. Ironically, the following year Liverpool FC's opponents in the European Cup Final were FC Bruges, a team which they had met in the final of the 1975/6 UEFA Cup! Liverpool FC won all four finals.

The first player to score a hat-trick of penalties in a European competition

In the 1980/1 UEFA Cup competition, Ipswich Town's John Wark scored a record-breaking 14 goals including four in his first game against Aris Salonika of Greece. This match was unique insofar as three of Wark's four goals were from the penalty spot. This was the first penalty hat-trick to be scored in a European competition. Ipswich Town FC went on to win the trophy that year.

10 THE EUROPEAN CUP-WINNERS CUP

The European Cup-Winners Cup was the last of the three European trophies to be established. Intended to be for national cup winners, it suffered initially because of the basic lack of proper knockout cup competitions in Europe. A whole range of different rules applied to the individual cup competitions in Europe with, for instance, Italian games being midweek fixtures, French games being played on neutral grounds, Portuguese games on a home-and-away basis and a number of countries without a cup competition.

Regardless of the problems of qualification and uniformity, the idea of a European Cup-Winner's Cup competition was first raised in 1958 but, as only six countries were then interested in the project, an Executive Committee meeting on 5 March 1959 decided to hold the matter in abeyance. In 1960, with the Mitropa Cup out of action, the number of possible entries rose to ten and it was decided to establish the European Cup-Winners Cup for the 1960/1 season. The Mitropa Cup committee was entrusted with the task of organizing the tournament. Arranged on a similar basis to the European Cup with a single match final (other than the first year), the competition took a severe dip in popularity in the mid-1970s but, aided by television coverage, has pulled back to become the most important European club competition other than the European Cup.

The first European Cup-Winners Cup match

ASK Vorwarts of Berlin beat the Czechoslovakian side Red Star Brnö 2–1 in the first match played in Berlin on 1 August 1960 but lost 2–0 in the away-leg ten days later.

The first British club to play in the European Cup-Winners Cup competition

Rangers FC, feeling that they had a score to settle with European clubs (after losing 12–4 on aggregate to Eintracht Frankfurt in the previous year's European Cup competition), met Ferencvaros of Hungary in the qualifying round of the first competition. Winning 5–4 on aggregate, they proceeded to the quarter finals against Borussia Moenchengladbach and after winning 3–0 in Germany, took Borussia apart at Ibrox Park winning the game 8–0 and the tie 11–0. Brand scored the first European Cup-Winners Cup hat-trick in his side's rout of the West German cup-holders.

The first English club to play in the European Cup-Winners Cup competition

Wolverhampton Wanderers FC were England's representatives in the first competition and were drawn against FK Austria in the first game. Losing the first leg in Vienna 2–0, Wolves stormed back at Molineux with the first English goal coming from Kirkham in the very first minute. They comfortably won the match 5–0 and the tie 5–2 on aggregate.

The first British clubs to play one another in the European Cup-Winners Cup competition

Rangers FC were drawn against Wolverhampton Wanderers FC in the semi finals of the 1960/1 competition and, in front of a crowd of 80 000 won the home leg 2–0. Taking over 10 000 of their fans with them, Rangers then turned the second game at Molineux into another 'home' fixture. For once, the famous 'Molineux roar' was overwhelmed and Rangers won through to the first final with a 1–1 draw (winning 3–1 on aggregate).

The first winners of the European Cup-Winners Cup

The first final of the European Cup-Winners Cup was played over two legs and Rangers, representing Britain, were, needless to say, the first British finalists. Their opponents, the Italian club, Fiorentina, won both legs with Milani scoring the first European Cup-Winners Cup Final goal in Glasgow on 17 May 1961. The scores were 2–0 in Glasgow and 2–1 in Florence. Milani scored in the second tie to become the first (and only) player to score in both legs of a European Cup-Winners Cup final.

The first English club to participate in the European Cup-Winners Cup competition as beaten finalists

The 1960/1 season was Tottenham Hotspur's double-winning year and, as they qualified to represent England in the European Cup they were unable to do so additionally in the European Cup-

THE EUROPEAN CUP-WINNERS CUP

Winners Cup. Leicester City FC, who were the beaten FA Cup finalists, took their place but were unable to progress beyond the second round when they went out to Atletico Madrid.

The first European Cup-Winners Cup Final to go to a replay

In 1961/2 UEFA's Executive Committee took over the organization of the European Cup-Winners Cup and the number of entries rocketed to twenty three. The final, between the holders Fiorentina (the first club to play in two consecutive finals) and Atletico Madrid, was the first to be played as a single match and was staged at Hampden Park, Glasgow before a meagre crowd of 27 389. The scores were level 1–1 after extra time and the first replay had to be arranged. This was not scheduled until 5 September 1962 and was the first European final to be held over to the following season. Atletico Madrid won the replay 3–0 in Stuttgart.

The first British club to win a European trophy

Unable to play in the 1961/2 European Cup-Winners Cup because they were participating in the European Cup, Tottenham Hotspur FC won the 1961/2 FA Cup and represented England in the 1962/3 competition. Disposing of Rangers FC, Slovan Bratislava and OFK Belgrade, they went on to become the first English club to reach the final, facing the holders Atletico Madrid. Goals by Greaves (2), White and Dyson (2) gave them a deserved 5–1 victory and they became the first British club to win a European trophy. Collar of Atletico Madrid scored their goal from the penalty spot to become the first penalty goalscorer in a European Cup-Winners Cup Final.

The first preliminary round tie to go to a replay in the European Cup-Winners Cup

Bangor City, the non-League winners of the Welsh Cup, beat AC Napoli (the Italian Cup-winners) 2–0 in Wales who went on to level the tie in Naples with a 3–1 scoreline. The replay was staged at Arsenal's Highbury stadium and the Italians won with a lucky goal five minutes from time.

The first meeting between English clubs in a major European competition

In the second round of the 1963/4 European Cup-winners Cup competition, Tottenham Hotspur FC (the holders) were drawn against Manchester United FC. After taking a 2–0 lead at White Hart Lane, Spurs, playing without Mackay who had broken a leg, or Blanchflower who had retired at the end of the previous season, struggled on the return match at Old Trafford and, thanks to a brilliant Charlton performance, went down 4–1 (4–3 on aggregate).

The first non-League club to win a European Cup-Winners Cup tie

Bangor City's staggering display in the 1962/3 competition when they only went out to Napoli after a replay was, if anything, bettered by the Welsh representatives in the 1963/4 competition. Borough United, opponents of Bangor City Reserves in the Northern Welsh League, beat Sliema Wanderers 2–0 on aggregate to become the first non-League team to win a tie. They lost to (but were by no means disgraced by) Slovan Bratislava in the next round.

The first double-figure score in a European Cup-Winners Cup competition match

In the 1963/4 competition Sporting Lisbon (the eventual winners) beat Neil Franklin's Cypriot team, Apoel Nicosia 16–1 in the home leg of their first-round tie. The Lisbon player Mascarenhas scored the first double hat-trick of the competition and, despite several subsequent high-scoring games, the 16–1 scoreline remains the highest yet achieved.

The first European Cup-Winners Cup tie to be decided on the toss of a coin

The 1963/4 preliminary-round tie between ASK Linz and Dynamo Zagreb was drawn 2–2 at the end of a replay and Dynamo Zagreb proceeded to the next round on the toss of a coin. Clearly this was an unacceptable method of deciding a tie and in 1965/6, the away-goals rule was introduced.

The first player to concede an own goal in a European Cup-Winners Cup Final

In the 1963/4 final which was played at Brussels between Sporting Lisbon and MTK Budapest, a paltry crowd of only 9000 were present to see the match end in a 3–3 draw. The MTK player Dansky conceded the first own goal in a final and Sporting Lisbon went on to win the replay 1–0.

The first European Cup-Winners Cup Final to be played at Wembley

A full house of 97 974 (usually recorded as 100 000) watched the 1964/5 European Cup-Winners Cup Final between West Ham United FC and TSV Munich 1860—quite a contrast to the previous season! This first Wembley final ended in a 2–0 victory for the 'Hammers' with Sealey scoring both goals.

The first English club to lose a European Cup-Winners Cup Final

In 1965/6 Borussia Dortmund defeated Liverpool 2–1 in the final, thanks to a Yeats own goal, and Liverpool became the first English club to lose in a European Cup-Winners Cup Final.

THE EUROPEAN CUP-WINNERS CUP

The first 'Eastern European' club to win the European Cup-Winners Cup

Slovan Bratislava of Czechoslovakia who defeated the Spanish club Barcelona 3–2 in the 1968/9 final were the surprise winners of the Cup and the first Communist country to be victorious. It is indeed ironical that in the year that the early stages of the competition were redrawn to keep Western and Eastern European countries apart (following Russia's invasion of Czechoslovakia) a Czechoslovakian team should have won the trophy!

The first Scottish club to win the European Cup-Winners Cup

In 1971/2 it was a case of 'third time lucky' for Rangers FC who had lost in 1960/1 and 1966/7. Their opponents were the Russian club Dynamo Moscow and the game in Barcelona ended in a 3–2 victory for Rangers. This game was marred by an orgy of violence indulged in by the hordes of drunken Scottish supporters which left one person dead and hundreds of others injured and arrested.

The first European Cup-Winners Cup holders to be banned from defending their title

Following the disgraceful behaviour of their fans at the 1971/2 final, Rangers FC were banned from competing in the 1972/3 competition. The reputation of the competition took a further blow, when the 1972/3 final referee, Michas, was suspended by his own association and UEFA, following an absolutely disgracefully biased piece of refereeing. Michas's contacts with the Italians were well known before the match and his punishment after the event was little consolation for Leeds United FC who lost 1–0 to AC Milan thanks to blatantly unfair decisions by the referee.

The first club to appear in three consecutive European Cup-Winners Cup Finals

Anderlecht appeared in their first final in 1975/6 when their opponents (in Brussels) were the English club West Ham United who had, themselves, won the Cup in 1964/5. They won this game 4–2 and defended the trophy unsuccessfully in the following year's final against SV Hamburg in Amsterdam, going down 2–0. In 1977/8 Anderlecht made it three finals in a row when they won back the trophy with a 4–0 victory over FK Austria WAC to become the first club to win the trophy twice.

The first club to win the European Cup-Winners Cup on penalties

The first three finals which were tied after extra-time all went to replays but the competition rules were changed in the late seventies to provide for a penalty 'shoot-out'. The Spanish club, Valencia, were matched against Arsenal FC and the score after extra-time was tied at 0–0. Graham Rix missed a penalty and Valencia took the cup 5–4 on penalties. Arsenal, who did not lose a single game en route to the final, thus became the first club to be undefeated whilst failing to win the trophy.

The first British club to participate in 20 European competitions

Rangers FC of Glasgow, having already appeared in nine European Cup, seven European Cup-Winners Cup and three UEFA Cup competitions, entered their 20th competition in 1979/80 when they went out in the second round of the European Cup-Winners Cup to the eventual winners Valencia.

The first British club to play a European match behind closed doors

In the 1980/1 European Cup-Winners Cup competition, West Ham United FC's supporters were involved in a violent riot at Castille in Spain and UEFA decided to ban all spectators from the return tie at Upton Park. Despite the lack of home support 'the Hammers' won the second leg 5–1 to take the tie 6–4 on aggregate.

The first British club to win the European Cup-Winners and their national cup in the same season

Aberdeen FC who took the 1982/3 Cup-Winners Cup by beating Real Madrid 2–1, went on to win the Scottish FA Cup ten days later (beating Rangers FC 1–0) to become the first British club to achieve this 'double'.

International soccer matches were first staged in the 1870s in Britain and, for the first 30 years, were confined to the Home Countries. The British Home International competition began in 1883/4, some 46 years before the World Cup, and a number of the 'firsts', which are recorded in this section, relate to that competition.

The South American championship began as early as 1916 and is now the longest-running international championship—the British Home International series having been discontinued.

Soccer was unofficially introduced into the Olympics for the first time in Paris in 1900, when an exhibition match between a Great Britain side (represented by Upton Park) and a French side, ended 4–0 to Great Britain. The 1908 Olympics saw the game accepted as an official Olympic sport.

Many internationals are, and have been, friendlies but overseas tours, which were intended to cement harmonious relations between nations, have often, in the past, succeeded in fostering the reverse—such can be the effect of soccer competition!

The first international match

On 5 March 1870, the English FA organized a game between Englishmen and Scotsmen at Kennington Oval which, theoretically, was the first international match. Looking objectively, however, since the FA selected both sides, and since many of the Scots were chosen because of their 'Scottish' names or family connections, this could not be regarded as a proper International. The final score was 1–1, and a further four unofficial 'internationals' of this type were staged at Kennington Oval in 1870 and 1871.

The first official international match

Not surprisingly between Scotland and England, the first ever international was played at the West of Scotland cricket ground at Partick on 30 November 1872. The Scottish team was selected by the captain of Queens Park FC, Robert Gardner, who chose eight current Queens Park players plus the brothers James and Robert Smith (two former Queens Park players who had moved to London) and W Ker, a Granville player. The Smith brothers became the first brothers to play together in a full international and they and their Scottish team-mates faced a talented English team who had travelled north 'to teach the Scots a thing or two about the game'.

Playing before a crowd of 4000 spectators the Scots proved to be perfectly capable opponents and the English were surprised to be held to a 0–0 draw (the next such result between the two countries was 98 years later in 1970!).

The first player to score a goal in an international match

In the second match between Scotland and England, played at Kennington Oval on 8 March 1873, the English captain Kenyon-Slaney scored the first international goal and then added another in his side's 4–2 defeat of the Scots.

The first player to represent more than one country in an official international

JH Edwards of Shropshire Wanderers played for England against Scotland on 3 March 1874 in the third full international between the countries (which the Scots classify as their first 'all-tartan' win—2–1) then went on to play for Wales against Scotland on 25 March 1876. This match was the first international not to involve England and the Scots won 4–0.

The first brothers to play in both an international side and an FA Cup-winning side

Frederick and Hubert Heron who played for England against Scotland on 4 March 1876 (England lost 3–0) appeared two weeks later for the Wanderers side which beat Old Etonians 3–0 in the FA Cup Final replay.

The first player to score a hat-trick in an official international match

The Vale of Leven player J McDougall scored the first international hat-trick on 2 March 1878 at Hampden Park, Glasgow, when Scotland achieved their heaviest win over England with a 7–2 scoreline.

The first player to represent England at both rugby and soccer

Reginald Halsey Birkett (appropriately a goalkeeper) represented England at soccer on 5 April 1879 (against Scotland) and, additionally, represented his country on the rugby field. Similarly, the Honourable Alfred Lyttleton, who represented England against Scotland on 3 March 1877 (scoring England's goal in a 3–1 defeat) went on to represent his country at cricket against Australia in 1880, to become the first player to do so in both sports.

The first country to score double figures in a full international match.

Ireland's first international was against England and was played on 18 February 1882 at Belfast. Although no record of the attendance remains available, the gate receipts were a princely

£12.19s.7d (£12.98). The Irish were thrashed 13–0 with the first-ever English hat-trick falling to Vaughton (who, in fact, scored 5) and a further hat-trick falling to A Brown (who scored 4). This score still ranks as the highest by an English team at full international level although England beat Australia 17–0 in a 'B' international at Sydney on 30 June 1951.

The first winners of the British Home International competition

The first British Home International series was staged in 1883/4 and was won by Scotland with three wins from the three games. England came second by registering wins over Ireland (8–1) and Wales (4–0).

The first-ever all-ticket soccer match

The first clash in the Home International competition (15 March 1884) between Scotland and England at the first Cathkin Park was restricted to ticket-holders only. This was the very first time that such a restriction had been applied and a sizeable crowd saw Scotland win the game 1–0.

The first professional player to represent his country

In 1885, the Football Association legalized professional soccer, despite protests that such a move would 'place more power in the hands of betting men and would encourage gambling'. Nineteen-year-old James Forrest of Blackburn Rovers is credited with being the first professional to play for his country, although, since his first international appearance against Wales on 17 March 1884 was some time before the legalization of professionalism, one must assume that his £1 match fee was an unofficial payment.

The first international match when all players received payment

At the Scotland v England international, played at the second Hampden Park, Glasgow on 27 March 1886, all the players were paid a fee of ten shillings (50 pence) for their efforts. Commonly described as 'the first professional international match', the game ended in 1–1 draw.

The first man to use the word soccer to describe association football

Charles Wreford-Brown, who made his international debut for England against Ireland on 2 March 1889 is reputed to have been the inventor of the word 'soccer'. When asked one day if he intended to play 'rugger' that afternoon he replied, distorting the word 'association', 'No, I am going to play soccer'.

The first ever substitute

The Rhostyllen goalkeeper A Pugh is reputed to have become the first substitute when, during the Wales v Scotland match on 15 April 1889, he replaced SG Gillam in the Welsh goal. Since the final scoreline was 0–0 he succeeded in doing what no previous Welsh goalkeeper had achieved—keeping a clean sheet.

The first international to be played outside the two competing countries

The 1890 British Home International match between Ireland and Wales was played in England, at Shrewsbury on 8 February. Wales won the game 5–2.

The first country to play two full internationals on the same day

On 15 March 1890, England played both their Wales and Ireland fixtures (in the British Home Championship) on the same day. In effect, two completely different English sides competed that day, one in Wrexham and the other in Belfast! Since Wales were the stronger opposition, it is generally assumed that the 'first team' played them and, although they won 3–1, as the 'other team' won 9–1 in Ireland, the strength in depth that the English enjoyed was apparent.

The first mass football disaster

On 5 April 1902 the British Home International match between Scotland and England took place at Ibrox Park, Glasgow before a huge crowd. With heavy rain falling, more spectators surged into the ground, spilling onto the grass at the side of the pitch and pushing to the top of the Western Terrace for an improved view. Disaster struck when a 70 ft by 12 ft (21 m by 3.6 m) length of terracing collapsed, hurling hundreds of people to the ground. Twenty-five people lost their lives and hundreds of others were injured but, incredibly, after only 20 minutes the game was restarted and ended in a 1–1 draw. The game did not count for the British Home International competition and a replay was played at Birmingham on 3 May 1902. The match ended 2–2 and Scotland won the championship.

The first international match to be played outside Britain

In the first full international between two non-British nations, Austria and Hungary (then both member states of the Austro-Hungarian Empire) played one another in Vienna in 1902. Austria won the game 5–0.

The first international match to be played in South America

In South America, the neighbouring countries of

INTERNATIONALS

Argentina and Uruguay played the first full international in 1905. This match ended 1–1 and was the forerunner of many matches including Olympic finals and the first World Cup Final.

The first international match between England and a non-British country

England went on their first overseas tour in June 1908 and, in only one week, played no fewer than four internationals. The first match was against Austria on 6 June (in Vienna) and the superiority of the English was emphasized with a 6–1 win. Two days later a rematch ended in an 11–1 win for England and with wins over Hungary (7–0) and Bohemia (4–0), England became the first touring side to be undefeated.

The first 'official' Olympic soccer series

Although soccer had featured in the 1900, 1904 and 1906 Olympics when individual club sides had represented their countries, it was not until the 1908 games in London, that the sport became an official event. France entered two teams, both of which were soundly thrashed by Denmark, the 'B' team losing 17–1. Sophus Nielsen of Denmark scored ten goals in this game—a feat, unbelievably repeated by Germany's Gottfried Fuchs in the 1912 Olympics!

The first country to win officially the Olympic soccer title

The Great Britain team beat Denmark (the unofficial winners in 1906) 2–0 in the first official final and in the next Games, in 1912, met and beat them again (this time 4–2).

The first winners of the South American championship

The first competition was contested in Buenos Aires in 1916 between Argentina, Brazil, Chile and Uruguay who, during the first series, formed the Confederacíon Sudamericana de Futbol. This body still runs the tournament today and although the competition was an annual event for most of the first ten years, it is now staged four-yearly. As such there was no 'final match' in the competition during the first series and Uruguay became the first winners of the 'Copa America' trophy with five points from their three games.

The first international team to 'walk off' in an Olympic Final

The 1920 Olympic Final in Antwerp saw Belgium, the home team, matched against a Czechoslovakian side which had soundly thrashed all its opponents en route. The home side took a 2–0 lead and, because of a series of controversial decisions against them, the Czechs walked off in protest and threw the tournament into chaos. With Czechoslovakia disqualified, the French (who had been defeated by the Czechs in the semi finals) were invited to play-off for second place but refused and Spain eventually became runners-up.

The first British club to provide both team captains in a full international match

On 16 February 1924 (during the Home International match between Wales and Scotland at Ninian Park, Cardiff) Cardiff City FC provided both the captain of Wales, Fred Keenor, and the captain of Scotland, Jimmy Blair. Wales won the game 2–0.

The first international to be played at Wembley

In the first-ever soccer match to be played at Wembley, on 12 April 1924, England met Scotland in the Home International series. Walker scored the first goal by an Englishman at Wembley and the game ended 1–1.

The first player to score a hat-trick at Wembley

Alex Jackson of Huddersfield Town FC scored the very first Wembley hat-trick whilst playing for Scotland against England on 31 March 1928. A member of the smallest forward line to appear for Scotland, he shocked the 81 000 crowd with his well-taken goals and helped the predominantly 'Anglo-Scottish' team to a 5–1 victory, which left England pointless at the bottom of the Home International table for the first time.

The first South American country to win the Olympic title

In 1924, Uruguay met Switzerland in the Olympic Final in Paris and, in so doing, became the first non-European team to reach the final stages. The match was played before a capacity crowd of 60 000 and Uruguay won 3–1.

In 1928, the first Olympic final match to be drawn was played between the holders Uruguay and their South American neighbours Argentina, in Amsterdam. The replay ended with Uruguay confirming its place in the forefront of world soccer with a 2–1 victory.

The first player to score directly from a corner in a full international match

In 1924, at a meeting of the International Board, the rules of soccer were altered to allow goals to be scored directly from corners. Alex Cheyne of Aberdeen FC scored the first international goal directly from a corner in the 88th minute of Scotland's Home International match against England at Hampden Park on 13 April 1929.

INTERNATIONALS

Scotland won the game 1–0 and in a Scottish FA Cup tie between Aberdeen FC and Nithsdale Wanderers FC on 1 February 1930, Cheyne went on to become the first player to score two goals directly from corners in one game!

The first foreign team to defeat England in a full international

England's early record against overseas sides was truly impressive with 20 wins and 1 draw in 21 games. Belgium became the first foreign team to win a point with a 2–2 draw on 2 November 1923 and it was not until 15 May 1929 that, in their 22nd game, they suffered a defeat. Playing in Madrid, the English team went down to a strong Spanish side 4–3 but, at Highbury two years later, gained their revenge with a 7–1 victory.

The first British player to score a double hat-trick in a full international match

Joe Bambrick, a Linfield FC player, achieved this feat when he scored six goals in Northern Ireland's 7–0 Home International competition defeat of Wales on 1 February 1930.

(Right) Alec Jackson, the Huddersfield Town winger. (Boys Magazine)

Joe Bambrick, pictured during his Chelsea days. (Colorsport)

The first match to have two referees

In an international trial match between England and 'the Rest' at West Bromwich on 27 March 1935 'dual-control' by two referees was tried out. The game ended 2–2 but the experiment was not a success.

The first winners of the British Home International Championship trophy

Although the competition commenced in 1883/4, it was not until 1935/6 that a trophy was made available. Scotland won that year's series to become the first winners of the trophy.

The first match to be televised live

On 15 November, 1936, German television showed the whole of the Germany v Italy international match live. Although the number of TV sets was still very small, there was keen interest in the 'showcase' meeting between the two fascist sides. Italy's reputation as a hard, uncompromising side was emphasized firstly by their victory in the 1934 World Cup and secondly by their incredibly arrogant and violent tactics against the United States of America in the 1936 Olympics, (this was the game in which the Italians blatantly intimidated the German referee who was trying to enforce his decision to dismiss an Italian player who had severely injured an opponent).

The televised game itself was without serious incident and ended in a face-saving 2–2 draw.

Walter Winterbottom outside the FA Headquarters on 1 January 1963 — the day that he was awarded the CBE for his services to sport. (Photosource)

The first occasion that 150 000 tickets were sold for an international match

On 17 April 1937, just one week before the Scottish FA Cup Final between Celtic and Aberdeen FC, which attracted a record attendance (147 265), Scotland played England in front of a record crowd in excess of 160 000. Although 150 000 tickets were sold and the official attendance was given as 149 415, at least 10 000 fans entered without paying when a gate was broken down!

The first full-time manager of the England international team

After the Second World War, English soccer entered a new era with many more games per season and it was therefore decided to appoint a full-time manager. Walter Winterbottom took up the appointment in 1946 and remained in control until replaced by Alf Ramsey in 1963.

The first foreign country to defeat England at home

England's first 14 home internationals against non-British opponents all ended in victory for the home side and it was not until 21 September 1949 that Eire inflicted their first home defeat upon them. The match, which was played at Goodison Park, Liverpool, ended 2–0 to Eire and was the first game that Eire had played in the UK.

The first substitute to appear for England in a full international

Wolverhampton Wanderers' player Jimmy Mullen became England's first substitute on 18 May 1950 during a friendly international against Belgium (in Brussels). Replacing the injured Jackie Milburn, he achieved a further distinction by becoming the first substitute to score a goal when he notched up England's first goal. The match ended in a 4–1 victory for England.

The first foreign country to play England at Wembley

Amazingly, it was not until 9 May 1951 that any country, other than Scotland, played England at Wembley. Argentina, the first South American team to play in England, lost 2–1 in a hard-fought game. On 28 November 1951, Austria became the first foreign country to win a point at Wembley when they held England to a 2–2 draw. During this game Alf Ramsey, later appointed manager of the England team, became the first player to score a penalty for England at Wembley with the first of his country's goals.

The first player to be sent off whilst playing for Scotland in a full international

In Scotland's 217th international match on 27 May

INTERNATIONALS

Alf Ramsey, England's soccer supremo, shortly after the 1966 World Cup win. (ASP)

1951, Dundee's Billy Steel became the first player to be sent off whilst representing Scotland. The match, against Austria in Vienna, ended in a 4–0 defeat for the Scots.

The first international soccer match to be played by a side with 12 players

On 11 November 1952 when France played Northern Ireland at the Stades Colombes, in Paris, an injured player, Bonifaci, although substituted inadvertently returned to the field of play after treatment. All 12 French players continued until half-time when the error was discovered. France won the game 3–1.

The first international involving a British Home Country to be abandoned

On 17 May 1953, in the first match of their American tour, England met Argentina in Buenos Aires. Torrential rain stopped play after only 23 minutes when the score was 0–0, and play did not resume again.

The first international involving England to be played under floodlights

On 8 June 1953 England met the United States of America for the first time since the Americans had achieved that incredible 1–0 World Cup win in Brazil. Played at the Yankee Stadium in New York, this was the final game in England's American tour and was the first floodlit game to be played by a British international side. Any hopes which the United States team may have harboured for a repeat of their Belo Horizonte result were quickly dashed as England cruised to a 6–3 victory.

The first foreign country to beat England at Wembley

On 25 November 1953 Hungary's Ferenc Puskas skippered the 'Magical Magyars' to a resounding 6–3 victory over England. England were handed a lesson in constructive football as the Hungarians outplayed them in all departments, and Nandor Hidegkuti became the first overseas player to score a hat-trick against England as Hungary won the game 6–3.

The following year England played a return match in Budapest prior to the 1954 World Cup series in Switzerland and were again humiliated by a 7–1 scoreline.

The first hat-trick by an England player in a full international at Wembley

Ray Bentley became the first England player to score a hat-trick in a full international at Wembley when England defeated Wales 3–2 on 10 November 1954.

The first international at Wembley to be completed under floodlights

On 30 November 1955 England's friendly match with Spain was completed by floodlight for the first time. Bill Perry, a South African who played for Blackpool FC, represented England that day (his second appearance) and scored two goals in England's 4–1 victory.

The first time that all of the British Home Countries finished level in the Home International Championship

Although the Home International Championship had been tied by two nations a couple of times, it was not until the 1955/6 competition (the 73rd) that all four countries finished level with three points each.

South African Bill Perry —
Blackpool's goalscoring
ace of the early 1950s.
(D C Thomson Ltd)

(Above) Puskas of Hungary and Wright of England
lead out their respective countries on 25 November
1953 before a packed home crowd. (Photosource)

The first player to represent his country in 100 full internationals

Billy Wright of Wolverhampton Wanderers FC first played for England on 28 September 1946 and won his 100th cap against Scotland at Wembley on 11 April 1959 in a game which England dominated but only won 1–0.

The first Fourth Division player to represent his country in a full international

Vic Rouse of Crystal Palace FC became the first Football League Fourth Division player to represent his country on 22 April 1959. He appeared for Wales against Northern Ireland at Belfast in a game which Wales lost 4–1. Prior to August 1958 there had been a regionalized Third Division (North and South) and a number of players from these divisions had represented their respective countries.

The first player to be capped for England whilst on the books of a Scottish League club

Scottish footballers began journeying down to the more lucrative English 'pastures' almost from the first kick-off and in the 1880s and 1890s many English soccer scouts made annual pilgrimages north of the border in search of 'salmon'. Movement in the opposite direction by English players was almost unheard of and it was not until 18 November 1959 that Joe Baker of Hibernian FC represented England against Northern Ireland in a full international. Despite his broad Scots accent he was born in Liverpool (although he lived in Scotland from an early age) and he made an impressive goal-scoring debut in England's 2–1 win.

The first British Home International to be played entirely under floodlights

It was not until 8 November 1961 that a British Home International match was played in the evening completely by floodlight. This game at Hampden Park, Glasgow, between Scotland and Wales ended in a 2–0 win for Scotland.

The first player to be capped for England whilst on the books of a foreign club

Gerry Hitchens, an Aston Villa FC player, first appeared for England against Mexico on 10 May 1961 and, after playing excellently against Italy a fortnight later (when he scored two goals) was

Billy Wright at a training session before his 100th game for England in April 1959. (Photosource)

(Below) An unusual 1961 shot of Gerry Hitchens training at Lesser Hampden, prior to appearing for the Italian League against the Scottish League. (D C Thomson Ltd)

Joe Baker later in his career in 1971. (D C Thomson Ltd)

A youthful-looking Jimmy Greaves seen in action for Spurs against West Ham on 26 August 1967. (ASP)

After gaining his 100th cap in 1983, Pat Jennings carried on to make a number of further appearances for his country. (ASP)

subsequently transferred to Inter-Milan. During his tenure with them in 1962 he was capped on several further occasions by England.

The first British Home International match to be played completely under floodlights at Wembley

Effectively the first evening Home International, this took place between England and Northern Ireland on 20 November 1963 and England won the game 8–3 with hat-tricks for Paine and Greaves (four goals).

The first player to be sent off in a British Home International

On 22 October 1966, (in England's first game after becoming World Champions) Northern Ireland's Billy Ferguson of Linfield FC became the first player to be dismissed in a Home International match. He 'achieved' a double-first that day by additionally becoming the first Northern Ireland player to be dismissed in a full international.

The first England player to be sent off in a full international

In a European Nations Cup Finals match, played in Florence, Italy on 5 June 1968, Alan Mullery of Spurs became the first Englishman to be dismissed in a full international. Retaliating against a bad foul by the Yugoslav player, Trivic, Mullery lashed out and, despite the blow failing to find its mark, the referee was convinced (by Trivic's agonized

writhing) that a sending-off was justified. England lost the game 1–0.

The first official women's international match to be played in Britain

Female participation in soccer has been restrained rather more by the physical demands of the game itself than it has by officialdom. Clearly, it would not be practicable to encourage mixed teams as the relative weight/size ratios would inevitably result in male domination. The first official international match in Britain between two teams of women was played at Greenock on 18 November 1972 between representatives of Scotland and England. England won the game 3–2.

The first 'All-Ireland' international match

Friendly rivalry between Northern Ireland and Eire simply does not exist so far as soccer is concerned. Throughout the world most neighbouring countries participate in friendly matches, but no such rapport exists in Ireland. It was not until the 1978 European Championship that the two countries met one another for the first time (at Landsdowne Road, Dublin) and the match ended in a 0–0 draw.

The first 'All-Anglo' Scottish international side

Our previous comments upon the habitual 'drift' of Scottish players to the Football League were

Dundee United's Gough scores Scotland's goal in the first Sir Stanley Rous Trophy game. (ASP)

more than emphasized on 25 October 1978 when all the 11 players appearing for Scotland were on the books of English clubs. The game at Hampden Park, Glasgow (a European Championship match against Norway) ended 3–2 to Scotland.

The first international team to have the players' names inscribed on their shirts

In the friendly game between Scotland and Peru, which was played at Hampden Park, Glasgow, on 12 September 1979, Scotland experimented with this 'personalized shirts' idea. Contrary to popular belief, this was not because the Scots could not remember the names of their team-mates! The game ended 1–1.

The first full international match to be postponed at Wembley

On 20 November 1979, England's European Championship qualifying game against Bulgaria was postponed because of fog and by the time that it was actually played the following day (thanks to Northern Ireland's 1–0 victory over Eire) England were already through to the finals. Regardless of this they still won the match 2–0.

The first Irishman to win 100 international caps

Pat Jennings, the Northern Ireland goalkeeper, in addition to recording a huge number of League and other senior competition appearances, became, on 21 September 1983, the first Irishman to represent his country 100 times. In the process, he became the first goalkeeper in Britain to achieve the century of caps and achieved the satisfaction that day of seeing Northern Ireland beat Austria 3–1 in a European Championship qualifying tie.

The first winners of the Sir Stanley Rous Trophy

Following the decision of Scotland and England to discontinue the British Home Championship, it was decided to hold an annual match between the two 'old enemies' and the 'Sir Stanley Rous Trophy' was instituted for the winners. The first game which was originally scheduled to be played at Wembley, was switched to Hampden Park, Glasgow, following a season of crowd violence in England and was played on 25 May 1985. Gough of Dundee United FC gave Scotland victory by scoring the only goal of the game.

The seven original member countries of FIFA: Belgium, Denmark, France, Holland, Spain, Sweden and Switzerland, meeting for the first time in Paris in 1904, included a provision in the FIFA constitution that only FIFA could organize a World soccer tournament. In 1920 FIFA progressed further when the principle of establishing the cup was agreed at their Antwerp Congress, but it was not until 1928 that it was decided to hold a four-yearly championship. At Barcelona in 1929, it was decided to stage the first World Championship in Uruguay in 1930. On the face of it, this may seem to have been an odd venue to choose, but, considering that the Uruguayans had been the reigning Olympic Champions since 1924 and were prepared to pay every team's full expenses, perhaps they were the logical hosts.

Only four European countries: France, Belgium, Rumania and Yugoslavia, decided to make the long sea voyage (the four British sides were ineligible having left FIFA in 1928) and the 13 participating countries also included the USA.

The first competition was played with three pools of three teams and one pool of four teams, each providing a semi finalist and thence to a straight knockout system. The 1934 finals in Italy and the 1938 finals in France were 'sudden-death' knockouts from the start and half of the teams journeying to these finals found themselves playing only one game. This was obviously unsatisfactory and a pool basis was reinstituted for the 1950 finals in Brazil, when there was even a 'final pool' and no final match as such. In the 1954 finals in Switzerland, the present system of groups, leading to a final match, was established. The venues of the later finals were: Sweden 1958; Chile 1962; England 1966; Mexico 1970; West Germany 1974; Argentina 1978; Spain 1982 and Mexico 1986.

The first nine World Cup competitions were for the 'Jules Rimet' Trophy which was then won outright and from 1974 'The FIFA World Cup' trophy has been awarded.

The first World Cup match

France, one of only four European sides that made the journey to the finals in Uruguay, won the opening game of the first-ever World Cup competition 4–1 on 13 July 1930. Their opponents were Mexico and the French forward Louis Laurent scored the first-ever World Cup goal early in the first half. The other French goals were by Langiller and Maschinot (2) (who thus became the first player to score more than one goal), and the Mexican scorer was Carreno.

The first player to be sent off in the World Cup

De Las Casas of Peru was dismissed during his country's first World Cup match against Rumania in Group 3 of the 1930 tournament. Rumania won the match 3–1, but were denied a semi-final place after being soundly beaten 4–0 by Uruguay.

The first player to score a hat-trick in a World Cup match

Guillermo Stabile of Argentina (the leading scorer in the 1930 competition with eight goals) scored the first-ever World Cup hat-trick when Argentina defeated Mexico 6–3 in an incident-filled match in which no fewer than five penalties were awarded. Trouble seemed to follow the Argentinians, with a crowd invasion in their opening match against France and further violence during their game against Chile, with police being called onto the pitch to stop fighting!

The first country to win the World Cup

The first World Cup Final involved the traditionally bitter rivals of Uruguay and Argentina who had faced one another two years earlier in the 1928 Olympic Final which Uruguay won 2–1. Boatloads of Argentinians, who had crossed the River Plate to support their country, were searched for arms and there was even a dispute about which match ball should be used. Eventually, different match balls, one made in Argentina and the other in Uruguay, were used each half. In an explosive game, Pablo Dorado of Uruguay scored the first-ever goal in a World Cup Final but, after an equalizer by Peucelle, Argentina's Stabile (the top scorer of the series with eight goals) gave his team a half-time lead. Three second-half goals gave Uruguay a deserved victory, Montevideo 'erupted' and the following day was declared a national holiday!

The first holders of the World Cup to fail to defend it

The first winners, Uruguay, greatly beset by internal strife and annoyed by the lack of European support for the 1930 series, declined to play in the 1934 series, and are the only holders ever to elect not to defend their title.

The first player to appear for different countries in a World Cup Final

Luisito Monti who played for Argentina in the 1930 final, was 'signed' by a wealthy Italian club and, being of Italian extraction, played for Italy in the 1934 final. Fearing further 'defections' the Argentinians did not field their best players for the

THE FIFA WORLD CUP

(Above) Uruguay, the first winners of the World Cup, pictured before the final in 1930. (Below) Vittorio Pozzo being carried off by his victorious Italian team after they had won the 1934 World Cup. (Photosource)

THE FIFA WORLD CUP

1934 series and were eliminated in the first round by Sweden.

The first European country to win the World Cup

The first final match to go into extra-time, the 1934 final was inevitably going to provide the first European world champions, as Italy were playing against Czechoslovakia. (Indeed, not a single non-European country progressed beyond the first round). The Czechs took the lead late in the second half and Orsi (an Argentian 'import') equalized eight minutes from time. Meazza scored the winner for Italy in extra-time.

The first country to retain the World Cup

The 1938 final between Italy and Hungary was the first one in which the host country failed to appear and, indeed, was the first one which the host country failed to win. The match at Stades Colombes was watched by 65 000 people, mainly Frenchmen, who turned up in large numbers to support the Hungarians because the Italians had beaten France 3–1 in the second round. This did not, however, deter the reigning champions from becoming the first country to retain the World Cup and with a 4–2 win, they did just that.

French referee Capdeville watches Italy's Meazza shake hands with Hungary's Sarosi prior to the 1938 World Cup Final. (Photosource)

The first England player to score a hat-trick in a World Cup match

Jackie Milburn of Newcastle United FC scored a hat-trick in England's 4–1 victory over Wales at Cardiff on 15 October 1949. Although the game was played as part of the 1949/50 Home International Championship it also doubled as a World Cup qualifying match and Milburn's feat, therefore, became England's first World Cup hat-trick. His team-mate Stan Mortensen had scored the first goal to become England's first World Cup scorer and later went on to become the scorer of England's first final series goal, against Chile.

The first Briton to referee a World Cup Final

Strictly speaking, there was no 'final match' in the 1950 series with Uruguay, Brazil, Sweden and Spain forming a 'Final Pool'. However, the final game in the Pool is generally regarded as the 'Final' with Spain and Sweden already in third and fourth places. Refereed by George Reader from Southampton, the match ended 2–1 with Uruguay winning the Cup for the second time in two appearances and Brazil becoming the first host country to be beaten in the final.

The first international match to be televised live in Scotland

The World Cup Group 3 match between Uruguay and Scotland was televised live from Basle, Switzerland on 19 June 1954. The Scottish team manager, Andy Beattie, had just resigned after Scotland's 1–0 defeat by Austria and a demoralized team crashed to a 7–0 defeat.

The first country to win the World Cup after losing earlier in the competition

In their second game in Group 2 of the 1954 series, West Germany crashed 8–3 to Hungary. This defeat seems to have been contrived by Sepp Herberger, the West German manager, because he fielded no fewer than six reserves in the West German side. It is assumed that he did so because he felt certain that his side could easily overcome Turkey in a play-off for the second qualifying place and thus would face weaker opposition in the quarter final when drawn against the second team in Group 1. His reasoning prevailed and West Germany thrashed Turkey 7–2 in the play-off. Strangely, they went on to meet Hungary in the final and, despite going two down, won the game 3–2. Two brothers, Fritz and Otmar Walter, both played in the West German team that day and became the first brothers to gain World Cup winner's medals.

Scotland's first hat-trick in a World Cup match

In a qualifying match at Hampden Park on 8 May

Jack Milburn, 'Wor Jackie' to Magpie fans, in
goalscoring action. (Colorsport)

1957 the Blackpool FC player, J K Mudie, scored
Scotland's first World Cup hat-trick in his
country's 4–2 win over Spain.

The first country to win the World Cup in a different continent

In the 1958 final at Stockholm, Sweden took an
early lead against Brazil but the South American
side powered back to beat the host side 5–2. Thus,
they became the first South American side to win
the Cup in Europe and, indeed, the first country to
win the Cup in a different continent.

The first occasion that all four British Home Countries qualified for the final series

In 1958 all four Home Countries reached the
finals—England qualified by topping a group with
Eire and Denmark, and both Scotland and
Northern Ireland qualified by a similar method
(with Northern Ireland disposing of both Italy and
Portugal). Wales qualified by beating Israel in a
play-off, after East Germany's withdrawal from the
group headed by Czechoslovakia. The
performances in the final series were somewhat
mixed with quarter-final places for Northern
Ireland and Wales after plays-offs with
Czechoslovakia and Hungary respectively.

The first player to score in two World Cup Finals

In 1962 Brazil became the first South American
country to retain the World Cup when they beat
Czechoslovakia 3–1 in Santiago, Chile. Vava
(Edwaldo Izidio Neto), their top scorer in the
earlier World Cup final series competitions, scored
their third goal and became the first player to score
in two World Cup Finals.

The first Asian country to win a World Cup final series match

In the 1966 finals in England, North Korea first of
all earned a point with a 1–1 draw against Chile,
then achieved the shock of the series by beating
Italy 1–0 to become the first Asian country to win
a final series game.

THE FIFA WORLD CUP

The first player to appear in five consecutive World Cup final series

The Mexican goalkeeper Antonio Carbajal became the first player to achieve this distinction in the 1966 series. His first game on 24 June 1950 was against Brazil, when he conceded four goals but, in his last game against Uruguay at Wembley, he kept a clean sheet.

The first professional footballer to be sent off at Wembley

Considering the large number of games that had been played at Wembley it was quite surprising that there were no dismissals before 1966. On 23 July 1966, in a bad-tempered World Cup quarter final between England and Argentina, Anton Rattin, the Argentinian captain, was sent off for dissent. After eight farcical minutes in which the Argentinians threatened to leave en masse, he eventually left the field of play. The first amateur footballer to be sent off at Wembley was Boris Stankovic, the Yugoslav captain, whilst playing for his country in the 1948 Olympics against Sweden.

The first person to manage two different countries in the World Cup finals

Rudolf Vytlacil, a Czech, managed his country's 1962 World Cup team which lost 3–1 to Brazil in the final, and then managed the less successful Bulgarian team that came bottom of Group 3 in the 1966 finals.

The first British home country to win the Cup

In the 1966 World Cup Final at Wembley, England became the first British team to win the Cup when they defeated West Germany 4–2 after extra-time. Geoff Hurst's three goals were the first-ever hat-trick to be scored in a World Cup Final.

The first country to defeat England after they had won the World Cup

England's arch-enemy, Scotland, playing at Wembley on 15 April 1967 in the 1966/67 Home International Championship, inflicted a 3–2 defeat on the World Cup holders—the first country to do so after they had won the World Cup.

The first country to win both the World Cup and the European Nations Cup

Italy, previous winners of the World Cup in 1934 and 1938, became the first country to have won both the World Cup and the European Nations Cup, when they won the European title in 1968.

Pele, pictured with his team-mates Santos (left) and Zito (centre) during a training session prior to his country's friendly game against England on 7 May 1963. (Photosource)

THE FIFA WORLD CUP

The first player from one of the British home countries to be sent off in a World Cup match

Celtic's Tommy Gemmell, representing Scotland against West Germany in a World Cup qualifying match at Hamburg on 22 October 1969, became the first British player to be sent off in a World Cup match. West Germany won the match 3–2 and Scotland failed to qualify for the 1970 finals.

The first country to win the World Cup outright

The 1970 final series provided quite an assortment of interesting firsts. The most significant one, of course, was Brazil's permanent capture of the Jules Rimet Trophy by winning the Cup for the third time. Had they lost to their opponents, Italy, instead of winning 4–1, Italy themselves would have achieved this honour.

The other firsts were:

Brazilian manager, Mario Zagalo, who had played in both the 1958 and the 1962 finals, achieved the unusual distinction of becoming the first person to play for and to manage a World Cup winning side.

Italy's Roberto Boninsegna, who scored Italy's only goal, became the first World Cup Final goalscorer to be substituted, when he was replaced by Gianni Rivera.

Pele (Edson Arantes Do Nascimento), who scored

(Above) The full-bearded Trevor Hockey in a typical commanding stance. (ASP)

(Left) Brazil's Jairzinho, scorer in every game of Brazil's 1970 World Cup final series. (Allsport)

Brazil's first goal, became the first player to be a member of three World Cup-winning sides and Jairzinho, who scored seven goals in Brazil's six matches, became the first player to score in every one of his country's games in a World Cup final series.

The first Welshman to be sent off in a full international

Trevor Hockey of Norwich City FC became the first player to be sent off whilst playing for Wales. This happened on 26 September 1973 at Katowice, Poland during a World Cup qualifying match against that country. Wales lost 3–0 and subsequently failed to qualify for the 1974 finals.

The first player to score from a penalty in a World Cup Final

Surprisingly, it was not until the 1974 World Cup Final between Holland and West Germany that a

penalty was awarded in a final. Straight from the kick-off the Dutch attacked, Cruyff was brought down in the area and the referee pointed to the penalty spot. Johan Neeskens took the kick which flashed straight into the West German net. Neeskens became the first player to score a penalty in a World Cup Final and West Germany became the first team to concede a World Cup Final goal without even touching the ball! Strangely, 25 minutes later West Germany themselves were awarded a penalty which Breitner scored to set them on track for a 2–1 win.

The first country to be eliminated from a World Cup final series without losing a match

In the 1974 series in West Germany, Scotland drew with Brazil and Yugoslavia and beat Zaire but, because they had a goal difference of +2 against Brazil's +3, were eliminated.

(Left) Cabrini's penalty shot goes wide in the 25th minute of the 1982 World Cup Final. (ASP)

The first substitute to score a hat-trick in a World Cup final series

In Hungary's first game in Group 3 of the 1982 series their opponents were the surprise Central American qualifiers, El Salvador. Completely outclassing them, Hungary won the game 10–1 to notch up the first-ever World Cup finals double-figure win. Laszlo Kiss came on as a substitute and became the first substitute to score a World Cup hat-trick.

The first occasion that penalty kicks were used as tie-breakers in the World Cup

The 1982 semi-final game at Seville between France and West Germany was tied 3–3 after extra-time and was decided on penalty kicks. France, who had held a 3–1 lead at one time, missed two kicks and West Germany went through to the final 5–4.

The first player to miss a penalty in a World Cup Final

In the Bernabeu Stadium in Madrid, Mr Arnold Cesar Coelho from Brazil became the first South American to referee a World Cup Final when he was selected for the 1982 game between Italy and West Germany. Italy were awarded a penalty in the 25th minute and Antonio Cabrini hit the ball wide of Schumacher's left post to become the first player to miss a penalty in a World Cup Final. Not dispirited by the miss, Italy went on to record their third win by a 3–1 margin.

The first country to host the World Cup twice

Colombia was originally chosen as the venue for the 1986 finals but finding itself lacking the huge financial resources necessary to organise the event, it withdrew in 1984. Thus it was that Mexico was selected once again and although violent earthquakes shook the area late in 1985, the stadia were unaffected and the finals went ahead. The torrid heat and the high altitude affected the play but the reintroduction of a 'Knockout' second stage lifted the overall footballing standards well above the rather boring levels of 1978 and 1982. West Germany became the first country to reach a fifth World Cup Final game and their opponents were Argentina who, fielding the man of the tournament, Diego Maradona, won the final 3–2.

The first African country to win a match in a World Cup final series

Unrated Tunisia provided the first sensation of the 1978 finals by beating Mexico 3–1 and became the first African country to win a World Cup finals match. They went on to prove that their performance was no fluke by losing by only 1–0 to Poland and drawing 0–0 with the holders, West Germany.

THE FIFA WORLD CUP

World Cup final series firsts

ALGERIA   First final series: 1982

First Final Competition match v West Germany in Group 1 of the series.

Underdogs Algeria pulled off one of the biggest surprises of the competition by recording their first World Cup final series win against the formidable West German team. Deserving 2–1 winners, their first World Cup goal was scored by Madjer with the other coming from the impressive Belloumi. Their next game, against a strong Austrian team, ended with them recording their first World Cup defeat by a 2–0 margin, but, in their third and final Group 1 game, they richly deserved their 3–2 victory over Chile. Had they been in any of the other five preliminary groups, they would have reached the quarter finals with their four points, but, because they had an inferior goal difference to Austria and West Germany, they failed to proceed further in the competition. By the time that the 1986 finals had arrived, Algeria were already a declining force. Although they began with their first draw (1–1 against Northern Ireland) it was apparent that they were not likely to achieve much success and, losing their other two games, failed to reach the next round.

ARGENTINA   First Final Series: 1930

First Final Competition match v France in Group 1 of the series.

Beaten finalists in the 1928 Olympics, Argentina got off the mark with a 1–0 victory over France, thanks to a second-half goal by Monti. Their second game against Mexico saw their striker Guillermo Stabile (the top scorer in the 1930 competition with eight goals) score their first World Cup hat-trick in a fiery 6–3 victory in which no fewer than five penalties were awarded. Winning Group 1 with six points, they met the USA in their first semi-final game and after being held to only one goal by Monti in the first half, they ran out 6–1 winners to earn their first final match place. Facing their neighbours and arch-rivals, Uruguay, in Montevideo, Carlos Peucelle scored their first final goal to level the score and by half-time they had taken a 2–1 lead. Uruguay, the Olympic champions stormed back to win 4–2.

In the 1934 series they fielded a much depleted side, preferring to leave their top players at home, rather than risk further defections to the wealthy Italian clubs and, consequently, lost their only game against Sweden. They fared badly in 1958 with only one win from their three games and little better in 1962 with only one win again, although they did notch up their first World Cup draw, 0–0, when playing Hungary. In 1966 they reached the quarter finals, losing in the notorious game against England at Wembley and fared similarly in 1974 coming bottom of their quarter-final group.

Hosts for the 1978 series, they stormed through to the final with four wins and a draw from their six matches and, thanks to Kempes, achieved their first championship by beating Holland 3–1 after extra-time. Through to the quarter finals in the 1982 series, they found themselves in the same group as Italy and Brazil and, losing both games, saw their hopes of retaining the Cup vanish.

Mexico 1986 was virtually, for Argentina, the series of Diego Maradona. Argentina won their first round group by beating South Korea and Bulgaria and drawing with Italy. After eliminating Uruguay in the second round they met England in the quarter finals (the first such meeting since the Falkland's War) and won 2–1 thanks to two goals from Maradona (one with his hand). In the semi final against Belgium, Maradona again scored twice and Argentina progressed to meet West Germany in their third World Cup Final. After taking a two-goal lead, Argentina allowed West Germany to fight back level but then went on to win the championship by a 3–2 scoreline.

AUSTRALIA   First Final Series: 1974

First Final Competition match v East Germany in Group 1 of the series.

Australia's Curran set East Germany on course for a 2–0 win when he conceded an own goal in the second half of the game. After losing their second match to West Germany, his country finished the series by earning their first World Cup point with a creditable 0–0 draw against Chile.

AUSTRIA   First Final Series: 1934

First Final Competition match v France in the first round of the series at Turin.

Hugo Meisl's Austrian 'Wunderteam', although past its peak, was still a force to be reckoned with and France performed remarkably well before going down 3–2. Sindelar scored Austria's first World Cup goal and the win earned them a tie against Hungary in the second round. After overcoming Hungary, they went on to meet their arch-rivals, Italy, in their first semi final and incurred their first defeat by a 1–0 margin. Despite qualifying for the 1938 series Austria were forced to withdraw when Germany 'combined' the two countries and dissolved the Austrian FA. Several Austrian players appeared for the German team.

In their 1954 Group 3 match against Czechoslovakia, Probst (their all-time top scorer with six goals) scored their first World Cup hat-trick in a 5–0 win, and a further quarter-final victory over the host nation, Switzerland, led them to their second semi-final defeat against their other neighbours, West Germany. Their first draw, 2–2 against England in the 1958 series, was their only point of that series and it was not until 1978 that they participated again. In both 1978 and 1982 they enjoyed a fair amount of success and reached both quarter finals.

THE FIFA WORLD CUP

BELGIUM   First Final Series: 1930

First Final Competition match v USA in Group 4 of the series.

Surprisingly 'seeded', the United States proved their superiority by handing Belgium their first World Cup defeat, scoring three goals without reply. Although they participated in both the 1934 and 1938 series and Voorhoof scored their first goals (2) against Germany in 1934, they did not collect their first point until they held England to a 4–4 draw in the 1954 series. Another 16 years elapsed before they registered their first win, 3–0 against El Salvador in 1970. The 1982 series proved to be a most successful one for Belgium when they made the quarter finals for the first time.

Belgium provided the biggest surprise of the 1986 series by progressing to their first semi final. They achieved this, reaching the second round after finishing in only third place in Group B, before beating the USSR in the Second Round and Spain in the quarter final. Their semi-final opponents, Argentina, won 2–0 thanks to a superb Maradona display and, in their first third-place play-off, Belgium lost 4–2 to France after extra-time.

BOLIVIA   First Final Series: 1930

First Final Competition match v Yugoslavia in Group 2 of the series.

Bolivia's participation in the first series was by invitation rather than qualification and their two games both ended in 4–0 defeats. In 1950 they were unfortunate to be drawn in the same group as Uruguay (the eventual winners) and lost their only game 8–0.

BRAZIL   First Final Series: 1930

First Final Competition match v Yugoslavia in Group 2 of the series.

Brazil's first World Cup game ended in a surprising 2–1 defeat by the unseeded Yugoslavs. Neto scored his country's first World Cup goal in the second half of the Yugoslavian game, and two further goals in their other match in the group, a 4–0 win over Bolivia.

Their next win was not until the first round of the 1938 series when their opponents in Strasbourg were Poland. Leonidas scored his country's first World Cup hat-trick and chalked up four goals in a remarkable 6–5 extra-time win. In the next round, their first drawn game, 1–1 against Czechoslovakia, led to their first semi-final appearance in which they lost 2–1 against Italy.

In 1950, when they were the host nation, they reached the final pool. Appearing in the unofficial final match at the Maracana Stadium in Rio de Janeiro, before a world-record crowd of just under 200 000, they went down 2–1 to their great South American rivals, Uruguay. After a moderately successful 1954 series when they reached the

quarter finals, in 1958 they began a remarkable run of victories. Reaching their first official final against the hosts, Sweden, they ran out superb 5–2 winners, with their powerful forward, Vava, scoring their first World Cup Final goal. In 1962 their run continued and, appearing in their second consecutive final, they crushed Czechoslovakia 3–1 to retain the Cup. A brief pause in their domination in the 1966 series enabled England to win their first title, but in 1970, they stormed back to beat Italy 4–1 in the final in Mexico and, as a result, won the Jules Rimet Trophy outright.

Their remarkable consistency continued in both the 1974 and the 1978 series when they again reached the semi finals. In 1982, after a storming start with three wins in three games, they went out to the eventual winners, Italy, in the quarter finals.

Brazil began the 1986 series as firm favourites and, in their first round Group D matches, made an impressive start by winning all three games without conceding a goal. In the second round, they also won without letting any in (4–0 against Poland) and looked to be heading for another final. However, France, their opponents in the quarter finals, had other ideas and deservedly held them to a 1–1 draw after extra-time and knocked them out of the series on penalties.

Brazil have appeared in every final series and have been by far the most successful nation overall.

BULGARIA   First Final Series: 1962

First Final Competition match v Argentina in Group 4 of the series.

In an uninspiring match at Rancagua, Bulgaria's first game became also their first defeat (0–1). Despite their first World Cup goal coming from Sokolov in their next game against Hungary, they did not earn a point until they registered their first draw (0–0) against England in the last game in Group 4.

In 1986, Bulgaria made their fifth appearance in the World Cup Finals and, for the first time, progressed beyond the first round. They achieved this, however, by playing two drawn matches and, losing to Mexico in the second round, have yet to win a World Cup Final series game.

CAMEROON   First Final Series: 1982

First Final Competition match v Peru in Group 1 of the series.

Rank outsiders, Cameroon surprised everyone when, in their first game, they earned a point with a 0–0 draw. In their second game, they did incredibly well to hold the ultimate winners, Italy, to a 1–1 draw. Their goal, which was scored by M'Bida was their first and, to date, their only goal in a final series. Despite not losing a single game, they failed to progress further because Italy had scored one more goal!

THE FIFA WORLD CUP

CANADA   First Final Series: 1986

First Final Competition match v France in Group C of the series. In their first game, Canada could have wished for easier opposition than the European champions, France, but, nevertheless, they soon unsettled the French with their solid defending. Papin scored the first and only French goal in the 79th minute and denied Canada any reward for their efforts. Canada's other two games against Hungary and the USSR also ended in defeat but although they were unable to score a single goal, they were by no means disgraced. Without doubt, when the proposed Canadian soccer league begins, Canada will become a force to be reckoned with.

CHILE   First Final Series: 1930

First Final Competition match v Mexico in Group 1 of the series.

Vidal, scoring Chile's first ever World Cup goal, gave his side the half-time lead, which, with two further goals from Subiabre, culminated in Chile's first World Cup win (3–0). After scoring a further goal in his country's 1–0 win over France, Subiabre added one more in their first defeat (3–1 by Argentina) to become his country's equal top World Cup scorer with four goals.

In the 1950 series Cremaschi scored Chile's first hat-trick in their 5–2 victory over the United States, but it was not until the 1962 series that they reached their first semi final. Playing against the holders, Brazil, on their home ground in Santiago they went down 4–2 before the biggest crowd of the series (76 594). They appeared in three subsequent series but failed to win another match.

COLOMBIA   First Final Series: 1962

First Final Competition match v Uruguay in Group 1 of the series.

Unfancied Colombia took a half-time lead with their first World Cup goal from Zaluaga, but Uruguay struck back to win 2–1. Precisely the opposite happened when, in their next game, they trailed 4–1 to USSR before fighting back magnificently to win their first (and only) World Cup point with a 4–4 draw. This must have drained the players who went down in their last game with Yugoslavia 5–0.

CUBA   First Final Series: 1938

First Final Competition match v Rumania in the first round of the series.

The biggest surprise of the first round of the series came when Cuba fought out a 3–3 extra-time draw against Rumania. Tunas scored their first-ever World Cup goal, and Cuba went on to win their first game, when beating Rumania 2–1 in the first-round replay. At Antibes, Cuba's dream of success came to an abrupt end when they suffered their first World Cup defeat, going down 8–0 to Sweden in their last game to date.

CZECHOSLOVAKIA   First Final Series: 1934

First Final Competition match v Rumania in the first round of the series.

Two superb saves by their keeper Planicka, their first-ever World Cup goal from Puc and another by their World Cup top scorer, Nejedly, gave Czechoslovakia their first World Cup win. Eliminating Switzerland in the second round, they went on to their first semi final against Germany and comfortably won 3–1. In the final, against Italy, Puc put them into the lead but Italy equalized eight minutes from time and won by scoring in extra-time.

In the 1938 series they played their first draw with a 1–1 score against Brazil but did not win another game until they beat Argentina in the 1958 series.

In 1962, they played magnificently to reach their second final in which they lost 3–1 to Brazil but failed to earn another point until they drew 1–1 with Kuwait in 1982.

DENMARK   First Final Series: 1986

First Final Competition match v Scotland in Group E of the series. Denmark played with great flair against Scotland and thanks to a first goal from Elkjaer went on to achieve their first win by a 1–0 margin. Elkjaer scored their first World Cup hat-trick in their next game, a magnificent 6–1 victory over the notoriously defensive Uruguayans, and Jesper Olsen scored their first penalty in their next game, a 2–0 victory over West Germany. Their next game against Spain ended in their first defeat by a surprising and undeserved margin of 5–1. In their first series Denmark had promised so much, and played so well but in the end were knocked out by Spain's superior tactics.

DUTCH EAST INDIES   First Final Series: 1938

First Final Competition match v Hungary in the first round of the series.

Representing Asia in the series, the Dutch East Indies played only one game and were thrashed 6–0 by the eventual runners-up.

EAST GERMANY   First Final Series: 1974

First Final Competition match v Australia in Group 1 of the series.

An own goal by Australia's Curran set East Germany on course for their first World Cup win and Streich scored their second goal—the first by an East German player. Their next game, against Chile, brought them their first World Cup draw with a 1–1 scoreline and they then beat West Germany 1–0 in the first-ever meeting between the two countries. This victory resulted in their progressing to a really strong final group and they recorded their first World Cup defeat at the hands of Brazil (1–0) and were then soundly beaten by Holland (2–0).

THE FIFA WORLD CUP

EGYPT   First Final Series: 1934

First Final Competition match v Hungary in the first round of the series.

In a straight knockout competition, Egypt went down at Naples, in their only World Cup game, despite a spirited performance. Fawzi scored their first-ever World Cup goal in the first half and added a further goal later in the match, but the Hungarians won comfortably 4–2.

EL SALVADOR   First Final Series: 1970

First Final Competition match v Belgium in Group 1 of the series.

Clearly outclassed, El Salvador were extremely fortunate not to lose their first game by a considerably greater margin than the 3–0 score and, despite playing gamely in their other two matches, went home without a goal or a point.

Their appearance in the 1982 finals resulted in their losing to the first-ever double-figure score (1–10) against Hungary and their other two games ended in defeat also.

ENGLAND   First Final Series: 1950

First Final Competition match v Chile in Group 2 of the series.

Both Scotland and England qualified for the 1950 series because that year's Home Championship was designated as a qualifying group with two teams going through. Unbelievably, Scotland refused, despite finishing second, stating that they would only go as Home Champions!

Stan Mortensen scored their first-ever World Cup goal and Mannion the second in a laboured 2–0 win over the Chileans. The second match at Belo Horizonte provided the biggest shock of the competition when a greatly unfancied United States team inflicted the first World Cup defeat upon England. The 1–0 scoreline was greeted with disbelief at home followed by astonishment and dejection and a wholesale reorganization was made to the team before their next match with Spain. This proved to be of no avail and, going down 1–0 again, the English squad packed their bags and returned home.

Their next appearance in the 1954 series was against Belgium and Dickinson's extra-time own-goal levelled the score at 4–4—England's first World Cup draw. In this series they progressed as far as the quarter finals, a feat which they failed to achieve in 1958, but which was again achieved in 1962.

As host country in the 1966 series, England were more than anxious to re-establish themselves as a world-beating side and Alf Ramsey had gathered together a powerful, hard-running team. Their series began with a nervy, uninspired 0–0 draw against Uruguay (the first occasion that a foreign side had prevented England from scoring at

Stan Mortensen, the scorer of England's first World Cup final series goal, was one of the most lethal headers of the ball that the game has ever seen. (D C Thomson Ltd)

Wembley) but with 2–0 wins over Mexico and France the quarter finals were reached with ease. Argentina, their quarter-final opponents, played cynical, bruising football and their captain, Rattin, became the first professional footballer to be sent off at Wembley. Hurst's 78th-minute header decided the tie and England progressed to their first semi final against Portugal. Although the Portuguese were appearing in their first final series their team was outstanding, including, as it did, Eusebio. In a rare treat of attacking football, two cracking goals from Bobby Charlton clinched victory for England 2–1. The final against West Germany proved to be an end-to-end game of attack and counter-attack and, after the West German's had taken a 13th-minute lead England fought back to reverse matters at 2–1 in the 78th-minute. The West Germans pressed hard and equalized from a free-kick in injury time. England took an extra-time lead with a contentious shot which hit the underside of the bar and bounced out

England's captain Bobby Moore and West Germany's captain Uwe Seeler watch the referee Dienst toss a coin before the 1966 World Cup Final. (Photosource)

again and in the dying seconds put the game beyond doubt at 4–2 with a Geoff Hurst goal—his third and the first World Cup Final hat-trick.

Defending the Cup in Mexico in 1970, England looked to be cruising to their second semi final when their opponents in the quarter finals were, once again, West Germany. However, the score was levelled 2–2 at full-time and Müller gave West Germany victory with an extra-time goal.

It was not until 1982 that England again qualified for the final series and, after an impressive three-win start, progressed to a quarter-final group with the hosts, Spain, and West Germany. Both games ended 0–0 and England failed to progress further despite conceding only one goal and without losing a game.

In 1986, England found themselves in the heat of Monterrey and began in a most indifferent manner losing 1–0 to Portugal. Facing Morocco in their next game, England again struggled to make an impression and were not helped when Wilkins became their first player to be dismissed in the finals after throwing the ball at the referee. After

drawing the Morocco game, England came good against Poland winning 3–0 thanks to a Lineker hat-trick and progressed through to the next round. Paraguay, their second round opponents, were despatched 3–0 and in the quarter finals England met Argentina — their first meeting since the Falklands War. Two goals from Maradona (one with his fist) gave Argentina a 2–1 victory and ended England's dreams of success, while Lineker's goal, his sixth of the series, resulted in his becoming the first England player to score in three consecutive World Cup games and the first English player to be the top scorer in a World Cup finals series.

FRANCE   First Final Series: 1930

First Final Competition match v Mexico in Group 1 of the series.

In the first-ever World Cup match, Laurent scored his country's first goal to put them on course for their first victory (4–1). Their next game against Argentina proved to be their first World Cup defeat with the only goal coming from Luisito Monti (one of the three Argentinians who 'defected' to Italy in the 1934 series).

France's first success in the 1958 series in Sweden came in their first game against Paraguay, when

Fontaine scored their first World Cup hat-trick in a thrilling 7–3 victory and then went on to score a further ten goals to become the all-time World Cup top scorer. They won their group and, eliminating Northern Ireland 4–0 in the quarter final, went on to their first semi final against Brazil. After losing this game 5–2 they trounced West Germany 6–3 in the third-place play-off.

It was not until the 1966 series that they recorded their first World Cup draw when Mexico held them to a 1–1 scoreline and they took their only point of the series.

They fared little better in 1978 but, in 1982, reached their second semi final against West Germany. The match ended level at 3–3 after extra-time and France became the first country to go out of the World Cup on penalties when they lost 5–4 in the penalty 'shoot out'.

France, the reigning champions of Europe, struggled to reach the 1986 finals but, once there, played some admirable football and qualified for the second round by beating Canada and Hungary and drawing with the USSR. In the second round, France easily defeated the holders, Italy, but it was in the quarter final against Brazil that they really came into their own. Playing magnificently, France held Brazil to a 1–1 score at the end of extra-time and went on to win 4–3 on penalties. Facing West Germany once again for the second

Just Fontaine, France's goalscoring genius, returning to Paris on a stretcher some while after breaking his leg during a French League game in 1961. (Photosource)

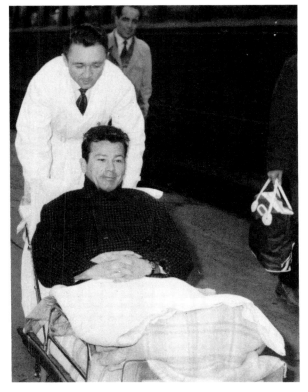

consecutive semi final, France went behind in the eighth minute and, despite valiant efforts, were once again eliminated by them. In the third place play-off France beat Belgium 4–2 after extra-time to achieve their best performance since 1958.

GERMANY (PRE-WAR) First Final Series: 1934

First Final Competition match v Belgium in the first round of the series.

The well-drilled German team came back strongly in the second half after trailing 2–1 at half-time. Conen, who became their first-ever goalscorer, grabbed two more in the second half to score their first hat-trick of the World Cup and Korbierski added two others to give Germany their first win (5–2). Disposing of Sweden in the second round, Germany met Czechoslovakia in their first semi final which also proved to be their first defeat (1–3). Their next game against Switzerland in the 1938 finals provided them with their first draw and the replay, which they lost 4–2, proved to be their last game before partition into East and West Germany.

HAITI First Final Series: 1974

First Final Competition match v Italy in Group 4 of the series.

Haiti gave Italy a thorough shaking by holding them to a 0–0 draw at half-time and then taking the lead with a goal by their centre-forward Sanon. This goal ended the Italian goalkeeper, Dino Zoff's record of having been unbeaten for 1143 minutes of playing time!

Despite this encouraging start, Haiti's dreams of glory were soon shattered and Italy won 3–1. Their two remaining games were mere formalities with defeats by Hungary (7–0) and Argentina (4–1).

HOLLAND First Final Series: 1934

First Final Competition match v Switzerland in the first round of the series.

Playing their first game in Milan, Holland were defeated 3–2 thanks to a freak goal in the second half. They fared no better in the 1938 series, going down 3–0 to Czechoslovakia, and it was not until 1974 that they played their next World Cup game. This time their opponents were Uruguay and, with two goals from Johnny Rep, they recorded their first World Cup win. Their first World Cup draw came in their next game—0–0 against Sweden and they cruised right through to the final with four more impressive wins. Appearing in their first final, against West Germany, they took an incredible first-minute lead through a penalty by Johan Neeskens—most incredible because no German player had actually touched the ball until Maier picked it out of the net!

In their first game in the 1978 series Rensenbrink notched up their first World Cup hat-trick in a 3–0 victory over Iran which set them on the road to another final place (against host country Argentina). The score was level 1–1 at the end of full-time and Holland went down 3–1 to extra-time goals from Kempes and Bertoni to become the first country to be runners-up in consecutive finals.

HONDURAS   First Final Series: 1982

First Final Competition match v Spain in Group 5 of the series.

With their first World Cup goal from Zelaya, Honduras shocked the host country, Spain, by winning their first World Cup point with a 1–1 draw. They went on to play Northern Ireland with a similar result and it was not until they played Yugoslavia that they lost their first World Cup game (1–0).

HUNGARY   First Final Series: 1934

First Final Competition match v Egypt in the first round of the series.

Over their first 29 World Cup matches, Hungary scored an average of almost three goals per game and scored four goals or more on ten occasions! Their first game against Egypt provided a taste of what was to come and, with Teleky scoring their first-ever World Cup goal, they ran out 4–2 winners. Their second round game against Meisl's Austrian team gave them their first defeat (1–2) and ended the 1934 series hopes.

In 1938 they reached their first semi final against Sweden in a game which saw Szengeller (who had scored two goals in their previous match) score his country's first World Cup hat-trick in a 5–1 win. Meeting Italy in their first final, their first final goal by Titkos levelled the score at 1–1 but Italy went on to a 4–2 win.

In the 1954 finals they again finished runners-up despite having trounced their opponents, West Germany, 8–3 in the opening group match and their next game, in the 1958 series (against Wales), was their first draw (1–1). Maintaining their high-scoring record they scored ten goals against El Salvador in the 1982 series (the first double-figure score) but still failed to reach the quarter finals!

1986 proved to be a series best forgotten for Hungary as they, for once, found themselves on the wrong end of a 6–0 scoreline (against the USSR). They went on to beat Canada but then lost to France and failed to qualify for the next round.

IRAN   First Final Series: 1978

First Final Competition match v Holland in Group 4 of the series.

Holland handed the spirited Iranian team their first World Cup defeat with a 3–0 scoreline and Peru went on to defeat them 4–1. Sandwiched between these defeats was their game against a Scottish side still reeling from the departure for home of Willie Johnston following a positive dope test. The Scots played terribly and Iran's Danaifard scored their first-ever World Cup goal and only an own goal by Eskandarian prevented them from winning the game.

IRAQ   First Final Series: 1986

First final competition match v Paraguay in Group B of the series. Surprising qualifiers, Iraq, still embroiled in a bitter war with its neighbour Iran, performed with credit against Paraguay but went down 1–0 to a goal by the South American 'Footballer of the Year' Romero. In their next game Rahdi scored Iraq's first Final Series goal but their opponents, Belgium, nevertheless won 2–1. The host country, Mexico, beat Iraq 1–0 in their last game and this left Iraq at the bottom of Group B without a single point.

ISRAEL   First Final Series: 1970

First Final Competition match v Uruguay in Group 2 of the series.

A full-strength Uruguayan team had little difficulty in beating Israel 2–0 in their first World Cup match but, in doing so, lost the services of Rocha who was carried off in the first 15 minutes of the game. Israel then played Sweden and Spiegler scored their first-ever World Cup goal in a creditable 1–1 draw. The shock result of the series came in their last match in Group 2 when they held the mighty Italian team to a 0–0 draw.

ITALY   First Final Series: 1934

First Final Competition match v United States in the first round of the series.

Schiavio scored Italy's first World Cup hat-trick in a cracking first game which saw them defeat a much depleted USA 7–1. Their second match in the series, against Spain, saw them fight back to their first World Cup draw (1–1) and they then went on to defeat them in the replay to earn a place in the semi final. This match was against their great rivals Austria and they won 1–0 to reach their first final. Their opponents, Czechoslovakia, took the lead and Orsi, scoring their first final goal, equalized eight minutes from time with Schiavio scoring their winner in extra time.

In the 1938 series, their hard uncompromising play excelled once again and they beat Hungary 4–2 in the final to become the first country to retain the Cup.

Despite appearing in the 1950, 1954 and 1962 series, they did not have much success and failed to progress beyond the first round on either occasion. In England in 1966 worse was to follow when they found themselves outplayed and outclassed by the unfancied North Koreans and they lost the tie 1–0 to fail again to reach the quarter finals.

In Mexico in 1970 the Italian fortunes took a decided turn for the better and after a somewhat

Italy's World Cup side, giving the Fascist salute to their leader, Benito Mussolini, during the 1934 Series. (Photosource)

shaky start with draws against Israel and Uruguay, they powered through the quarter finals and semi finals with wins over the host country, Mexico, and West Germany respectively. Appearing against a strong Brazilian side, in the Aztec stadium, Italy's negative tactics failed to curb their opponents who won the game 4–1 and consequently took the Jules Rimet Trophy outright.

After failing to make the 1974 quarter finals Italy stormed back in 1978 when they headed a strong Group 1 with three wins out of three. In the next round in Group A, they lost to Holland in a hard-fought game which distinguished itself more for the fact that Holland's Brandts scored an own goal for Italy in addition to one of his own country's goals (to become the first player to score for both sides) than for the calibre of the football. Finishing second in the Group, they lost the third-place play-off against Brazil 2–1.

In 1982 their dreams of the 1970 and 1978 series became reality when they reached their fourth final against West Germany. Arnold Cesar Coelho, a Brazilian, became the first South American to referee a final, and in the 25th minute, he awarded Italy a penalty for a foul on Conti. When Cabrini failed to score from the spot he registered the first World Cup final penalty miss, but, nevertheless, the Italians went on to become the first European country to win the Cup three times by winning 3–1.

On 31 May 1986, Italy, as holders played the first game of the competition against a dour Bulgarian side and only managed a 1–1 draw. In their next game they again drew 1–1 (against Argentina) and in their last first round game met South Korea needing a result to progress to the next round. With memories of their 1966 defeat by North Korea still lingering in their minds, they just scraped a 3–2 victory. France ended Italy's 1986 series with a 2–0 victory in a second round tie best forgotten by Italian fans.

KUWAIT   First Final Series: 1982

First Final Competition match v Czechoslovakia in Group 4 of the series.

Kuwait earned their first World Cup point with a 1–1 draw in their opening match, with their first World Cup goal coming from Al Dakheel. Controversy reared its head when they played France in their second game and appeared to be preparing to leave the pitch because someone in the crowd distracted them by blowing a whistle. Sheik Fahid, the head of their delegation, sorted the uproar out but they still lost 4–1. In their last game they soaked up England's pressure well, before going down 1–0.

MEXICO   First Final Series: 1930

First Final Competition match v France in Group 1 of the series.

In the first-ever World Cup match Mexico went down 4–1 with their first goal coming in the second half from Carreno. They fared similarly in their other two matches of Group 1 and, despite participating in both the 1950 and 1954 series, it was not until 1958 that they earned their first World Cup point. This game against Wales ended in a 1–1 draw and gave Mexico their only point of the 1958 series.

Their first World Cup win came in the last game in Group 3 of the 1962 series when they beat the eventual runners-up, Czechoslovakia, 3–1. Before their home crowd in 1970 they reached the quarter finals with two wins and a draw, before losing 4–1 to Italy.

Convinced that 1986 was to be their year, Mexico began by beating Belgium 2–1 and went on to qualify for the next round by drawing with Paraguay and beating Iraq. In the second round they beat Bulgaria and progressed to a quarter-final tie with West Germany. This ended 0–0 after extra-time but Mexico then went out of the competition 4–1 on penalties.

MOROCCO   First Final Series: 1970

First Final Competition match v West Germany in Group 4 of the series.

Morocco shocked West Germany by taking an early lead through Houmaine and were unlucky to lose the game 2–1. They held out bravely against Peru until the 66th minute and lost 3–0. Their promise of better things was realized in their third and last game when they earned their first World Cup draw with a 1–1 score against Bulgaria.

In 1986, Morocco surprised everybody by finishing top of Group F after drawing with Poland and England and beating Portugal. This ensured that they became the first African country to progress beyond the first round but, facing West Germany in their next game, they went out 1–0 to a last-minute goal.

NEW ZEALAND   First Final Series: 1982

First Final Competition match v Scotland in Group 6 of the series.

Had Scotland managed to beat New Zealand by more than the 5–2 margin that they actually achieved, they might have pipped USSR for a quarter final place. However, it was not to be and New Zealand's two goals (the first from Sumner) effectively put paid to Scotland's hopes. New Zealand's two other games both ended in defeat and so ended their only World Cup final series.

NORTH KOREA   First Final Series: 1966

First Final Competition match v USSR in Group 4 of the series.

In the opening match of Group 4 (at Middlesbrough) North Korea's boundless energy and enthusiasm won them the immediate support of the home crowd despite losing the game 3–0. Their second match against an under-par Chilean side earned them their first draw (1–1) with their first goal being scored by Pak Seung Jin. The sensation of the series and, indeed, the biggest upset since England's defeat at the hands of the United States in 1950, came in their next game against Italy. Taking a 1–0 half-time lead, North Korea held on against a demoralized Italian side to

record their first World Cup win. Italy reacted in the customary manner and greeted the return of their team with a fusillade of rotten tomatoes! Faced with an on-song Portugal, in the quarter final, it was not surprising that North Korea went down 5–3 — thanks to four goals (including 2 penalties) from Eusebio.

NORTHERN IRELAND   First Final Series: 1958

First Final Competition match v Czechoslovakia in Group 1 of the series.

With all four British home countries through to the final series for the first time, Northern Ireland became the first of the four to win when Cush scored his country's first World Cup goal to give them a 1–0 win. Their next game against Argentina proved a big disappointment when they lost 3–1. Two goals from McParland against West Germany earned them their first World Cup draw and, after a play-off (against Czechoslovakia) they progressed to their first quarter finals. In their quarter final game against France, Harry Gregg, the Northern Ireland keeper, was far from fit and the unstoppable Fontaine grabbed two of his country's four goals to end the Irish run.

In the 1982 series Northern Ireland shrugged off draws against Yugoslavia and Honduras and beat the host country Spain 1–0 to top Group 5 and to progress to Group D of the quarter finals. After a creditable 2–2 draw against Austria, the Irish luck ran out against France and the 4–1 defeat ended their Cup aspirations.

Stalwart defence linked with sparkling performances from their veteran goalkeeper, Pat Jennings, earned Northern Ireland a place in Mexico in 1986. Jennings, by far the oldest player in the series, continued to play commandingly but, although Northern Ireland earned a draw against Algeria, even he was unable to prevent them from losing their other two games.

NORWAY   First Final Series: 1938

First Final Competition match v Italy in the first round of the series.

Norway's one and only game in the World Cup finals against the holders, Italy, almost provided the upset of the series. Their outside-left, Brustad, scored his country's first World Cup goal early in the second-half, levelling the score at 1–1. Had his second goal not been ruled offside, Italy would have been unable to score their extra-time winner.

PARAGUAY   First Final Series: 1930

First Final Competition match v USA in Group 4 of the series.

The United States proved why they had been chosen as one of the four 'seeds' when, in their second game, they chalked up their second successive 3–0 win—against Paraguay. In their second match, Paraguay's Pena scored his country's first World Cup goal in their 1–0 victory over Belgium. Their next game, in the 1950 series in Brazil, gave them their first World Cup draw with a 2–2 scoreline against Sweden.

In 1986, Paraguay surprised many by taking the fourth South American place in the finals and then went on to prove that this was no fluke by qualifying for the second round for the first time. This was largely achieved through the perseverance of Romero, the 1986 South American Footballer of the Year, and left them facing England for a quarter-final place.

England ended their hopes by beating them 3–0.

PERU   First Final Series: 1930

First Final Competition match v Rumania in Group 3 of the series.

Peru lost their first game against Rumania with a 3–1 scoreline, Souza scoring their first and only goal of the series, and in their second game lost 1–0 to the ultimate winners, Uruguay. Their next appearance, in 1970, saw them achieve their first World Cup win with a 3–2 victory over Bulgaria but it was not until the 1978 series that they played their first World Cup draw—0–0 against Holland, and in their next game Cubillas notched up their first World Cup hat-trick in their 4–1 victory over Iran. They reached the quarter finals for the first time that year but lost all three of their games in the group.

In the 1982 series, although they managed to draw with the ultimate winners, Italy, they earned only one other point and finished at the bottom of their group.

POLAND   First Final Series: 1938

First Final Competition match v Brazil in the first round of the series.

In an absolutely thrilling game, Poland's Williamowski scored their first World Cup goal, then went on to score three more, notching up his country's first World Cup hat-trick. With a 4–4 full-time score Poland were beaten in the closing minutes of extra-time in just about the highest scoring match ever played in the World Cup (6–5). They then had to wait for a further 36 years before they played their next World Cup game against Argentina and, in the process, recorded their first win with a 3–2 margin. Winning four and losing just one game saw them through to their first third-place play-off (there were no semi finals as such in the 1974 series). With the only goal of the match scored by Lato, they overcame the reigning champions, Brazil, to achieve third place.

In the first match of the 1978 series they recorded their first draw 0–0 (against West Germany) and won their group to progress to the final Group B. Defeats by the eventual winners, Argentina, and by Brazil ended their aspirations for the series.

In the 1982 series, they again made a good start by

After winning eight Irish League Championship medals with Glenavon, Wilbur Cush, the scorer of Northern Ireland's first World Cup final series goal began his Football League career with Leeds United in 1957. (D C Thomson Ltd)

topping their first-round group and, after winning Group A of the next round progressed to their first semi final. Their opponents, Italy, the eventual winners, beat them 2–0 but in the third-place play-off, Poland beat France 3–2 to cap a fine series.

The 1986 series proved to be a great disappointment for Poland who scored only one goal but, nevertheless, qualified for a second tie against Brazil. They lost this 4–0 and bowed out of the tournament without showing any flair or drive whatsoever.

PORTUGAL   First Final Series: 1966

First Final Competition match v Hungary in Group 3 of the series.

Portugal's Augusto scored his country's first World Cup goal in an interesting match against Hungary at Old Trafford, Manchester. Goalkeeping errors by Hungary's Szentmihayl let him in for a further goal in the second half and Portugal won the game 3–1. Beating both Brazil and Bulgaria saw them through to a memorable quarter-final match against North Korea when Eusebio, with four goals, scored their first World Cup hat-trick and effectively won the game 5–3

A youthful Bobby Charlton pictured during his early days at Old Trafford. (Allsport)

after they had trailed 3–0. Their first semi-final appearance came against England in a superb free-flowing match at Wembley.

Bobby Charlton scored two goals to Eusebio's one in an end-to-end thriller, which ended in their registering their first World Cup defeat. Their third-place play-off two days later, against USSR, was a drab, bad-tempered game in which Torres scored the winner (2–1) in the dying minutes to spare the crowd extra-time.

Qualifying for only their second finals in 1986, Portugal met England (their conquerors in the 1966 semi final) in their first game. There had been great dissention amongst the Portuguese players with threats of walkouts and arguments over pay and, to everyone's surprise Portugal beat England 1–0. This was, however, their last moment of glory as they lost first to Poland and then to Morocco and came bottom of their group.

RUMANIA   First Final Series: 1930

First Final Competition match v Peru in Group 2 of the series.

Staucin gave them their first World Cup goal in the first-half and scored another in the second half in a 3–1 win. Their next opponents, Uruguay, brought them down to earth, handing them a thumping 4–0 defeat to end their hopes for the series.

They made a quick exit from the 1934 series, being eliminated by Czechoslovakia in the first round,

and, appearing in the 1938 series, registered their first draw with a 3–3 scoreline against Cuba before being eliminated in the replay.

In the 1970 series they were drawn in the same group as Brazil and England and, although they won a game against the other member of the group, Czechoslovakia, they did not progress beyond the first round.

SCOTLAND   First Final Series: 1954

First Final Competition match v Austria in Group 3 of the series.

As in 1950, the British Home International Championship was designated as a preliminary group with the top two teams qualifying. Once again the Scots qualified after finishing runners-up, but, this time, they agreed to participate although they had to do so without any Rangers players (Rangers considered a club tour to be more important). Playing the seeded Austrians, Scotland were unfortunate to go down 1–0 and when their team manager Andy Beattie resigned following criticism, they were left in disarray to face the powerful Uruguayans in their next game. Perhaps not surprisingly, they were thrashed 7–0 and so ended their first final series. Their next appearance against Yugoslavia in the 1958 series, earned them their first World Cup draw when Murray scored the equalizer (Scotland's first World Cup goal) in the second-half. They lost the other two games in the series and did not qualify again until 1974. Their first game in this series was against Zaire and goals by Lorimer and Jordan gave them their first World Cup win (2–0). Two further draws left them in equal top place with four points but they failed to qualify for the final rounds on goal difference (the first country to be eliminated without defeat).

The 1978 series saw Scotland embark full of confidence but, with a disastrous opening game against Peru (which they were fortunate to lose only 3–1), their dreams of championship were soon dashed. Worse followed when their winger Willie Johnston was given a dope test which proved positive and, protesting that he had merely taken two tablets for hay fever, was sent home in disgrace. Manager Ally MacLeod's inexperience became evident when he was unable to bring harmony to the side who, feuding amongst themselves, were only able to draw with Iran, thanks to an own goal from Eskandarian. The final game of the group saw Graeme Souness brought into the team against Holland and, with an inspired performance, Scotland won the game 3–2 but failed to progress further because of Holland's superior goal difference.

In 1982, for the third successive series, Scotland finished in equal second place with USSR in the preliminary group but, because of a poor goal difference, failed to progress further.

In 1986, Scotland found themselves in the

THE FIFA WORLD CUP

toughest first-round Group of the competition and lost their first two matches, to Denmark and West Germany respectively. Their third game was against the ruthless Uruguay team who, despite having a player sent off in the first minute of the tie, held out for a 0–0 draw to relieve Scotland of any further interest in the series.

SOUTH KOREA   First Final Series: 1954

First Final Competition match v Hungary in Group 2 of the series.

South Korea's two World Cup games in the series highlighted the great chasm between the standards of Asian and European football. Hammered 9–0 by Hungary and then 7–0 by Turkey, they bowed out of their first final series without impressing anyone.

It would have been difficult for South Korea to fare as badly in 1986 and in their first game against Argentina, Park Chang Sun scored their first World Cup goal, although they still lost 3–1. In their next game they won their first World Cup point by drawing 1–1 with Bulgaria but, in their last game to date, went down 3–2 to Italy.

SPAIN   First Final Series: 1934

First Final Competition match v Brazil in the first round of the series.

Spain's first World Cup goal came from a penalty kick by Iraragorri early in the first half which, together with two goals from Langara, despatched Brazil from the series by a 3–1 margin. In the next round they were somewhat unfortunate to draw the most improved team in Europe, Vittorio Pozzo's Italy. With a superb display from Zamora, Spain held them to a 1–1 draw (their first in the World Cup) in a match that is remembered for its violence above all else. Indeed, when the tie was replayed the following day, no fewer than seven Spaniards and four Italians were too badly injured to play! Italy won the replay 1–0 in a hard match that was refereed so badly that M Mercet, the Swiss official, was suspended by his national federation.

Spain next participated in the 1950 finals when they beat England, Chile and USA to reach the final pool and went on to finish the series in fourth position.

Participating in both 1962 and 1966, they failed to reach the quarter finals, winning only two of their six games and it was not until 1982, when they were the host country, that they again reached the finals. In 1982 they progressed to a quarter-final group with West Germany and England and with only one draw from the two games finished bottom of the group.

After a rather disappointing 1982 series, Spain performed much better in 1986 and, despite undeservedly losing 1–0 to Brazil in the opening game, qualified for the second round with victories over Northern Ireland and Algeria.

Facing Denmark in the second round, Spain surprised everyone by commanding play throughout the game as Butragueno notched up their first World Cup hat-trick (he scored 4 goals) enabling them to run out 5–1 winners. In the quarter final they drew 1–1 with Belgium but went out 5–4 on penalties.

SWEDEN   First Final Series: 1934

First Final Competition match v Argentina in the first round of the series.

Sweden won their first World Cup game with their first goal coming from Jonasson who then scored another in his side's 3–2 victory. (Without any of their 1930 final team at all to avoid further 'poaching' by Italian clubs Argentina, in fact, performed as well as could be expected.) Sweden's second-round tie against Germany saw them struggling with only ten men for much of the game and they suffered their first World Cup defeat (2–1).

Sweden's first-round game in the 1938 series was cancelled when their opponents, Austria, were forcibly withdrawn, following the German takeover of their country. England were, generously, offered Austria's place, but they refused and Sweden were given a bye through to the quarter finals. In the quarter finals they thrashed Cuba 8–0 with their first World Cup hat-trick coming from Wetterstroem who, in fact, scored four goals that day. Facing Hungary in their first semi final, they went down 5–1 and then lost the third-place match 4–2 to Brazil.

In the 1950 series they again played well to reach the final pool at the expense of Italy and Paraguay and then went on to take third place overall. They were the hosts for the 1958 series and, after winning their preliminary group, beat USSR in the quarter final and West Germany in the semi final to reach their first final game against Brazil. Liedholm gave them a great start by scoring after only 5 minutes but the brilliant Brazilians put on a marvellous display to win the game 5–2.

They next reached the finals in 1970 but were pipped on goal average for a quarter-final place by Uruguay. In the 1974 series they gained their revenge when beating Uruguay for a quarter-final group place, but, winning only one of their Group B matches failed to proceed further.

In 1978 they reached the finals, but failing to win a single game, had their worst final series ever.

SWITZERLAND   First Final Series: 1934

First Final Competition match v Holland in the first round of the series.

Switzerland's first goal was scored by Kielholtz who went on to score a further goal in their 3–2 victory over Holland. In the best match of the second round, they played Czechoslovakia in Turin. The Czech goalkeeper, Planicka, had a superb game as Switzerland kept up the pressure and only a goal seven minutes from time gave Czechoslovakia the tie (3–2). Their next World Cup game, in the 1938 series, was against Germany, a team strengthened by the addition of four Austrians (following Hitler's takeover of that country and their withdrawal as a separate World Cup team). Andre Abegglen, who, only two weeks earlier, had scored Switzerland's winning goal against England in Zurich, scored their only goal in this, their first World Cup draw. In the replay five days later, despite being 2–0 down at half-time the Swiss came back strongly to win 4–2 and progressed to a second-round tie against Hungary at Lille. Still tired after their replay, they went down 2–0. Of their appearances in later series, their 1954 quarter-final game (as hosts) against Austria was perhaps the most memorable. After taking an early 3–0 lead, they found themselves 5–4 down at half time in a game which produced some magnificent end-to-end football. The final score, 7–5 to Austria, is the record for the number of goals scored in a World Cup match. They have not won a World Cup game since, despite appearing in two further series.

TUNISIA   First Final Series: 1978

First Final Competition match v Mexico in Group 2 of the series.

Tunisia provided the first surprise result of the competition by soundly beating the Mexican team 3–1 with their first World Cup goal coming from Kaabi. They went on to prove that this was no freak result when they gave the powerful Polish team a hard fight before going down to their first World Cup defeat 1–0. Their third and last World Cup game, against the reigning champions West Germany, was perhaps their best performance of all and they recorded their first World Cup draw in a tight goalless match.

TURKEY   First Final Series: 1954

First Final Competition match v West Germany in Group 2 of the series.

Suat gave Turkey their first World Cup goal in the first half but they went down 4–1, despite being level at half-time. Facing South Korea in their next match, Turkey recorded their first World Cup win with an emphatic 7–0 scoreline. Burhan scored their first World Cup hat-trick in the game which was very much one-way traffic. The grouping in the 1954 series was such that they did not face the group winners Hungary but, tieing on points with West Germany, had to face them again in the play-off for a quarter-final place. It is widely assumed that West Germany contrived at this confrontation by fielding, in their previous match, the much-weakened side which lost 8–3 to Hungary.

If this was so, then it proved to be a successful ploy as they walloped Turkey 7–2 in the replay— Turkey's last World Cup game.

URUGUAY   First Final Series: 1930

First Final Competition match v Peru in Group 3 of the series.

Reigning Olympic champions, Uruguay, the host country for the 1930 series, got off to a somewhat shaky start, scraping a 1–0 victory thanks to their first World Cup goal from Castro. Gaining their stride, they despatched Rumania 4–0 to reach their first semi final, against Yugoslavia. With their first World Cup hat-trick coming from Cea they easily won the game 6–1 and went through to their first final against their bitter rivals and neighbours Argentina. In a fiercely fought game, Dorado put them into the lead with the first-ever World Cup Final goal but Argentina, urged on by thousands of their own supporters fought back to lead 2–1 at half-time. Cea levelled the score after a superb run and two further goals gave them a deserved 4–2 victory.

Because of internal strife and other arguments, they did not participate again until the 1950 series when they dropped their first World Cup point with a 2–2 draw against Spain the final pool. This was, however, their only set-back, and they emerged as champions once again by beating the favourites, Brazil, 2–1 in the deciding match of the final pool. This game, played at the Maracana Stadium in Rio de Janeiro was watched by a crowd of 199 854!

In the 1954 series, they appeared once more to be cruising to the final with 2–0, 7–0 and 4–2 wins until they met the on-song Hungarian side in the semi final. Fearing trouble after the violent melees of the 'Battle of Berne' quarter final between Brazil and Hungary, steel-helmeted police ringed the pitch. They were not needed in a game which proved to be an absolute delight of footballing skills and which ended in Uruguay's first-ever defeat in the World Cup, with a 4–2 score. In the third-place play-off they went down, again, to Austria (3–1). The other milestone in their World Cup career came in 1970 when they met Brazil in the semi finals—the first World Cup meeting between the two since Brazil's defeat in the 1950 final-pool decider. In a thrilling and, at times, violent match, they went down 3–1 giving Brazil their 'revenge' at last.

Entering the 1986 finals as South American Champions, Uruguay found themselves in the toughest first round group. After drawing their first game against West Germany they were thrashed 6–1 by Denmark and were fortunate to draw 0–0 with Scotland after having a man sent off in the first minute. In the second-round they went out somewhat meekly, losing 1–0 to Argentina.

USA   First Final Series: 1930

First Final Competition match v Belgium in Group 4 of the series.

McGhee scored the first World Cup goal in the

opening minutes of the game and then notched up another in his country's 3–0 victory over Belgium. With a similar score in their second game the USA proved that the experts had been correct in seeding them and they progressed to their first semi final against Argentina. The skilful Argentinians exposed the Americans' limited abilities and beat them 6–1 with the USA's goal coming from Brown in the second-half.

Drawn against the powerful Italian side in the 1934 series they made a swift exit, losing 7–1, and it was not until the 1950 series that they next appeared. When losing their first game against Spain 3–1, they gave no hint of what was to follow in their next game against England. In what was probably the greatest shock in any World Cup series they defeated the 'mighty' English team 1–0 at Belo Horizonte and effectively ended England's World Cup aspirations. Their only other game against Chile ended in a 5–2 defeat.

USSR   First Final Series: 1958

First Final Competition match v England in Group 4 of the series.

Russia had drawn 1–1 against England in a game at Moscow only three weeks earlier and, not surprisingly, this first World Cup match, too, ended all-square at 2–2 with Simonian scoring his country's first World Cup goal. Their following game against Austria earned them their first World Cup win (2–0) and, losing their next game against Brazil (2–0), they went on to play England again, for a quarter-final place. They won the play-off 1–0 and faced the host country Sweden in the quarter finals. Sweden won 2–0.

In 1962 they again lost in the quarter finals and reached their first semi final against West Germany in 1966. Playing at Goodison Park, they seemed to be gaining the upper hand until Haller scored for West Germany two minutes before half-time and seconds later Chislenko was sent off after kicking Held. With only nine fit men (Sabo had injured himself whilst trying to foul Beckenbauer) Russia fought bravely but went down 2–1. Their third-place match against Portugal also ended in a 2–1 defeat. In the 1970 series they again reached the quarter finals, losing to Uruguay, and in 1982 went through to the quarter-final group and only failed to reach the semi finals on goal difference.

In 1986, the USSR played the most thrilling football of the first round, in thrashing Hungary 6–0, drawing with France and beating Canada 2–0. Facing Belgium in the second round, Belanov scored Russia's first World Cup hat-trick but, in the most exciting game of the series, they went down 4–3 in extra-time.

WALES   First Final Series: 1958

First Final Competition match v Hungary in Group 3 of the series.

In their first World Cup match John Charles scored Wales' first World Cup goal to give them a 1–1 draw and, with two further draws against Sweden and Mexico, they went into a play-off for a quarter-final place against Hungary. In an over-physical match which saw Hungary's Sipos sent off, Ivor Allchurch and Terry Medwin both scored to give Wales their first World Cup victory (2–1) and a quarter-final place against Brazil. Without the dominating John Charles, who was injured by harsh Hungarian tackling in the play-off, Wales held out until Pele scored the only goal of the match in the second-half.

WEST GERMANY   First Final Series: 1954

First Final Competition match v Turkey in Group 2 of the series.

West Germany were not seriously troubled by the Turkish side and Klodt gave them their first World Cup goal in the first-half and, with three more coming in the second-half, they won 4–1. Sensationally, in their next game, they fielded at least six reserves against the full strength Hungarian side and were thrashed 8–3. This

John Charles, a tower of strength as a defender and a penetrating sharp-shooting forward, was in 1957 transferred to Juventus for £65 000.
(D C Thomson Ltd)

appears to have been a tactical ploy by the West German manager, because his team then played Turkey for a quarter-final place and an easier passage in the final rounds. It certainly worked and, with Morlock scoring his country's first World Cup hat-trick, they thrashed Turkey 7–2 to ensure a quarter-final tie against Yugoslavia. They disposed of Yugoslavia 2–0 and went on to play their first semi-final game against their Austrian neighbours at Basle. Schaefer gave them a 1–0 half-time lead but they ran away with the game in the second-half to win 6–1, to reach their first final game against Hungary—their conquerors in the first round. Playing against a Hungarian side that had gone four years and 29 games without a defeat, the West Germans certainly had their hands full! They were helped, however, by the fact that Ferenc Puskas, the Hungarian's key player was suffering from an ankle injury and although he scored Hungary's first goal and had another disallowed, he did not stamp the game with his usual authority. Morlock scored West Germany's first World Cup Final goal after the Hungarians had gone two up and a brace of goals from Rahn gave them their first championship win.

Their record in subsequent series has been exceptional, with a semi-final defeat in 1958, a quarter-final defeat in 1962, runners-up in 1966 and a third place in 1970. In the 1974 series they were the host nation and once again progressed to the final, this time against Holland. Despite suffering an incredible set-back when Holland took a penalty-goal lead before any West German player had even touched the ball, they came back with a Breitner penalty of their own and a Müller goal clinched the championship once again.

In 1982 they reached their fourth final which they lost to Italy 3–1.

1986, despite early forebodings, proved to be a highly successful series for West Germany as they progressed to become the first country to reach a fifth World Cup Final match. Their progress en route was somewhat halting and they reached the second round despite losing to Denmark and drawing with Uruguay. Nor did they excel in either the second round or the quarter finals when they narrowly defeated Morocco and Mexico respectively. It was not until the semi final against France (the first ever 'repeat' semi final) that they at last came into form and destroyed France's dreams of revenge for 1982 by winning the game 2–0. Argentina were, oddly enough, their first South American final opponents and, fielding Diego Maradona, proved more than a match for West Germany by beating them 3–2 in the final.

YUGOSLAVIA   First Final Series: 1930

First Final Competition match v Brazil in Group 2 of the series.

Yugoslavia shocked the seeded Brazilians by taking a 2–0 half-time lead with their first goal coming from Tirnanic. Despite pulling a goal back, Brazil were unable to prevent Yugoslavia registering their first World Cup win and Yugoslavia then progressed to the semi final after beating Bolivia 4–0. In their first semi final, Yugoslavia met the powerful Uruguayan team and were soundly beaten 6–1 after opening the scoring through Seculic.

They had a moderately successful 1950 series with two wins and one defeat and, in the 1954 series, beat France 1–0 before playing their first World Cup draw, 1–1 against Brazil. In 1958 they went out to West Germany in the quarter finals. In 1962 they had their most successful series, winning two of their Group 1 matches (including a 5–0 victory over Colombia in which Jerkovic, scored their first hat-trick) to progress to a quarter-final tie against West Germany, once again. This time they won the tie to reach their first semi final against Czechoslovakia.

Playing at Vina del Mar in Chile they were unfortunate to lose the game 3–1 very much against the run of play. Their only semi-final goal was scored by Jerkovic, their top World Cup scorer.

The 1974 series saw Yugoslavia register their highest win when they beat Zaire 9–0 with no fewer than seven different players scoring goals. Despite topping their first-round group, they failed to win a single game in the quarter-final group.

In 1982 they scored three points to finish level with Spain on both points and goal difference but failed to progress further because Spain had scored one more goal (3 instead of 2).

ZAIRE   First Final Series: 1974

First Final Competition match v Scotland in Group 2 of the series.

The underdogs of the Group, Zaire, held Scotland to a 2–0 margin which effectively ended Scotland's quarter final-aspirations. Other defeats by Yugoslavia (9–0) and Brazil (3–0) concluded their only final series.

13 EUROPEAN FOOTBALL CHAMPIONSHIP

Sometimes referred to as the Henri Delaunay Cup, the European Football Championship was inspired by Henri Delaunay the secretary of the French Football Association who proposed the tournament in the mid-1950s. The competition began in 1958 but M Delaunay did not live to see its commencement.

The first two competitions were organized on a similar basis to the European club competitions with a home and away aggregate knockout system leading to quarter finals, semi finals and a single-legged final. Prior to 1966, the competition was officially known as 'The European Nations Cup' but in 1966 the name was changed and the knockout system was replaced by a group system akin to the World Cup.

The first country to win the European Football Championship

The 1958/60 championship series is best remembered for the 'absentee' countries with Italy, West Germany, Holland, Belgium and all four British home countries declining the invitation to participate. Only 17 nations took part and, although Eire became the first country to win a match when they beat Czechoslovakia 2–0, Czechoslovakia took the away leg 4–0 to progress to the next round.

France hosted the first finals and the two participants in the final game were Russia and Yugoslavia. Russia were fortunate to be given a walk-over in the quarter finals when their opponents, Spain, became the first country to withdraw from the championship (because of political reasons dating back to the Spanish Civil War).

The first final goal

This was an own goal conceded by the Russian player Netto and his team-mates Metreveli and Ponedelnik scored in their opponent's goal to win the first championship for Russia 2–1. The winning goal was scored during extra-time—the final being the first to go beyond the 90 minutes.

The first host country to win the European Football Championship

The second competition in 1962/4 was much better supported with 29 nations participating (including all the home countries except Scotland). England's first game in the competition was played at the Hillsborough stadium in Sheffield and their opponents, France, held them to a creditable 1–1 draw, then easily won the return game in Paris (Alf Ramsey's first game as team manager), 5–2. Northern Ireland became the only British side to progress beyond the first round when they beat Poland 4–0 on aggregate but they lost 2–1 to the final's host nation, Spain, in the next round.

The final match was between the host country Spain and Russia and, played in Madrid, was watched by a partisan crowd of 120 000. Political objections shelved, Spain won the game 2–1 to become the first host nation to take the championship.

The first European Football Championship final match to be replayed

The 1966/8 championship saw the introduction of the first grouping preliminary competition and all four home countries entered for the first time. In fact, the four home countries formed Group 8 and, as in earlier World Cup qualifying games, the two year's Home Championships seconded as European Championship games. England won Group 8 and beat the champions, Spain, 3–1 on aggregate in the quarter finals. Their sudden-death semi-final game ended in a 1–0 defeat by Yugoslavia in a match which saw Alan Mullery become the first England player to be sent off in a full international.

Meanwhile, Italy, the final series hosts, went through to their first final on the toss of a coin, after drawing the semi final against Russia 0–0. The final game between Yugoslavia and Italy ended 1–1 after extra time and the first final replay took place two days later. Italy with five different players in their team, proved the fresher side and won the replay 2–0 with goals from Riva and Anastasi.

The first country to qualify for the European Football Championship finals on goal difference

In Group 1 of the 1970/2 preliminary series, Rumania and Czechoslovakia tied with nine points each and Rumania progressed to the quarter finals thanks to a superior goal difference.

EUROPEAN CHAMPIONSHIPS

The first country to appear in three European Football Championship finals

In the 1970/2 series, England were, once again, the only one of the home countries to reach the quarter finals and thanks to the familiar problems created by clubs refusing to release key players, Alf Ramsey fielded a makeshift team against West Germany at Wembley. West Germany won the game and ultimately the tie 3–1 and progressed to their first final. Their opponents, Russia, became the first country to appear in three finals but were comprehensively beaten 3–0.

A choice piece of acting by the Yugoslav, Trivic, earned Alan Mullery the distinction of becoming the first England player to be sent off, on 5 June 1968. (ASP)

The first player to score in consecutive European Football Championship finals

West Germany's Müller scored twice in the 1972 final (having already scored against every country which West Germany had met in the competition), then scored his country's first goal in the 1976 final against Czechoslovakia to become the first player to score in two finals and in consecutive finals. The score after extra-time was Czechoslovakia 2 West Germany 2 and the final became the first to be decided on a penalty shoot out. Czechoslovakia won the penalty shoot out 5–3.

The first country to appear in three consecutive European Football Championship finals

Italy became the first country to qualify for the finals because they were the host country when, in the 1978/80 series, the preliminary groups were limited to seven in number. Indeed, after being the hosts in 1968, they also became the first country to stage the finals twice. With the finals arranged on a group basis for the first time, West Germany reached their third consecutive final by heading Group 1 and Belgium were, surprisingly, their opponents after heading Group 2. West Germany won the game 2–1 and became the first country to win the trophy twice.

The series was marred, from the English point of view, by the 'Battle of Turin' when English supporters were taunted by Italian spectators following Belgium's equalizing goal. An angry reaction by English fans was violently quelled by Italian riot police wielding batons and firing teargas and, with several players affected by the gas, England could only manage a draw. It would not be difficult to theorize that much of the bitterness between English and Italian supporters which culminated in the Brussels tragedy in 1985 began at Turin that day.

The first double-figure score in the European Football Championships

Needing to beat Malta by 11 goals in their final qualifying game, Spain won the match 12–1 to top their group and pip Holland for a final-series place. Many eyebrows (particularly Dutch ones) were raised at this surprising scoreline, but television replays suggested that any doubts were groundless.

Country-by-country firsts
ALBANIA First series entered 1962/4

Albania's first European Championship match against Greece was never played because Greece (technically at war with their Albanian neighbours since 1912) withdrew leaving Albania a walkover into the second round. Denmark were their second round opponents and won 4–0 in Copenhagen in the first leg of the tie. The return game in Tirana, four months later, ended in a 1–0 victory to Albania, Pano scoring the first Albanian goal of the competition. Although Albania have competed in four further championships, they have never progressed to the final stages. However, they achieved a major surprise on 17 December 1967 by holding West Germany to a goalless draw, effectively ending the Germans' hopes of progressing to the quarter finals.

AUSTRIA First series entered 1958/60

Austria won their first European Championship game in Oslo 1–0, thanks to a fine goal by Hof who scored two more goals in the second leg of the tie in Vienna which Austria won 5–2. Their second-round opponents were France who had finished in third place in the 1958 World Cup tournament scoring the highest number of goals, thanks to goal ace Just Fontaine. Fontaine continued in his goalscoring ways and hammered a hat-trick in France's 5–2 victory and France also won the return-leg in Vienna 4–2. Austria have never reached the final stages of the competition.

BELGIUM First series entered 1962/4

Belgium went down 3–2 in their first European Championship game in Yugoslavia, Stockman scoring their first goal and also lost the home leg of the tie 1–0. In the 1970/2 series Belgium reached the final stages of the competition for the first time after knocking Italy out in the quarter finals. Belgium was selected as the venue for the finals but the home team went down 2–1 to West Germany in the semi finals and had to settle for third place, after beating Hungary by the same margin in Liège. In the 1978/80 series, Belgium went one better and reached their first final, again facing West Germany but lost 2–1, thanks to a last-minute goal by Hrubesch.

BULGARIA First series entered 1958/60

Bulgaria lost the away leg of their first European Championship game in Yugoslavia 2–0 and could only draw the home leg 1–1, thanks to a Diev goal. In the 1962/4 series Bulgaria beat Portugal 3–1 at home only to lose the away leg by exactly the same margin and thus became one of the first two countries to participate in a play-off. This took place in Rome and Bulgaria won 1–0 to progress to the second round for the first time. Their opponents, France, won the two games 3–2 on aggregate and Bulgaria have been unable to go beyond the first round since, although they almost made it in 1987 when Scotland's late winner robbed them of a place in the West German finals.

CYPRUS First series entered 1966/8

Although Kostakis gave Cyprus the half-time lead in their first European Championship game against Rumania, the Rumanians stormed back after the break to win 5–1. The next four of their Group 6 games also ended in defeat but on 17 February 1967, Cyprus achieved their first victory by beating Switzerland 2–1. Cyprus have never reached the final stages of the competition but in 1987 were involved in an extraordinary incident when their keeper Charitou was injured by a smoke bomb thrown by a Dutch hooligan. Because of this attack, the result was declared void and a replay was ordered, behind closed doors. The Dutch won the replay 4–0 and went on to take the championship.

CZECHOSLOVAKIA First series entered 1958/60

For their first European Championship game Czechoslovakia were faced by Eire in the only preliminary round ever played in the competition. The first leg of the tie in Dublin went Eire's way 2–0 but, in the return leg, after Dolinsky had given Czechoslovakia a half-time lead with their first goal, the Czechs went on to

The victorious Czechoslovakian team—in the shirts of their defeated opponents.

Soren Lerby in action against France in the 1984 European Championship Finals. (Colorsport)

goal, they were hammered 5–1 in the away leg of the tie. In the next series, the Danes were more than a little lucky in drawing Malta, Albania and Luxembourg *en route* to their first semi final but, with the USSR as their semi-final opponents soon ran out of luck and went down 3–0. In the third-place match, they held Hungary 1–1 thanks to a Berthelsen goal, but then conceded two extra-time goals to lose 3–1. Denmark reached the semi finals again in the 1982/4 series when they faced Spain. Despite an early goal by Lerby, the score at the end of extra-time was still tied 1–1 and Spain won the penalty shoot-out 5–4.

EAST GERMANY First series entered 1958/60

East Germany performed well, away to Portugal in the first leg of their first European Championship game and were unfortunate to lose 3–2, Vogt scoring their first goal in the competition. The return leg of the tie proved a great disappointment and East Germany lost the game 2–0. In the 1962/4 series, East Germany knocked out Czechoslovakia 3–2 on aggregate to progress to the second round for the first and only time but their opponents, Hungary, took the tie 5–4.

EIRE First series entered 1958/60

Eire won their first European Championship match in Dublin when, thanks to goals by Tuohy and Cantwell they beat Czechoslovakia 2–0 in a

Noel Cantwell, the scorer of Eire's first penalty goal in the European Championship. (Colorsport)

win 4–0 to progress to the first round proper. After disposing of Denmark and then Rumania, Czechoslovakia reached the first semi finals on 6 July 1960 when they lost 3–0 to the USSR in Marseille. Three days later they won the third-place match against France by a margin of 2–0. In the 1974/6 series, Czechoslovakia progressed to the quarter finals after topping Group 1 ahead of England and gained their revenge over the USSR by beating them to progress to a semi-final tie.

After winning this 3–1, Ondrus scoring their first semi-final goal, the Czechs met West Germany in their first final on 20 June 1976. Svehlik put them ahead in the first half but, even after extra-time, the final score was still tied 2–2 and Czechoslovakia went on to become the first country to win the trophy on penalties. In the next series, Czechoslovakia almost reached the final again but, because no semi finals were played in the 6th series, had to settle for an appearance in the third-place match against the host country, Italy. Ironically this game, as the previous final, went to a penalty shoot-out which Czechoslovakia won 9–8 to become the first country to gain third place on penalties.

DENMARK First series entered 1958/60

Although Denmark managed to draw their first European Championship match against Czechoslovakia 2–2, P Pedersen scoring their opening

Ron Flowers of Wolves and England, whose penalty goal against France was England's first goal in the European Championship. (Popperfoto)

Michel Platini (right) the scorer of France's first goal in a European Championship Final. (Allsport)

preliminary-round tie. A little over a month later, the Irish lost the return leg 4–0. In 1962/4 Eire met Austria in the second round, having easily beaten Iceland in the first and progressed to their first quarter finals by winning the tie 3–2. Their quarter-final opponents, Spain, made short work of the Irish who failed to progress beyond the first round again until the 1986/8 series. In that series Eire pulled of an extraordinary feat by beating England 1–0 and were only denied a semi-final place when Holland, the eventual winners, scored a lucky goal nine minutes from the end of their last game.

ENGLAND First series entered 1962/4

England faced France in their first European Championship game at an unusual venue, Sheffield Wednesday's Hillsborough Stadium. Flowers scored England's first goal in the competition when he equalized from the penalty spot in the second half of the game, after Goujon had given the French a first-half lead. The return-leg of the tie was played on 27 February 1963 and was Alf Ramsey's first game as the England manager. France won 5–2 thanks largely to a poor display by England's keeper Ron Springett who was struggling to regain match-fitness after injury. In the 1966/8 series, the British Home International Championship seconded as a qualifying group and, despite losing 3–2 to Scotland at Wembley, England reached the quarter finals by drawing 1–1 at Hampden Park in front of the biggest crowd (134 000) ever to attend a European Championship match. England then progressed to their

first semi final by beating Spain in both legs of the quarter final — the first clash between reigning World Champions and reigning European Champions. Yugoslavia were England's first semi-final opponents and they took the tie with the only goal of the game late in the second half after Alan Mullery had become the first British player to be sent off while playing for his country. In the third-place match Bobby Charlton put England ahead against the USSR and a further goal by Geoff Hurst made the final score 2–0 to secure England's highest-ever position in the Championship. England have been unable to reach the semi finals since, despite winning through to the finals on three further occasions.

FINLAND First series entered 1966/8

Finland's first European Championship game against Austria ended in a goalless draw and the honour of scoring the first goal fell to Makipaa, in the next game in Greece which the Finns lost 2–1. Finland ended at the foot of their group table in the 1966/8 series, a feat which they emulated in 1970/2 and 1974/6. They have never yet progressed beyond the first round of the competition.

FRANCE First series entered 1958/60

Fresh from a high-scoring performance in the 1958 World Cup in Sweden, France hammered Greece 7–1 in their first European Championship game. Raymond Kopa opened the scoring for France and Cisowski scored the first-ever European Championship hat-trick. In the quarter finals, the French continued their high-

Ruud Gullit, the scorer of Holland's first goal in a European Championship Final. (Allsport/David Cannon)

scoring performances beating Austria 9–4 on aggregate to progress to the first semi finals of the competition. As one of the four semi finalists, France was selected as the venue for the finals but bowed out to Yugoslavia 5–4 despite leading 4–2 only a few minutes from the end. France met Czechoslovakia in the third-place match, losing 2–0 and did not progress to a further semi final until 1984, ironically again on home soil in Marseille. This time their opponents were Portugal and France won through to their first final due to a goal by Michel Platini in the last minute of extra time which made the score 3–2. In the final in Paris, France faced Spain and Platini scored their first goal as they went on to win the Championship 2–0.

GREECE First series entered 1958/60

Greece were over-run by France's high-scoring forward line in their first European Championship match and were lucky to keep the score down to 7–1, Yfantis scoring their goal. In the return leg, two months later, the Greeks redeemed their honour somewhat by holding the French to a 1–1 draw. In the 1962/4 series, Greece were drawn against neighbouring Albania, a country against whom they had been technically at war since 1912 and, fearing for the safety of their players, withdrew from the competition. Greece have reached the final stages on only one occasion, in 1978/80, when they played remarkably well to top their first round group ahead of the USSR, Hungary and Finland. Despite playing some excellent football, Greece came bottom of their quarter-final group but had the satisfaction of holding the ultimate winners, West Germany, to a 0–0 draw.

HOLLAND First series entered 1962/4

The Dutch had little difficulty in disposing of Switzerland in their first European Championship game, winning 3–1, Van der Linden scoring their first goal. Their second-round opponents, Luxembourg, achieved one of the greatest shocks in the history of the competition when, playing both legs of the tie in Holland, they overcame the Dutch 3–2 on aggregate. It was not until the 1974/6 series that Holland again progressed beyond the first round and they did this by topping Group 5 above Poland, Italy and Finland. After beating their arch-rivals, Belgium, in the quarter finals they faced Czechoslovakia in the semi finals in Zagreb. After 90 minutes the match was tied 1–1, Ondrus of Czechoslovakia having scored both goals, his own goal for Holland being their first semi-final goal! Czechoslovakia clinched a place in the final with two extra-time goals and Holland had to settle for third place after beating the hosts, Yugoslavia, 3–2 in the third-place match in Zagreb. In 1986/8 Holland reached the semi finals again, against West Germany and, thanks to an 88th minute goal by Marco Van Basten, won the tie 2–1 to reach their first final. Their opponents in the final, the USSR, had beaten Holland 1–0 in a Group 2 game two weeks previously but, after Ruud Gullit had opened the scoring in the 32nd minute, Van Basten clinched their first Championship win with a 53rd minute goal.

HUNGARY First series entered 1958/60

In their first European Championship game Hungary faced the USSR in Moscow's huge Central Stadium. The game itself was the first ever game in the 'European Nations Cup' proper and, within ten minutes, Hungary were two goals behind. Gorocs struck back with Hungary's first goal in the second half but the scoreline finished 3–1 in Russia's favour. In the 1962/4 series, Hungary reached the semi finals by defeating Wales in the first round, East Germany in the second round and France in the quarter finals. Their semi-final opponents were the host country, Spain and, although Bene scored for Hungary in the second half, his goal was not enough to defeat the Spanish who won 2–1. Their third-place fixture against Denmark was tied 1–1 after 90 minutes but Hungary scored twice in extra-time to gain third place. Hungary reached the semi finals again in 1972 but went down 1–0 to the USSR in Brussels.

Inter-Milan's Angelo Domenghini, whose late equaliser earned Italy a final replay against Yugoslavia. (Popperfoto)

EUROPEAN CHAMPIONSHIPS

ICELAND First series entered 1962/4

Iceland travelled to Dublin to play Eire in their first European Championship game but, despite scoring twice through Jonsson, lost the match 4–2. The return leg ended in a 1–1 draw and, although Iceland have achieved some surprising results in subsequent series, they have yet to progress beyond the first round.

ITALY First series entered 1962/4

Orlando scored Italy's first European Championship goal against Turkey in their first game in the competition and went on to score three more in his country's 6–0 victory. In the second round Italy met the reigning champions, the USSR, and went out 3–1 on aggregate. After topping Group 6 in the 1966/8 series, Italy beat

Northern Ireland's Derek Dougan pictured in his Blackburn days. (Popperfoto)

Bulgaria in the quarter finals to progress to the semi finals. Selected as hosts, Italy faced the USSR in the semi finals and, after the game had ended 0–0, became the first country to progress to a European Championship Final on the toss of a coin. Their opponents in the final were Yugoslavia and the Italians scored a late equalizer through Domenghini to tie the game 1–1. Thus Italy progressed to the first Final Replay and, fielding a much-changed team won the trophy with a 2–0 victory.

LUXEMBOURG First series entered 1962/4

After receiving a bye in the first round, Luxembourg met their neighbours, Holland, in the second round. The Grand Duchy FA decided to play both legs of the tie in Holland and stunned the Dutch by drawing the 'away' leg 1–1 thanks to a goal by May. In the second leg, Luxembourg pulled off one of the biggest surprises that the competition has ever seen by beating Holland 2–1 to progress to the quarter finals. Their quarter-final opponents were Denmark and Luxembourg proved that their second-round performance had been no fluke by drawing both legs of the tie. The play-off ended 1–0 in Denmark's favour and Luxembourg have failed to progress beyond the first round in all the subsequent series.

MALTA First series entered 1962/4

Malta's first game in the European Championship was against Denmark in Copenhagen and Ole Madsen, the Danish centre-forward scored a hat-trick in his country's 6–1 victory, Theobald scoring Malta's goal. The Maltese have never progressed beyond the first round and have conceded over six goals on five occasions.

NORTHERN IRELAND First series entered 1962/4

Derek Dougan put Northern Ireland ahead in their first European Championship game in Poland and Humphries scored a second to give the Irish a deserved but unexpected 2–0 victory. After winning the second leg by the same margin, Northern Ireland looked set to spring another surprise when they held the reigning European Champions, Spain, to a 1–1 draw in Spain in the second round but then lost the home leg 1–0. Northern Ireland have failed to progress beyond the first round in any subsequent series.

NORWAY First series entered 1958/60

Norway were somewhat unfortunate to go down 1–0 to Austria in their first European Championship game in Oslo but were soundly beaten 5–2 in the return leg four months later when Odegaard scored both of Norway's goals. Norway have never progressed beyond the first round of the competition.

EUROPEAN CHAMPIONSHIPS

POLAND First series entered 1958/60

For a country that has achieved relative success in the FIFA World Cup, Poland's record in the European Championship has been abysmal. Spain were Poland's visitors for their first European Championship game and, aided by an on-form Di Stefano, they achieved an easy 4–2 victory, Poland's goals coming from Pol and Brychczy. The return leg finished 3–0 to the Spaniards and Poland have yet to progress beyond the first round of the competition.

PORTUGAL First series entered 1958/60

Portugal travelled to East Germany for their first European Championship tie and surprised the Germans by taking a first-half lead through Matateu and going on to win 2–0. In the second round Portugal beat Yugoslavia 2–1 at home but were thrashed 5–1 in the away leg. Portugal faced Bulgaria in the first round of the 1962/4 series and after losing away 3–1, defeated Bulgaria by exactly the same margin to earn a place in the first-ever play-off of the competition. Bulgaria won the play-off by courtesy of a late Asparoukhov goal and Portugal failed to progress beyond the first round again until the 1982/4 series when they topped Group 2 above Poland, the USSR and Finland. In the finals in France, Portugal played remarkably well to progress to their first semi final, against the host country. Jordao scored Portugal's first semi-final goal when he equalized in the second-half and again in extra-time. France, however, hit back through Domergue and won the game with a last-minute Platini goal.

RUMANIA First series entered 1958/60

Rumania were held to a 0–0 half-time score by their visitors, Turkey, in their first European Championship game but, after Oaida had put them ahead in the second half, they surged to a 3–0 victory. Turkey won the second leg of the tie but Rumania progressed to the next round on a superior goal difference. Czechoslovakia ended Rumania's hopes of further success beating them at home and away in the second round. Rumania had to wait until the 1970/2 series before they again progressed beyond the first round when they got their revenge over Czechoslovakia by overcoming them in the first-round group matches. Their quarter-final opponents were Hungary and they were finally beaten in a play-off after both legs of the tie had been drawn. Rumania reached the finals again in 1984 but finished bottom of their group with a single point.

Alfredo Di Stefano leaves the pitch after representing a FIFA Rest of the World team against England in 1963. (Popperfoto)

EUROPEAN CHAMPIONSHIPS

SCOTLAND First series entered 1966/8

Scotland's first game in the European Championship was a British Home International match in Wales when Denis Law scored their goal in a 1–1 draw. Scotland then won against Northern Ireland before beating England at Wembley (England's first defeat as reigning World Champions) and, as a result, were expected to progress to the second round ahead of England. On 24 February 1968, however, Scotland could only manage a draw against England and thus narrowly missed their chance of a quarter-final tie against Spain. Since then, Scotland have failed to get within a stone's throw of the later stages, finishing third, third, fourth, fourth and fourth in the five succeeding first-round groups.

SPAIN First series entered 1958/60

Spain travelled to Poland for their first European Championship game and won an easy 4–2 victory after Di Stefano had opened the scoring. The home leg of the tie was won by an equally convincing margin (3–0) and Spain drew the USSR in the second round. However, 1959 was little over 20 years after the end of the Spanish Civil War and Franco's right-wing government, who were still pursuing an extreme anti-communist policy, forced the Spanish FA to withdraw from the tie. In the 1962/4 series, Spain was selected as the venue for the finals after reaching the semi finals by beating Rumania, Northern Ireland and Eire. Their semi final opponents were Hungary and a relatively modest crowd of 50 000 were in Real Madrid's magnificent Chamatin Stadium to see Pereda set Spain on course for a 2–1 victory with his first-half goal. Four days later, Spain faced the USSR in the final and, this time, there was no question of a Spanish withdrawal. A massive crowd of 120 000, including General Franco himself, packed into the Chamatin stadium and, in pouring rain, saw Spain take an early lead through Pereda. The Russians equalized but, late in the second half, Marcelino scored the winning goal as Spain became the new champions and the first team to beat the USSR in the competition. Spain reached the final again in 1984, overcoming Denmark 5–4 on penalties in the semi finals but lost 2–0 to the host country, France.

SWEDEN First series entered 1962/4

Sweden made the short trip to neighbouring Norway for their first European Championship game and had little difficulty in overcoming the Norwegians 2–0 thanks to two goals by Martinsson. The return leg ended all square at 1–1 and Sweden met Yugoslavia in the second round. After drawing the away leg 0–0, Sweden won through to the quarter finals by beating the Slavs 3–2 at home. Their quarter-final oppo-

nents were the USSR and, after drawing the home leg 1–1 thanks to a Hamrin goal, the Swedes were unlucky to lose the away leg 3–1. Sweden have failed to progress beyond the first round in any subsequent series.

SWITZERLAND First series entered 1962/4

Switzerland's first European Championship game was against Holland away and, although Hertig kept them in the game with a first-half goal, Holland ran out easy 3–1 winners. In the home leg of the tie the Swiss came back from a goal down to draw the game 1–1. Switzerland have never progressed beyond the first round of the competition.

TURKEY First series entered 1958/60

After losing 3–0 in the away leg of their first European Championship game against Rumania, Turkey played remarkably well to win the home leg 2–0 after two goals by Lefter and, with luck, might have earned a play-off. Turkey have never progressed beyond the first round of the competition.

USSR First series entered 1958/60

The USSR took a fourth-minute lead through Ilyin when they met Hungary in the first ever first-round game in Moscow's Central Stadium before an enormous crowd of 100 572. The match finished 3–1 in Russia's favour and, thanks to a brilliant display by Lev Yashin, the USSR took the away-leg 1–0 to progress to the second round. Spain were their second-round opponents but, because of long-standing political differences, the Spanish government forced their FA to withdraw, and this gave the USSR a walkover into the first semi finals in France. Czechoslovakia were Russia's semi-final opponents in a game played in blistering heat in Marseille and, after Ivanov had put the USSR ahead with a first-half goal, he and Ponedelnik scored again after the interval to make the result 3–0. Thus the USSR progressed to the first ever final when Metrevelli levelled the scores with a second-half goal after Yugoslavia had taken an early lead. The game went into extra-time and a goal by Ponedelnik was enough to win the first final for the USSR. In the 1962/4 series the USSR again progressed to the final (becoming the first country to reach two finals) but suffered their first defeat in the competition when they lost 2–1 to the host country, Spain. Russia's remarkable consistency in the competition continued with a semi-final appearance in the

Lev Yashin, the USSR's goalkeeping genius in training prior to playing for The Rest of the World against England in 1963. (Popperfoto)

1966/8 series (when they became the first country to reach three consecutive semi finals) and this was followed by a further appearance in the final in the next series in 1970/2 (when they became the first country to reach three finals). In 1986/8 the USSR went down 2–0 to Holland in their fourth final and became the first country to lose three final games in the process.

WALES First series entered 1962/4

Although Medwin scored a first-half goal for Wales in their first European Championship game in Hungary, the Welsh lost the game 3–1 and, only managing a 1–1 draw in the home leg, bowed out of the competition. In the 1974/6 series, Wales progressed beyond the first round for the first time and were rewarded with a quarter-final tie against Yugoslavia. After losing the away leg 2–0, Wales could again only manage a 1–1 draw at home and were unable to proceed further as a result. Wales has failed to progress beyond the first round in any subsequent series.

WEST GERMANY First series entered 1966/8

Muller was quickly off the mark against Albania in West Germany's first European Championship game and he went on to increase his tally to four goals as West Germany strolled to a 6–0 victory. Eight months later in the last game in their qualifying group, West Germany travelled to Albania for the return fixture, knowing that they required a victory by any margin to progress to the next round ahead of Yugoslavia. Albania, however, despite having lost their previous three games in the group, were not the pushovers that the West Germans thought they

Horst Hrubesch whose last-minute goal enabled West Germany to become the first country to win the European Championship twice. (Allsport)

were. Defending resolutely, Albania held West Germany to a 0–0 draw and might even have snatched a winner to add to the West German's embarrassment.

In the next series West Germany again found themselves up against Albania in their qualifying group but, this time, made no mistake and progressed to a quarter-final tie against England. After Hoeness had put West Germany ahead in the first half at Wembley, Netzer and Muller also scored to give West Germany a comfortable 3–1 victory. The home-leg ended goalless and West Germany progressed to their first semi final against host country Belgium in Antwerp. An enormous number of West German fans made the short trip across to Antwerp and virtually turned the semi final into a home tie for West Germany, drowning out the Belgian cheers with their hunting horns. Muller scored both goals in West Germany's 2–1 victory and notched up two more when his country overcame the USSR 3–0 in the final, four days later.

West Germany won the 1974 FIFA World Cup to become the first reigning European Champions to take that title and then reached the final of the next European Championship with little difficulty. Their opponents, Czechoslovakia, how-

Spurs Welsh International Terry Medwin, the scorer of his country's first European Championship goal. (Colorsport)

EUROPEAN CHAMPIONSHIPS

European champions, West Germany, celebrate their victory over Belgium in 1980.

ever, refused to be intimidated by the West Germans' apparent invincibility and won 5–3 on penalties after holding them to a 2–2 draw after extra-time. West Germany became the first country to appear in three consecutive finals when they met Belgium in Rome in the next series and, thanks to a last-minute Hrubesch goal became the first and, so far, only country to win the title twice.

YUGOSLAVIA First series entered 1958/60

At home to Bulgaria, Yugoslavia took the lead through Galic, in their first European Championship game, and went on to win 2–0. Five months later the away leg ended 1–1 and Yugoslavia faced Portugal in the quarter finals. Although they lost the first leg in Portugal 2–1, when they played the home leg they stormed ahead in the second-half and won 5–1 to earn a semi final tie against France, the hosts. With less than half-an-hour remaining in that game Yugoslavia were trailing 4–2 but, inspired by centre-forward Jerkovic, they came back strongly and progressed to the first ever final with a remarkable 5–4 victory. Four days later they faced the USSR in the final in Paris and shocked the Russians by taking a first-half lead through Galic. Metrevelli equalized for the USSR soon after the start of the second half and, with the game tied 1–1 at 90 minutes, extra-time was played. With just seven minutes of extra-time remaining, Yugoslavia conceded a goal and were unable to get back into the game. In the 1966/8 series, Yugoslavia reached the final again and were unfortunate to be held to a 1–1 draw by the hosts, Italy. Just two days later, Yugoslavia, with a depleted squad from which to choose, made just one team change in the first ever final replay, whereas the Italians were able to field five fresh players. The tired Yugoslavia team lost the replay 2–0 and became the first country to lose two finals. In 1974/6, Yugoslavia progressed to the semi finals once more and found themselves selected as the host country for the first time. Unfortunately, they went down 4–2 to West Germany in the semi finals and have failed to progress beyond the first round in any subsequent series.

14 AWARDS AND HONOURS

Throughout its history the game of soccer has not been renowned for its generosity towards individuals who have promoted the sport. All too often, years of sterling service have been cast aside without a single word of thanks and the national and international associations have been just as remiss as individual clubs in acknowledging outstanding contributions. There were exceptions, thankfully, and the introduction of various writer's and association's awards after the Second World War now serve to highlight outstanding performances.

The first person to be honoured by the Football Association

On Monday 6 February 1911, Lord Kinnaird was presented with the second FA Cup (the first had been stolen) after it had been replaced by the present trophy, in recognition of his outstanding services to soccer. He had then been the President of the Football Association for 21 years and to this day holds the record for the most FA Cup Final appearances.

The first 'Soccer Knight'

In 1927 J Clegg of Sheffield, who had been a member of the Football Association's council since 1886, was given a knighthood and, as President of the Football Association until 1937, was known as Sir Charles Clegg. Both John Charles Clegg and his brother William Clegg (later Sir William Clegg, Lord Mayor of Sheffield) had played for England and had figured prominently in the early years of soccer. Their greatest claim to fame was perhaps their participation on 14 October 1878 in the first ever floodlit match which was staged at Bramall Lane, Sheffield before an estimated crowd of 20 000. WE Clegg captained the winning team and JC Clegg the other team for the game which was, additionally, the first occasion that a crowd in excess of 10 000 attended a match outside Glasgow. Quite what proportion

A hard, low shot from Blackpool's Bill Perry beats Manchester City's Bert Trautmann during the 1954/5 season. (*Book of Football Champions*)

AWARDS AND HONOURS

Stanley Matthews shows the Stoke City 1948 'Player of the Year' trophy to a young fan. (Colorsport)

of the crowd were attracted by the game and what proportion by the novelty of electric floodlighting will never be known but, had the lighting around the ground been better, perhaps the 8000 fans who entered without paying would have been deterred.

The first winner of the 'Footballer of the Year' award

In 1948 the Football Writers Association introduced their 'Footballer of the Year' award for players from the Football League, and Stanley Matthews of Blackpool FC became the first winner after a sparkling season.

In 1949 the Irishman Johnny Carey of Manchester United FC became the first non-British winner of the award and in 1956 Bert Trautmann of Manchester City (whose bravery in the FA Cup Final had earned universal praise) became the first goalkeeper to win the award. In 1957 Tom Finney of Preston North End FC became the first player to win the title twice (he first won in 1954) and in 1965 Bobby Collins of Leeds Utd FC became the first Scottish winner.

The first winner of the 'European Footballer of the Year' award

In 1956, the French football weekly *France*

Football first conducted their annual poll of European soccer writers to establish this title and, as with the 'Footballer of the Year' award, Blackpool's Stanley Matthews was the first winner.

The legendary Alfredo Di Stefano of Real Madrid won the title in 1957 and, in 1959, became the first player to win twice. In 1964 Denis Law became the first Scottish winner of the award and in 1974 Johan Cruyff became the first player to win the award three times and also the first player to win in consecutive seasons.

The first Scottish footballer to be honoured by the Monarch

In HM the Queen's Birthday Honours List in 1980, Tommy Walker of Heart of Midlothian FC became the first Scot to be honoured for his services to the game, when he received the OBE.

The first soccer player to be knighted

In 1965, crowning an absolutely wonderful career in soccer, Stanley Matthews (who had already won practically every award going) was awarded a knighthood by HM The Queen. This incredible player, who had made his international debut for England in 1934, last played first class soccer in 1965 at the age of 50!

The first winner of the 'Scottish Footballer of the Year' award

Decided by the Scottish Football Writers

AWARDS AND HONOURS

Association, this award was not instituted until 1965 when Celtic's Billy McNeill became the first winner.

The first winner of the 'Golden Boot' award

Presented to Europe's leading league goalscorer, this was instituted at the end of the 1967/8 season. Eusebio Da Silva Ferreira of Benfica won the first award with 43 goals and in 1972/3 scored 40 goals to become the first player to take the title twice. Ian Rush became the first British winner of the award at the end of the 1983/4 season.

(Right) Iron man, Norman Hunter, who was selected as the first 'Player's Player' in 1973. (ASP)

(Below) Stanley Matthews before taking the field for Stoke City after reaching the age of 50! (Allsport)

AWARDS AND HONOURS

The first winner of the 'Player of the Year' award

Decided by the Professional Footballers Association, this was instituted in 1973 and the winner is generally described as the 'player's player'. Norman Hunter of Leeds United FC and England was the first recipient of the award in October 1973.

The first winner of the 'Young Player of the Year' award

Also decided by the Professional Footballers Association, this title was instituted in 1974 when Andy Gray of Aston Villa FC became the first

winner. In the same year he also won the 'Player of the Year' award to become not only the first winner of both titles, but also the first winner of both titles in the same year.

Andy Gray, pictured in November 1985, back in Aston Villa's strip, after spells with Wolves and Everton. (ASP)

15 | GOALKEEPING FIRSTS

By the very nature of their position, goalkeepers are often regarded as a breed apart from other soccer players and it is because of this that we have allocated them their own, albeit small, section.

The existence of goalkeepers was first acknowledged around 1870 in the 'Sheffield' Association's rules which stated that 'the goalkeeper is that player on the defending side who, for the time being, is nearest his own goal'. The 1878 FA rules first permitted the use of hands by the goalkeeper. R Gardner became the first goalkeeper to captain his country (Scotland) in the early 1870s whilst he was a Queens Park player and went on to make further international appearances after transferring to Clydesdale.

James McAulay of Dumbarton, who scored a goal whilst playing at centre-forward in the 1881 Scottish FA Cup Final, changed positions to become the most authoritative keeper of his day. He made eight international appearances for Scotland and was the first player to be regaled with the title 'The Prince of Goalkeepers'.

Defenders were allowed to tap goal-kicks straight into their keeper's hands (until 1936) and on 14 April 1900 in a match against Sunderland, Manchester City's goalkeeper, C Williams, became the first keeper (technically) to score from a goal-kick. Sunderland won the game 3–1.

Until the rules were changed in 1912, goalkeepers were allowed to handle the ball anywhere within their own half of the field and in 1910 J Brownlie of Third Lanark FC and C Hampton of Motherwell both took advantage of this rule to score goals in the same match!

The Middlesbrough goalkeeper, Williamson, making his international debut for England against Ireland on 25 February 1905, became the first goalkeeper to score an own goal in an international. No doubt this was a double embarrassment due to the fact that the game was played on his own club's ground!

Combi of Italy became the first goalkeeper to captain a World Cup winning side when he helped his country to defeat Czechoslovakia 2–1 in the 1934 final. Remarkably, Planicka, the Czech goalkeeper, was also the team captain that day.

Manchester City's Frank Swift became the first keeper to captain England on 16 May 1948, when he helped his country to a 4–0 victory.

A spectacular save by Crystal Palace's Vic Rouse gives some insight into the Welsh selectors' reasons for selecting a Fourth Division player. (Photosource)

16 TRANSFERS

The major difficulty in recording firsts for transfer fees paid by one club to another arises because there is no uniformly accepted method of quantifying the actual fees paid. Transfers are private contractual matters and since there is no published register of fees, we have found it necessary to rely upon press releases and statements by clubs and players which, because of the nature of public relations exercises, occasionally owe more to fantasy than fact!

In 1899 the Football Association suggested that there should be a maximum transfer fee of £10, but it was not until January 1908 that a fee limit (£350) was first imposed. The implementation of the limit proved impossible and, four months later, it was scrapped.

Unless otherwise stated, all transfers relate to British clubs.

The first £500 transfer fee and the first £1000 transfer fee

The link between these two fee thresholds is, quite simply, Alfred Common. This extraordinary player was transferred from Sheffield United FC to Sunderland FC in 1902 for £500 and again in February 1905 from Sunderland FC to Middlesbrough FC for £1000. His introduction into a struggling Boro side proved a success when they immediately chalked up their first away win for almost two years and avoided relegation to the Second Division.

The first £2000 transfer fee

During December 1912, Blackburn Rovers FC paid the Southern League club, West Ham United FC, £2000 for the services of Danny O'Shea and the following year Chelsea FC paid the first £2500 fee for T Logan from Falkirk FC.

The first £5000 transfer fee

There were no fewer than three different players who, in 1922, were transferred for fees of £5000 or more. Firstly, in February, Falkirk FC reversed the trend and bought an Englishman, Sid Puddefoot, from West Ham Utd FC and soon afterwards, Sunderland twice broke the £5000 barrier with the transfers of Mick Gilhooley from Hull City FC and W Cresswell from South Shields FC.

The first £10 000 transfer fee

The fee limits continued to rise steadily, despite the depression, as soccer attendances, too, began to climb and in October 1928 the first five-figure fee was paid. This was paid by Arsenal FC to Bolton Wanderers FC for David Jack and was variously quoted as being: £10 890; £10 340 and £10 670!

The first £50 000 transfer fee

In June 1957 Leeds United's Welsh international player John Charles was transferred to the Italian club Juventus for £65 000. This was the first occasion that a British player was transferred overseas and it was not until March 1960 that a fee in excess of £50 000 was paid by an English club (Denis Law when transferring from Huddersfield Town FC to Manchester City FC).

Globe-trotting Denis Tueart's £¼ million transfer to Manchester City in 1974 led a surge of fees of that magnitude. (ASP)

Seventeen-year-old Denis Law pictured before his transfer from Huddersfield Town to Manchester City. (Allsport)

The first six-figure transfer fee

Denis Law again figured in the transfer-fee spiral, when he was transferred from Manchester City FC to Torino in July 1961 for £100 000 and yet again in July 1962, when Manchester United FC brought him back to England for £115 000. An Argentinian, Enrico Sivori, had figured in the first £100 000 transfer as early as 1957 when he moved from the River Plate club to Juventus.

The first six-figure fee between two English clubs was paid in August 1966 when Alan Ball transferred from Blackpool FC to Everton FC, and the first between two Scottish clubs was the transfer of Colin Stein from Hibernian FC to Rangers FC in October 1968.

The first £¼ million transfer fee

In 1974 there was a rush of transfer fees in excess

of £250 000 with Denis Tueart's transfer from Sunderland FC to Manchester City FC leading the field. The first £¼ million transfer fee overseas was paid in 1968 when Haller moved from Bologna to Juventus.

The first £½ million transfer fee

In June 1977 Kevin Keegan was transferred for a fee of £500 000 when he moved from Liverpool FC to Hamburg, West Germany. Overseas, it was Paul Breitner (whose transfer from Bayern Munich to Real Madrid in 1975 had cost £675 000) who first passed the £½ million mark. It was not until 10 January 1979 that the £½ million mark was passed between two English clubs when West Bromwich Albion FC paid Middlesbrough FC £510 000 for David Mills.

(Right) Clive Allen in December 1980, while playing for Crystal Palace. (ASP)
(Below) Trevor Francis tightly marked by Sheffield United's Ted Hemsley in the Birmingham City colours some time before his £1 million transfer to Nottingham Forest. (ASP)

Colin McAdam after his transfer to Rangers. (D C Thomson Ltd)

Laurie Cunningham before his transfer from West Bromwich Albion to Real Madrid in 1979. (ASP)

The first £1 million transfer fee

Incredibly, just five weeks after the first £½ million transfer between two British clubs the £1 million mark was reached. On 14 February 1979, Nottingham Forest FC paid £975 000, plus VAT, plus player's percentage to Birmingham City FC for the services of Trevor Francis (a total of around £1 150 000!)

Overseas, the first £1 million transfer had taken place in 1975 when G Savoldi was transferred from Bologna to Naples for £1 100 000.

Clive Allen was the first British player to be transferred for £1 million on two occasions: from QPR to Arsenal in June 1980 and from Arsenal to Crystal Palace in August 1980.

The first player to have his fee set by a tribunal in Scotland

Partick Thistle's Colin McAdam was the first player to have his fee set by the arbitration tribunal when he transferred to Rangers FC in June 1980.

The first £1½ million transfer

After the meteoric rise in transfer fees between 1974 and 1980 (when average British fees rose by almost 500%) Bryan Robson's transfer from West Bromwich Albion FC to Manchester United FC heralded not only the passing of the £1½ million barrier but, thankfully (some will say), almost the last really huge fee between two British clubs. No doubt the legal changes which resulted from the player's new freedom of contract were a prime factor in the reversal of this trend and it is to be hoped that the days when striving clubs almost bankrupted themselves to buy players, have now passed.

The first player to have his fee set by an international tribunal

Pat Nevin, who joined Chelsea FC from Clyde FC in May 1983, was the first player, moving between separate national leagues, to have the transfer fee fixed by the tribunal.

The first £1 million player to be given a free transfer

Laurie Cunningham, whose transfer to Real Madrid in 1979 had funded West Bromwich Albion's purchase of David Mills, was given a free transfer by the Spanish club in 1984.

Aberdeen FC

Although the current Aberdeen FC was not formed until 1903, a forerunner (also named Aberdeen) was established in 1881 and was based at Pittodrie from 1899. Aberdeen FC was created in 1903 by the amalgamation of three major clubs from the 'granite city'. These clubs, Aberdeen FC, Victoria United FC and Orion FC combined under the Aberdeen FC name and, using Pittodrie as a base, joined the Northern League in 1903. In 1904, Aberdeen were elected into the Second Division of the Scottish League and, despite only attaining seventh place in that division, were promoted to the First Division the following season. Clyde FC who had finished the 1904/5 season as Second Division champions could feel some justification in being aggrieved by this decision but, since automatic promotion was not introduced until 1921/2 there was little that they could do.

At the end of the 1916/17 season when the League was reduced to only 18 clubs, Aberdeen FC were excluded from membership and were not reinstated until 1919/20. Although a consistent First Division side (they have never been relegated from the top division), Aberdeen did not really come right to the forefront until after the establishment of the Premier Division and the arrival of Alex Ferguson.

First game.

Although the Aberdeen club which preceeded the present one first played in 1881, the current Aberdeen FC's first match was their Northern League fixture against Stenhousemuir FC on 15 August 1903 which ended in a 1–1 draw.

First Scottish FA Cup match.

Aberdeen's first foray into the Scottish FA Cup took place at Alloa on 23 January 1904 when they went down 2–1 in the first round of that year's competition.

First Scottish League match.

Elected into the Scottish Football League Second Division for the 1904/5 season, Aberdeen's first game at home to Falkirk FC on 20 August 1904 ended in a 2–1 victory for Falkirk. It was not until 24 September 1904 that Aberdeen achieved their first victory, a 3–1 home win over Abercorn.

First Scottish FA Cup game win.

On 28 January 1905, Aberdeen FC, still only a Second Division side, knocked out First Division Queens Park who, although well past their best, were still a formidable side, and eventually progressed to their first quarter-final tie. Their opponents were Third Lanark FC who put paid to Aberdeen's Cup hopes and went on to win the trophy themselves.

First Scottish First Division game.

Elected into the First Division in only their second season in the Scottish League, their first game in the top division on 19 August 1905 ended in a 1–0 home defeat by Partick Thistle FC.

First Scottish FA Cup semi final.

In 1907/8 Aberdeen progressed to their first semi-final game but were defeated 1–0 by the holders Celtic FC who went on to retain the trophy.

First Scottish FA Cup Final.

In 1936/7 Aberdeen reached their first Cup Final when they faced Celtic FC at Hampden Park, Glasgow. Before a crowd of 147 365 (the largest official attendance for a British soccer match) Aberdeen went down 2–1.

First League Cup matches.

Having won the forerunner of the Scottish League Cup (the Scottish Southern League Cup) in 1945/6, Aberdeen FC were favourites for a place in the first final. Their first game was against Falkirk in the qualifying group and thanks to four goals from G Hamilton, they won the game 4–3 and topped their group table to reach the quarter finals. Wins over Dundee FC in the quarter finals and Hearts in the semi final saw them facing Rangers (who they had beaten in the previous year's Scottish Southern League Cup Final) in the first-ever League Cup Final on 5 April, 1947. Unable to match their form of the previous year, Aberdeen FC lost the game 4–0.

First Scottish FA Cup Final win.

Just two weeks after losing the first Scottish League Cup Final, Aberdeen FC met Hibernian in the Scottish FA Cup Final. In one of the few finals not to involve a Glasgow club, Aberdeen won their first trophy by a 2–1 scoreline.

First League championship win.

Although they had finished in the top four on a number of occasions, it was not until 1954/5 that Aberdeen achieved their first title win with one of the highest winning tallies ever recorded—24 wins from just 30 games.

First Scottish League Cup Final win.

Appearing in their second final on 22 October 1955, Aberdeen FC defeated St Mirren FC 2–1 to take the trophy for the first time.

First European competition.

Aberdeen's first game in Europe was a European Cup-Winners Cup tie against KR Reykjavik and was played on 6 September 1967. Winning 10–0, with a hat-trick from F Munro, Aberdeen took the tie 14–1 on aggregate but went out 3–2 to Standard Liege in the second round.

First Fairs/UEFA Cup tie.

Aberdeen's first appearance in the Fairs Cup was away to Slovia Sofia on 17 September 1968. This match ended in a 0–0 draw and Aberdeen won the home leg 2–0 to progress to the next round. In the second round they beat Real Zaragoza 2–1 at Pittodrie but lost the away leg 3–0.

First European Cup tie.

In an extremely close-fought tie Aberdeen beat Austria Vienna 1–0 at Pittodrie on 17 September 1980 and held on in Vienna to draw 0–0 and win the tie. Their 'reward' was a tie with Liverpool who won both legs to end Aberdeen's thoughts of European Cup success.

First European Trophy.

In 1982/3, after playing their best football ever to win the semi-final matches with Waterschei 5–2 on aggregate, Aberdeen met the legendary Real Madrid in the European Cup-Winners Cup Final in Gothenburg. In a close-fought encounter in pouring rain John Hewitt came on as substitute for Black (who had scored the first goal) and scored the winner in extra-time—2–1. They then went on to beat the European champions, Hamburg, to win the 'Super Cup' for the first time.

Arsenal FC

Arsenal FC were founded in 1886 by the workers at the Royal Arsenal and played a few games behind their workshops under the title 'Dial Square FC' before re-organizing as 'Royal Arsenal FC' and moving to play on Plumstead Common. In 1887

Aberdeen's 1954/5 Championship-winning team. (*Book of Football Champions*)

they moved to the Sportsman's Ground in Plumstead Village and then on the nearby Manor Field until 1890. Between 1890 and 1893 they played at the Invicta Ground, also in Plumstead, and during this time (1891) they changed their name to Woolwich Arsenal FC and turned professional.

In 1893 they became the first London club to be elected to the Football League and formed themselves into a limited company to buy their old Manor Field ground. What had started out essentially as a working men's club was, by 1910, struggling desperately to remain financially viable. That year, £3000 in debt, the company went into liquidation and were only saved from extinction by Henry Norris, the mayor of Fulham, who initially envisaged moving the club to share Fulham's Craven Cottage ground. However, the club played on at the Manor Ground until 1913 when, intent on improving their support, Norris moved the club 'lock, stock and barrel' across the river to their present Highbury site. Norris invested £125 000 to provide the club with a first-rate ground and after finishing a creditable third from top in Division Two, at the end of the 1913/14 season, changed their name to 'The Arsenal'.

Eric Black scores Aberdeen's first goal against Real Madrid in the 1983 European Cup-Winner's Cup Final. (Colorsport)

Arsenal's Parker carries off the FA Cup after his team's victory on 26 April 1930. (Photosource)

With the start of the First World War Arsenal were again plunged into financial despair when, having spent enormous amounts on their facilities, they found themselves without any income as a result of the abandonment of the League for the duration. By 1919 they were really in a fix until Norris, pulling every string at his disposal, scandalously secured Arsenal's promotion to the First Division at the expense of near-neighbours Tottenham Hotspur (who should, by rights, have retained their First Division status because of the increase in size from 20 to 22 clubs).

Despite being the only First Division club not to have qualified for their promotion from the Second Division, Arsenal went from strength to strength to consolidate their position and are now, rightly, placed amongst the best clubs in the land.

First FA Cup matches.

The first qualifying-round match was played on 5 October 1889 against Lyndhurst and resulted in an 11–0 win for Royal Arsenal, with W Scott achieving their first hat-trick of the competition by scoring four goals. Despite this win they did not qualify for the full competition until 17 January 1891 when they went out to Derby County in the first round with a 2–1 scoreline.

ARSENAL

First Football League match.

This Second Division match was played on 2 September 1893 against Newcastle United FC and ended in a 2–2 draw.

First Football League win.

Playing Walsall Town Swifts FC on 11 September 1893, they notched up their first victory by a 4–0 margin. Heath scored three of the goals that day to secure the clubs first League hat-trick.

First full FA Cup competition win.

On 9 February 1901, Second Division Woolwich Arsenal beat First Division Blackburn Rovers 2–0 to achieve their first win in the FA Cup first round. In the second round, they lost 1–0 to West Bromwich Albion.

First promotion to the First Division.

1903/4 was a very close-fought season with Preston North End (50 pts) first taking the Second Division championship from Woolwich Arsenal (49 pts) and Manchester United (48 pts). However, despite failing to take the championship, the Gunners were promoted to the First Division for the first time as runners-up. Four seasons later, still in the First Division, the Gunners and Blackburn Rovers achieved a unique first by ending the season equal 14th *both* with the statistics P38 W12 D12 L14 F51 A63!

First FA Cup semi final.

The Gunners' promotion to the First Division in 1904/5 heralded their first real success in the 1905/6 season, when they progressed beyond the second round for first time, and despatched Sunderland in the third round (5–0) and Manchester United (3–2) in the quarter final. In the semi final they were defeated 2–0 by Newcastle United FC. The following season they again went out at the semi-final stage, losing 3–1 to The Wednesday.

First FA Cup Final.

On 23 March 1927 it was a case of third time lucky when Arsenal beat Southampton 2–1 in the semi final to progress to their first final match. Cardiff City won the match 1–0 to end Arsenal's hopes of success in addition to becoming the first non-English club to win the Cup.

First FA Cup Final win.

On 26 April 1930 Arsenal achieved their first victory in an FA Cup Final when they beat Huddersfield Town 2–0. Alex James, who was transferred from Preston North End on 29 June 1928 for a fee of £9000, scored the first goal of the match. In October 1928, Arsenal became the first club to break the five-figure threshold when they paid more than £10 000 for David Jack from Bolton Wanderers.

more than £10 000 for David Jack from Bolton Wanderers.

First League championship win.

Arsenal's domination of the English game started with their first FA Cup victory and the following season saw them win their first championship by a margin of seven points from Aston Villa. In 1931/2 they had the misfortune of being both League and FA Cup runners-up but came back with a vengeance the following season when capturing their first of three successive League titles.

First substitute.

On 28 September 1965, against Northampton Town FC in the League, A Skirton became the first Arsenal player to come on as a substitute for the first team. Three years later, in the opening match of the season, B Gould, who came on as substitute against Leicester City FC, became the first 'sub' to score when he netted two goals.

First League Cup match.

It was not until 1966 that Arsenal entered the League Cup for the first time, and their first tie, on 13 September 1966 against Gillingham FC, ended in a 1–1 draw. On 28 September 1966 the return-tie ended in a 5–0 victory for Arsenal but it was the next season that they progressed through their first semi final (by beating Huddersfield Town FC 6–3 on aggregate) to their first final. In the final game at Wembley, Arsenal were beaten 1–0 by Leeds United.

First £100 000 transfers.

In January 1970, Arsenal paid their first six-figure fee for P Marinello from the Scottish club Hibernian and in July of the following year received their first six-figure fee when J Sammels was transferred to Leicester City FC.

First European competitions.

Arsenal have played over 50 games in the three European competitions beginning on 25 September 1963 when both Strong and Baker scored hat-tricks in their 7–1 victory over Staevnet Copenhagen in the Fairs Cup. They progressed to the 1970 Fairs Cup Final against Anderlecht when, despite losing the away-leg 3–1, they won the Cup with a 3–0 home victory.

In the European Cup they defeated Stromsgodset both home and away and were unfortunate to go out to an on-form Ajax in the quarter-finals.

Their one appearance in the European Cup-Winners Cup competition began on 19 September 1979 with a 2–0 victory over Fenerbahce and seven games later, Arsenal faced Valencia in the final in Brussels. The game remained goalless and Arsenal lost the penalty shoot-out 5–4.

Celtic FC

Unlike most clubs, which were formed to promote soccer, Celtic's origins were of a far more philanthropic nature. In November 1887, under the guidance of a Roman Catholic priest, Brother Walfrid, the club was established within the desperately poor Irish Catholic community in the east of Glasgow. Its main objective was to raise funds to feed and clothe the children of the community and its formation soon provided a source of inspiration to the poor of the area. Some six months afterwards, the first game was played against the Protestant club Rangers and the rivalry of 'Old Firm' confrontations, which has dominated Scottish football, was established.

Throughout the years, 'the Bhoys' have encountered adversity, particularly of a sectarian nature and, like Everton, were in the early 1890s confronted with an exorbitant rise in their rent (from £50 p.a. to £500 p.a.). Their reaction was predictable and they purchased the site of their present ground a short distance away in 1892. Their huge stadium was initially the venue for Scotland's home fixtures and was constructed with that aim in mind.

Within a short time, Celtic were quickly established in the forefront of Scottish football and have remained there ever since.

First game.

In May 1888 Celtic's first game was against Rangers FC and ended 5–2 to Celtic FC.

Jimmy McGrory was turned down by Bury but became the most consistent goalscorer that British football has seen. (Colorsport)

CELTIC

First Scottish FA Cup match.

Celtic began their first Scottish FA Cup campaign on 1 September 1888 by beating Shettleston FC of Glasgow 5–1 at the first Celtic Park. In the next round they continued in style by beating another Glaswegian club (Cowlairs) 8–0 with Michael Dunbar scoring their first hat-trick. By 12 January 1889 they had reached their first semi final and their opponents, Dumbarton, were despatched 4–1 to send Celtic through to the final against Third Lanark FC at their first attempt. On the day of the match the pitch was covered in thick snow and a friendly was played instead. The match was declared void because of the snowstorm and was replayed the following week when Third Lanark FC won 2–1.

First League match.

On the opening day of the Scottish League (16 August 1890) Celtic played at home to Renton who won the game 4–1. However, Renton were disqualified by the League after only a handful of games, and their record was expunged. Their next game on 23 August 1890 was against Heart of Midlothian FC at Tynecastle Park, Edinburgh and gave an indication of the successes which were to follow when Celtic won the game 5–0. The following week in their first home game, Peter Dowds scored their first League hat-trick in their 5–2 defeat of Cambuslang.

First Scottish FA Cup Final win.

On 12 March 1892 Celtic met Queens Park, the long-time giants of Scottish soccer, in their second Cup final. The match was played at the neutral Ibrox ground and Queens Park protested when encroachment by the capacity crowd resulted in Celtic scoring the only goal of the match. On 9 April 1892, the final was replayed before a greatly reduced all-ticket crowd and Celtic won their first trophy by a score of 5–1. McMahon scored Celtic's first final hat-trick that day.

First League championship.

After finishing third in 1890/1 and second in 1891/2, Celtic won their first title in 1892/3 by a single point from Rangers. The following season they retained the title and in 1895/6 they became the first club to win three championships.

The first international match to be played at Parkhead.

Soon after Celtic moved to their new home at Parkhead, Scotland beat Ireland 6–1 in the first international to be staged at the ground.

First League Cup game.

In the League Cup Celtic were unable to emulate their early performances in the Scottish FA Cup and their first game against Hibernian on 21 September 1946 ended in a 4–2 defeat. Indeed, it was not until they met Third Lanark FC at Hampden Park on 19 October 1946 (Cathkin Park was closed for repairs) that they recorded their first victory (3–2).

In 1951/2 they progressed to their first semi final, when they lost 3–0 to Rangers and it was 1956/7 before they reached their first final. Facing Partick Thistle, they drew the first game 0–0 but won the replay 3–0 to take their first League Cup trophy. The following year the first 'Old Firm' League Cup Final was played and, in one of the most one-sided meetings between the two sides, they retained the trophy with a 7–1 scoreline.

Between 1964 and 1978, Celtic appeared in a record-breaking 14 consecutive League Cup Finals winning six of them!

First Fairs/UEFA Cup match.

In their very first European tie, Celtic travelled to Spain to meet Valencia on 26 September 1962 and went down 4–2. They were unable, in the home-leg, to pull back the deficit and went out of the competition 6–4 on aggregate.

First European Cup-Winners Cup tie.

Celtic's first foray into the European Cup-Winners Cup soon produced success, when on 17 September 1963 they travelled to Switzerland to play Basle. Thanks to a hat-trick from John Hughes, they won the game 5–1 and the tie 10–1 and with victories over Dynamo Zagreb (4–2 on aggregate) and Slovan Bratislava (2–0 on aggregate) reached their first semi final against MTK Budapest. A 3–0 home victory was thrown away and they lost the tie 4–3 on aggregate.

First substitute.

In a Scottish League Cup tie at St Mirren on 3 September 1966, Willie O'Neill became the first substitute to be used and, three weeks later, in a League match at Dundee, Steve Chalmers became the first substitute to score a goal.

First European Cup tie.

1966/7 was a quite exceptional year for Celtic. First they won the League Cup by beating Rangers 1–0, then they won the Scottish FA Cup by beating Aberdeen 2–0 and then they won the League championship. It was perhaps not surprising that such a powerful team, (under the guidance of Jack Stein) should sample European success also. On 28 September 1966 they won their first home tie against Zurich 2–0 and powered to their first European Cup Final by knocking out Zurich, Nantes, Vojvodina Novi Sad and Dukla Prague. Their final opponents were Inter-Milan of Italy and despite going a goal down in the early stages, Celtic rallied to win 2–1 and crowned a truly magnificent season with Britain's first European Cup victory.

EVERTON

Everton FC

Formed as St Domingo's FC in 1878, Everton first played in Stanley Park, Liverpool and, playing in the Everton district, changed their name to Everton FC in 1879. In 1882 they moved to a fenced-in ground in Priory Road which proved to be inconveniently located and in 1884 moved to Anfield at the instigation of John Houlding, a wealthy supporter. Paying Houlding a rent of £100 p.a., Anfield proved to be a very satisfactory site and had he not increased their rent to £250 p.a., the club would probably still be playing at Anfield. Mr Houlding was a very important and wealthy person in the Liverpool area and, indignant that the club had refused to pay the increased rent, he served them with notice to quit and immediately formed a club, intending to retain the Everton name for his own club. The Football League would not allow Houlding to use the Everton name and so Liverpool FC was founded.

In the meantime Everton moved to their present Goodison site (which they purchased outright) and set about developing it into the superb stadium that it now is. As Liverpool FC improved in stature, rivalry between the two clubs commenced apace and success, both on and off the field, soon made Everton into one of the richest and best-supported sides in the country. With their League and Cup wins still increasing, Everton and their neighbours have ensured their city's continuing domination of the English scene.

First FA Cup match.

Everton's first foray into the FA Cup in 1886/7 saw them drawn against the Scottish club, Glasgow Rangers. Although Rangers won the match 1–0, it is sometimes recorded that Everton in fact scratched the tie on the grounds that certain ineligible players had been fielded. More controversy followed during the 1887/8 competition when, after losing their first game to Bolton Wanderers, Everton appealed that Bolton had fielded an ineligible player and the tie was replayed. Two replays still failed to produce a result and more controversy followed when the third replay ended in a 2–1 victory for Everton. This time Bolton protested because Everton had fielded seven ineligible players. As a result of the protest Everton were suspended, although they had already lost their 'second round' game against Preston North End before the ruling was made. Bolton were reinstated and received a bye into the fourth round when they, too, were thrashed by Preston North End.

In the 1888/9 competition Everton scratched to give Ulster a walkover into the second qualifying round and did not compete again until 1891/2 when, yet again, Everton protested after losing 4–2 to Burnley and a replay (which Burnley won 3–1) was ordered.

First Football League match.

Played at Anfield on 8 September 1888, Everton's first match was against Accrington. Two goals by Fleming gave Everton a 2–1 victory.

First Football League championship.

After finishing runners-up to Preston North End in 1889/90, in 1890/1 Everton turned the tables by taking the championship with Preston North End second.

First FA Cup Final.

Everton's record in the Cup had been far from impressive until they made amends in the 1892/3 season. Starting with their first FA Cup win (4–0 over West Bromwich Albion) they then knocked out Nottingham Forest (4–2) and Sheffield Wednesday (3–0) before reaching their first semi final against Preston North End. The first game ended in a 2–2 draw and Everton won the replay 2–1 to reach their first final.

Playing Wolverhampton Wanderers at Fallowfield, Manchester, Everton were unlucky to lose the game by a single second-half goal.

First FA Cup win.

Everton reached their third FA Cup Final in 1905/6 and faced Newcastle United, the previous year's League champions and beaten finalists. The game was played at the Crystal Palace stadium and ended in a 1–0 victory for Everton with the only goal of the match from their centre-forward Young. The following year Everton were beaten 2–1 in the final by The Wednesday (Sheffield Wednesday).

First Football League Cup game.

In 1960 Everton's opponents in the first round of the very first Football League Cup competition were Accrington Stanley and the match ended in a 3–1 victory for Everton. In the second round Everton were again drawn at home and defeated their opponents, Walsall, 3–1 to earn a third-round tie home to Bury. A 3–1 victory led them to a tie with their neighbours, Tranmere Rovers. They won this match 4–0 but went out 2–1 to Shrewsbury Town in the fifth round.

First European Cup tie.

Everton's first experience in Europe was not one to be relished. Facing the defensive might of the Italian club Inter-Milan, they were held to a 0–0 draw at Goodison Park and lost the away leg by the only goal of the match.

First Fairs Cup tie.

In 1962/3 Everton's first Fairs Cup appearance was at home to the Scottish club Dunfermline and ended in a 1–0 victory. However, the away-leg proved more difficult and Dunfermline won the leg 2–0 and the tie 2–1.

Johann Krankel of Rapid Vienna exchanges penants with Everton's Kevin Radcliffe before commencing the 1984/5 European Cup-Winners Cup Final in Rotterdam. (Allsport)

First European Cup-Winner's Cup tie.

In 1966/7 Everton won their first tie in the competition when they beat Aalborg BK 85 2–1 on aggregate. In the second round Real Zaragoza beat Everton 2–1 on aggregate.

First Football League Cup Final.

Everton's record in the Football League Cup has been far from inspiring and it was 1976/7 before they reached their first final. Facing Aston Villa, Everton drew the game at Wembley 0–0 and then drew the replay at Hillsborough 1–1. In the second replay Aston Villa won the game 3–2 after extra-time.

First European trophy.

1984/5 was a magnificent season for Everton. They broke Liverpool's domination of the English football scene by taking the League title and were unlucky to lose the FA Cup to Manchester United by a single goal.

In the European Cup-Winner's Cup they beat UC Dublin, Bratislava, F Sittard and Bayern Munich to reach their first final against Rapid Vienna in Rotterdam. Goals by Gray, Sheedy and Steven gave Everton a much-deserved 3–1 victory.

Liverpool FC

The story behind the formation of Liverpool FC is perhaps the strangest of all the English League clubs. In 1892 Everton rowed with their landlord (and enthusiastic supporter) John Houlding, after he had increased their rent to £250 p.a. and literally walked out from Anfield to play at another location, halfway through the season. Houlding decided to form his own club and, firstly, tried to keep the name Everton FC until prevented from so doing by the Football League. Charging a rent of only £100, he invested £500 and literally set the club up from scratch. Within a year Liverpool were admitted to the League and, by the turn of the century, were of a similar standard to Everton.

Success was not long in coming and Liverpool's fine record of championship wins commenced at the turn of the century and continued intermittently despite occasional spells in the Second Division. In the mid-seventies Liverpool's domination of the English scene was consolidated when they achieved an incredible seven out of nine championship wins and impressive cup victories to boot.

After exceptional achievements in European competitions, in 1985 the appalling loss of life at the European Cup Final between Liverpool and Juventus threw the entire professional game into turmoil. It will be several years before a proper assessment of the long-term results of this tragedy can be made, but there can be no doubt that the harrowing scenes which were televised throughout Europe will have an enduring effect upon the standing of the game.

First FA Cup tie.

On 15 October 1892 Liverpool began their FA Cup games with an easy 4–0 win away to Nantwich and followed up in the second qualifying round with a 9–0 win over Newtown in which McVean scored their first FA Cup hat-trick. In the third qualifying round, they lost 2–1 away to Northwich Victoria.

The following year, in their first season as a Football League club, they progressed to the quarter-final stages of the competition before losing 3–0 to Bolton Wanderers and in 1896/7 reached the semi finals for the first time, losing 3–0 to Aston Villa, the eventual winners.

First Football League match.

Liverpool's unorthodox formation coincided with the resignation from the Football League of neighbouring Bootle and, in 1893, they were elected in their place. Playing their first match away to Middlesbrough Ironopolis, the predominantly Scottish Liverpool team achieved a 2–0 victory on 2 September 1893. The following week, their first home game against Lincoln City ended in a 4–0 victory and, when the season ended, Liverpool were champions with 50 points from only 28 games. In fact, during this season, they became the first (and to date only) Second Division club not to lose a game.

Their first season in the First Division proved less successful and, finishing bottom with only 22 points, they were relegated back to the Second Division immediately. In 1895/6, undeterred, they rallied and, once again, won the Second Division championship.

First Football League championship.

In 1898/9 Liverpool, well established amongst the top clubs, finished runners-up to Aston Villa but in 1900/1 just pipped Sunderland for their first title by winning their final League game against the bottom club West Bromwich Albion.

First FA Cup Final.

In 1914 Liverpool gained revenge for their 1897 semi-final defeat by beating Aston Villa 2–0 and went on to meet Burnley in their first final match. Liverpool, fielding amongst others a player with the contradictory name Fairfoul, lost the game by a single goal scored by Burnley's centre-forward Freeman.

First League Cup match.

Unlike a number of the other better-known clubs, Liverpool, a Second Division side from 1954 to 1961, participated in the first League Cup competition in 1960. Their first game, home to Luton Town, ended in a 1–1 draw but they won 5–2 away to reach the next round. In the third round they lost 2–1 to Southampton. The following season Liverpool withdrew from the competition and did not participate again until 1967/8.

First European Cup match.

Liverpool's first European tie was an easy introduction, being drawn against KR Reykjavik of Iceland. After winning the away-leg 5–0 (on 17 August 1964), they won at Anfield 6–1 and then beat Anderlecht to reach their first quarter final. Facing IFC Cologne, Liverpool drew both the home and away legs 0–0 and after the play-off had ended 2–2 were fortunate to progress to their first semi final by winning the toss of a coin.

First FA Cup win.

On 1 May 1965, in their second Wembley Cup Final (they lost the 1949/50 game 2–0 to Arsenal), Liverpool met Leeds United. At full time the scoreline was 0–0 and with goals from Hunt and St John Liverpool won 2–1 in extra-time.

First substitute.

The first substitute to be used by Liverpool was G Strong who (against West Ham United on 15 September 1965) came on in place of Lawler and scored the equalizing goal just 14 minutes from the end.

First European Cup-Winners Cup match.

On 29 September 1965 in their first tie in the competition, Liverpool were matched against formidable opposition, Juventus of Italy, but despite losing the away-leg 1–0 they progressed to the next round thanks to a 2–0 home win. Wins over Standard Liege and Honved then led them to their first semi final against Celtic and a 2–0 win on the home-leg saw them through to their first European final. This was played on 5 May 1966 at Hampden Park, Glasgow, against Borussia Dortmund of West Germany and, after finishing level 1–1 at full-time, Liverpool lost the game 2–1.

First Fairs/UEFA Cup tie.

1967/8 was the season in which Liverpool first competed in this competition and on 19 September 1967 they beat Malmo FF 2–0 in Sweden and then won 2–1 at home to progress to the second round. Then, playing the West German club TSV Munich 1860, they dominated the home game winning 8–0 only to lose 2–1 away. In the next round their interest in the competition ended when they lost both games to Ferencvaros by a margin of 1–0.

The jubilant Liverpool team celebrate their capture of the European Cup in 1977. (Photosource)

competition began when, having drawn 1–1 with West Ham United in the final at Wembley, they won the replay at Villa Park 2–1. The following year, the competition was first sponsored by the National Dairy Council and Liverpool retained the trophy and won the first 'Milk Cup' by beating Tottenham Hotspur.

Manchester United FC

Originally formed in 1878 as Lancashire and Yorkshire Railway Company Newton Heath, the name was changed in 1892 to Newton Heath FC (which was the name of the company's main Manchester depot). The club first played at a 'mud-heap' of a ground in North Street and, a founder member of the Football Alliance, joined the Football League in 1892 when the Alliance and League merged. In 1893 they moved to Bank Street, Clayton, an equally 'salubrious' ground adjacent to a chemical works, and by 1902 went into liquidation. A local brewer, JH Davies, rescued the club, changed its name to Manchester United FC and upgraded the Bank Street ground.

The following year they went out in the first round to Atletico Bilbao on the toss of a coin.

First UEFA Cup win.

In the 1972/3 season, Liverpool reached their first UEFA Cup Final by beating Tottenham Hotspur in the semi finals. Facing Borussia Moenchengladbach, they went into a commanding 3–0 lead in the home-leg thanks to two goals from Keegan and a further one from Lloyd and just held on in the away-leg to win the cup with a 3–2 margin. This was Liverpool's first European trophy win.

First European Cup win.

On 25 May 1977, just one week after losing the FA Cup Final to Manchester United and so ending hopes of the coveted 'double', Liverpool reached their first European Cup Final. Ironically their opponents were once again Borussia Moenchengladbach (who were en route for their third successive West German championship) and an inspiring display by Keegan (who was playing his last game before transfer to Hamburg) helped his club to their first European championship by a 3–1 margin.

First League Cup Final.

It was not until the 1977/8 season that Liverpool reached their first final, having despatched Arsenal 2–1 in the semi final. Their opponents were Nottingham Forest who won the hard-fought game thanks to a single penalty goal from Robertson, then went on to take the League championship.

Three years later Liverpool's domination of the

Matt Busby during the days of his own youth while playing for Manchester City. (Pattrieoux)

MANCHESTER UNITED

After the club's FA Cup victory in 1909, Mr Davies purchased a site several miles away (next to the Lancashire County Cricket Ground), and in 1910 began constructing the 'Old Trafford' which we know today. During the Second World War German bombers inflicted severe damage on the stadium and United were forced to share Manchester City's Maine Road ground for a number of years until, in 1949, the stadium was rebuilt.

In the late 1950s the 'Busby Babes' carried all before them until the team was decimated by the 1958 'Munich disaster' in which the bulk of the first-team players lost their lives. As with the stadium, the 'phoenix' of Manchester United was, once again, forced to rise from the ashes and, through the dedication and skill of their management team, the club once more fought their way back to the forefront of the English soccer scene.

First FA Cup tie.

Drawn against Higher Walton in the first qualifying round of the 1890/1 competition, Newton Heath won the tie 2–0 to earn a second qualifying-round tie against Bootle. Bootle, Everton's chief rivals for the Merseyside crown, won the game 1–0.

In the first qualifying round of the 1891/2 competition, Newton Heath met their local rivals Ardwick (Manchester City) and won 5–1. They went on to beat Heywood in the second round (3–2) but went out 4–3 to Blackpool in the final qualifying round.

Their first match in the competition proper was played on 21 January 1893 when (as a First Division side) they were no longer required to qualify! Blackburn Rovers, their Lancastrian opponents, won the tie 4–0.

First Football League match.

Newton Heath were founder members of the Football Alliance in 1889 and remained in that competition until its amalgamation with the Football League in 1892 (when it became the Second Division). In fact, as the First Division was then increased in size, Newton Heath were elected straight into it, having been Alliance runners-up in the 1891/2 season. Their first fixture on 3 September 1892 was away to Blackburn Rovers and the game ended in a 4–3 defeat. Five more fixtures were played before they recorded their first League win—a thumping 10–1 victory over Wolverhampton Wanderers. Donaldson (who had scored in four of the previous six games) and Stewart both picked up hat-tricks in a game which still remains United's biggest League victory. Ironically, 41 years later, Wolves inflicted United's equal heaviest defeat (7–0). They ended their first League season at the bottom of the First Division but won the test matches to remain in the top

division until, in 1893/4, they finished bottom again and were relegated to the Second Division.

First Football League match as 'Manchester United'.

Their first fixture under their new name was played on 6 September 1902 and a single goal by Richards gave them victory over Gainsborough Trinity, their Second Division opponents.

First Football League championship.

In 1907/8, just two seasons after being promoted back from the Second Division, United romped to their first League championship, winning by nine clear points from Aston Villa.

First FA Cup Final win.

United experienced their first real success in the FA Cup in 1905/6 when they lost to Woolwich Arsenal in the semi finals and, in 1908/9, they reached their first final. The game was played at the Crystal Palace stadium and United beat their opponents, Bristol City, 1–0.

First FA Youth Cup win.

Matt Busby's policy of promoting the development of young players was highlighted when, in 1953, the Manchester United youth team met Wolverhampton Wanderers in the first FA Youth Cup final. United, fielding, amongst others, Duncan Edwards (who, in 1955, became the youngest-ever England international) won the home leg 7–1 and the tie 9–3 on aggregate. United went on to emphasize the brilliance of their young players by winning the next four FA Youth Cup finals.

First European competition.

On 12 September 1956 Manchester United became the first English club to appear in the European Cup (Chelsea withdrew from the 1955/6 competition) and were drawn against the Belgian club RSC Anderlecht. The first leg was played in Belgium and United recorded an impressive 2–0 victory. In the home leg, Dennis Viollet scored United's first European hat-trick and Tommy Taylor scored another as United attained the first ever double-figure scoreline in the competition (10–0). United progressed to their first semi final by beating Borussia Dortmund and Atletico Bilbao but then met the holders, Real Madrid. United lost the away-leg 3–1 but were unable to pull back the deficit at Old Trafford and lost the tie 5–3 on aggregate.

First floodlit match at Old Trafford.

This was played on 25 March 1957 between United and Bolton Wanderers in a Football League First Division match, which Bolton won 2–0.

Duncan Edwards, who, in 1955, won his first full cap for England when only 18, was one of eight players to die as a result of the Munich aircrash.
(D C Thomson Ltd)

The 'Munich' tragedy.

The 1956/7 season saw the 'Busby Babes' romp to the League championship by eight clear points and, representing England in the 1957/8 European Cup, got off to an excellent start by beating Shamrock rovers 9–2 on aggregate. In the next round, United eliminated Dukla Prague 3–1 on aggregate and in the quarter-final beat Red Star Belgrade 5–4 on aggregate before disaster struck. Returning from Yugoslavia after drawing 3–3 to win the quarter-final tie on aggregate, United's plane crashed on take-off at Munich. Amongst others, eight players, including the brilliant Duncan Edwards, lost their lives and United's European championship aspirations were crushed. In the semi finals AC Milan won 5–2 on aggregate against a hastily assembled team of reserves, and new buys.

In 1958/9 UEFA, with a much applauded gesture towards United's heroism, offered them a place in the finals. The Football League and the FA put considerable pressure on United, forcing them to refuse UEFA's kindness.

First Football League Cup game.

Manchester United were one of the few big clubs to compete in the first League Cup competition and on 19 October 1960 played their first fixture away to Exeter City. A goal by Dawson late in the game earned United a 1–1 draw and they then won the replay 4–1. In the second round, United lost 2–1 at Bradford City.

First European Cup-Winner's Cup match.

On 25 September 1963, United's first game in the competition was played away to the Dutch side Willem Tilburg 11 and ended in a 1–1 draw. In the home leg on 15 October 1963, Denis Law notched up their first hat-trick of the competition, as they won the game 6–1. In the next round their opponents were the holders, Tottenham Hotspur and United pulled back a 2–0 away-leg deficit to win the tie 4–3 on aggregate before losing the semi finals to Sporting Lisbon.

First Fairs Cup match.

On 23 September 1964 United's first opponents in the competition were the Swedish club Djurgaarden. United drew the away game 1–1 but took the tie 7–2 on aggregate thanks, once more, to Denis Law who scored a hat-trick at Old Trafford. United then stormed through to the semi finals against Ferencvaros but lost 2–1 in the play-off after drawing 3–3 on aggregate over the first two games.

First European trophy.

In 1967/8 United once again faced Real Madrid in the semi finals of the European Cup and, after winning the home-leg by a single goal, played superbly at the Charmartin Stadium, to draw 3–3 and win the tie 4–3 on aggregate. United were fortunate indeed that the final was to be played at Wembley but, facing Eusebio's Benfica, could have hoped for easier opposition. The game was drawn 1–1 at the final whistle and United stormed ahead in extra-time to win the game 4–1. Scenes of great emotion followed the victory when Matt Busby, together with Bill Foulkes and Bobby Charlton (all survivors of the Munich disaster), saw their team achieve what fate had torn away in 1958.

First Football League Cup Final.

The League Cup has not, over the years, proved to be a competition in which United have achieved much success. It was 1982/3 before they reached their first final; then, playing against Liverpool, the winners of the two previous competitions, they lost 2–1 after extra-time.

Rangers FC

Rangers FC were formed in 1872 and after playing a number of games at Glasgow Park moved to Kinning Park, Glasgow, the venue for the 1881 Scottish FA Cup Final. In 1887 they moved to their present ground at Ibrox Park which was opened on 20 August 1887 with a friendly against the dominant English club, Preston North End. With a

RANGERS

Third time lucky — Rangers' players celebrate victory over Moscow Dynamo in the 1971/2 European Cup-Winners Final. (Photosource)

less than friendly scoreline of 8–0 to Preston, Ranger's supporters invaded the pitch to end the humiliation and to give a foretaste of violence to follow.

Although Rangers quickly established themselves in the forefront of Scottish football, their rivalry with Celtic soon became a byword for aggressive confrontations. Whilst it was not only Celtic that incurred the wrath of Rangers' partisan supporters and players (in 1879 little Vale of Leven won the Scottish FA Cup when Rangers refused to appear for the replay!) nevertheless 'Old Firm' meetings still are justifiably renowned for their hostility.

In 1902 Rangers' ground was the scene of the first major loss of life at a football match when, during a Scotland v England international, a section of the terracing collapsed, killing 25 people. Sixty-nine years later, 66 people died in the second Ibrox Park tragedy, when spectators leaving the ground lost their footing.

It is not, however, such tragedies for which Rangers are renowned; rather they are famed for their domination of the Scottish football scene and their development (along with Queens Park) of the close-passing game.

Today they have one of the finest stadiums in the country and rightly occupy a dominant position in Scottish and European football.

First game.

In May 1872 Rangers drew with Callendar FC in their first ever game and later the same year first played in blue when beating Clyde FC 11–0.

First Scottish FA Cup game.

Playing at Queen's Park in September 1874, Rangers' first Scottish FA Cup tie was against Oxford and ended in a 2–0 victory for Rangers. In the next round, Rangers drew 0–0 with Dumbarton at Glasgow Green but lost the replay 1–0.

First Scottish FA Cup Final.

In 1876/7 Rangers defeated Lennox 3–0 in the quarter finals and were fortunate indeed to receive a 'bye' in the semi finals. Facing Vale of Leven in the final, Rangers were forced to two replays before a result (3–2 to Vale of Leven) was obtained. Two years later Rangers, once again, were given a bye in the semi finals and, once again, faced Vale of Leven in the final. The game ended 1–1 but, maintaining that they had a legitimate 'winning goal' disallowed in the first game, Rangers refused to turn up for the replay and Vale of Leven were awarded the trophy.

First English FA Cup tie.

Although Rangers entered the 1885/6 English FA Cup competition, they withdrew without playing a game because of a dispute over 'professionalism'. The following year they played their first game against Everton and won 1–0 and then won a number of other games to reach their first semi final against Aston Villa. The game was played at Crewe and ended in a 3–1 defeat for Rangers.

First Scottish League match.

In August 1890, their first fixture in the League was at home to Heart of Midlothian and Rangers won the game 5–2. The season ended with Rangers and Dumbarton tied on 29 points and, after a championship play-off had ended 2–2, the clubs were declared 'Joint Champions'.

In 1898/9 Rangers were undisputed champions when they won the League title with the first ever 100% record.

First Scottish FA Cup Final win.

After appearing in the controversial finals in 1876/7 and 1878/9, it was 14 seasons before they appeared again in 1893/4. In the first 'Old Firm' final, Rangers beat Celtic 3–1 to win the trophy for the first time.

First Scottish League Cup game.

Rangers, who had appeared in the final of the Scottish Southern League Cup in 1945/6 began the first ever Scottish League Cup campaign in style with a 4–0 home victory over St Mirren. They progressed without difficulty to the first final when their opponents were Aberdeen who had beaten them in the 1945/6 'Southern Final' mentioned above. Rangers won the final 4–0 and in 1948/9 took the trophy again, becoming the first club to win twice.

First European Cup tie.

In 1956 Rangers first sampled European competition by beating OGC Nice 2–1 at Ibrox Park and went on to lose the away-leg by the same score. This led to a replay which ended 3–1 to Nice.

The following season Rangers again drew a French club (St Etienne) but this time won the tie 4–3 on aggregate. In the next round Rangers were thrashed 6–1 on aggregate, by the Italian club AC Milan.

First European Cup-Winners Cup tie.

Competing in the first competition in 1960, Rangers' first game was at home to Ferencvaros of Hungary and they won the game 4–2 and the tie 5–4 on aggregate. In the next round of the competition Rangers beat Borussia Moenchengladbach 8–0 at Ibrox (Brand scored the first-ever hat-trick in the competition) and 3–0 away. After defeating Wolves in the semi final, they reached the final and became the first British club to reach a major European final.

In 1960/61 the final was played over two legs and facing a strong Italian team, Fiorentina, Rangers lost both legs.

First Fairs Cup tie.

In 1967 Rangers first competed in the Fairs Cup and after beating Dynamo Dresden 3–2 on aggregate, beat IFC Cologne and then received a bye into their first quarter final. Facing the holders, Leeds United, Rangers could only draw the home leg 0–0 and went down 2–0 away.

First European trophy.

Appearing in their third European Cup-Winners Cup Final in 1971/2, Rangers met the Russian club Moscow Dynamo at Barcelona. The final, renowned for the appalling behaviour of the Rangers fans off the field, ended 3–2 to Rangers and they were fortunate to be allowed to retain the trophy when UEFA met afterwards to take disciplinary action.

Tottenham Hotspur FC

Formed as Hotspur FC in 1882, Spurs first played on the Tottenham marshes and, in 1884, changed their name to Tottenham Hotspur FC. In 1888 they moved to play at Northumberland Park in Trulock Road and played there to increasing attendances until 1899 when they moved to their present ground. At that time the site was a run-down nursery complete with greenhouses and sheds, and was owned by Charringtons, the brewers, who also owned the nearby White Hart Inn. After a very successful season, in which they won the Southern League championship, Spurs bought the freehold of the ground from Charringtons and, several years later, after their election to the Football League in 1908, they developed it into the superb stadium that it now is.

Although they ended the 1914/15 season at the bottom of the First Division, with the resumption of the Football League after the Great War in 1919, Spurs felt very rightly aggrieved when they were relegated to the Second Division despite the enlargement of the First Division by two teams. Arsenal, their local rivals who had finished in fifth place in the Second Division, pulled strings to obtain Spurs' First Division place and although the antagonism caused by this move created much unrest in North London, Spurs immediately took the Second Division championship and stormed back into the First Division. Since that time, the club has enjoyed mixed fortunes with relatively regular visits down into the Second Division, although their level of support has always remained extremely high and they have literally 'reached the heights' on many occasions.

First FA Cup tie.

The name 'Spurs' carries with it memories of successful FA Cup campaigns but success did not arrive immediately. In their first venture into the competition in 1894, they won their first qualifying match against West Herts 3–2 (Hunter scored their first goal). They failed to reach the full competition, losing 4–0 to Luton in the fourth

TOTTENHAM HOTSPUR

(Left) Martin Chivers, Spurs' long-serving centre forward. (ASP)

qualifying round (after drawing the first match 2–2).

First FA Cup hat-trick.

In 1896, during a first round qualifying match, RW Clements notched up the club's first FA Cup hat-trick, scoring three of the goals in their 4–0 defeat of St Stephens and, two seasons later, the club reached their first quarter final going down 4–1 to Stoke. (Ironically, Stoke's withdrawal from the League at the end of the 1907/8 season opened the door for Spurs' entry.)

First FA Cup Final.

Spurs' 1900/1 FA Cup campaign still ranks as one of the most outstanding achievements of the competition. Having won their first Southern League championship in 1899/1900, Spurs progressed through their first semi final by beating West Bromwich Albion 4–0 thanks to four goals from Brown, their brilliant centre-forward. In the final at Crystal Palace, which was played before the first ever six-figure crowd (officially 110 820) Brown grabbed two more goals to earn his club a 2–2 draw.

The match was replayed at Burnden Park, Bolton and Spurs became the first and only non-Football League club to win the trophy after the formation of the League. That man Brown scored another of the club's goals in their 3–1 win and they then became the first club to tie their colours to the trophy—a tradition which is still upheld.

First Football League match.

Elected to the Football League in 1908, Spurs defeated Wolves 3–0 in their first match (Woodward scored the first goal) and won 20 games to achieve promotion to the First Division at their first attempt. The following season, in their 70th Football League match, Minter scored their first League hat-trick when, on 29 March 1910, they defeated Blackburn Rovers 4–0.

First Football League championship.

After an eight-season spell in the Second Division, in 1949/50 Spurs won the Second Division championship by a nine-point margin and the following season stormed on to win their first League championship by four clear points.

First double.

In 1960/61, starting with a record-making run of consecutive wins, Spurs took the League by siege, winning no fewer than 31 of their 42 matches and scoring 115 goals, then went on to win the FA Cup by beating Leicester City 2–0. This was the first 'double' this century and, the following season, Spurs retained the FA Cup by beating Burnley 3–1.

First European competition.

Spurs began their extremely successful string of appearances in Europe somewhat ignominiously on 13 September 1961 when they lost 4–2 to Gornik in Poland. However, they redeemed themselves in the home-leg and won 8–1 thanks mainly to a hat-trick from Cliff Jones and two goals from Bob Smith. In their first semi final, they beat Benfica (the eventual champions) 2–1 at home but lost the away-leg 3–1.

In 1962/63, Spurs drew Glasgow Rangers in their first European Cup-Winners tie and won both legs to progress to the next round. Further success followed and, on 15 May 1963 they reached their first final, against Atletico Madrid. Goals by Dyson (2), Greaves (2) and White gave the club a 5–1 victory and Britain its first major European trophy.

First substitute.

On 11 September 1965 in the home First Division 'derby' match with Arsenal, Roy Low replaced Derek Possee to become the club's first substitute. Cliff Jones became the first substitute to score when he came on against Liverpool in an FA Cup tie on 12 March 1968.

First League Cup match.

One of the last clubs to enter the competition, Spurs' first match was against neighbouring West Ham United on 14 September 1966 and ended in a 1–0 defeat. Indeed, it was not until 4 September 1968 that they achieved their first victory when they beat Aston Villa 4–1 and Martin Chivers scored their first hat-trick in the competition. Having achieved that first win, they then progressed to their first semi final, losing 2–1 on aggregate to Arsenal, their arch rivals.

First League Cup Final.

On 27 February 1971 Spurs reached their first League Cup Final against Aston Villa and, maintaining their tradition of winning cup finals, achieved a 2–0 victory. Two years later, they beat Norwich City 1–0 to become the first club to win the trophy twice.

First UEFA Cup competition.

On 14 September 1971 Spurs met Keflavik of Iceland in the away-leg of a tie which is remembered more for the fact that Graeme Souness then made his only appearance for the club (when coming on as substitute for Alan Mullery) than for the 6–1 victory or Alan Gilzean's hat-trick. The return-leg ended in a 9–0 victory and set Spurs on course for their first UEFA Cup Final. Played against Wolverhampton Wanderers, this first European final between two British clubs ended in a victory for Spurs (3–2 on aggregate) and enabled them to become the first British club to win two different European trophies.

Spurs' Medwin, seen in action during their European Cup semi-final tie with Benfica on 5 April 1962. (Photosource)

ASTON VILLA

Aston Villa FC

Aston Villa Football Club was founded in 1874 by the young men of the Aston Wesley Chapel in Lozells, a district of Birmingham. Originally playing at Aston Park, the club moved to Perry Barr in 1876, at the instigation of their captain, Scotsman George Ramsay, who later became Villa's secretary.

Scots figured prominently in Villa's early development, none more so than William McGregor whose drive and enthusiasm led to the formation of the Football League in 1888. Naturally, Villa were one of the founder members of the League and enjoyed great success in the competition's formative years. By the time they moved to their present home at Villa Park (then called the Aston Lower Grounds) in 1897, Villa had won the League championship three times and the FA Cup three times.

Indeed, that very season of 1896/7 they became only the second club to do the League and Cup double, following in the footsteps of Preston North End who achieved that feat in the League's first season.

Villa recorded three more League championships and three more FA Cup wins before being relegated for the first time in 1936. They won the Second Division title in 1937/8 and, apart from one season, remained in Division One until 1967 when they began an eight-season spell which took them down to Division Three for the first time.

Villa returned to the First Division in 1975 and in 1980/1 surprised everyone by taking their seventh League title. Twelve months later they were European Cup holders and although relegated in 1987, Villa soon made a concerted effort and achieved a swift return to the top flight.

First game.

The Villans' first game was a peculiar 'hybrid' affair against Aston Brook St Mary's Rugby Club in March 1875, the first half of which was played under Rugby Laws and the second half under Association Laws! There was no score in the first half but Jack Hughes scored the only goal of the game to give Villa a 1–0 victory.

First FA Cup match.

Andy Hunter scored Aston Villa's first FA Cup goal when they drew 1–1 with Stafford Road Works FC on 13 December 1879. The replay a little over a month later gave them their first FA Cup victory when they won 3–0.

First FA Cup Final.

After defeating Glasgow Rangers 3–1 in their first FA Cup semi final on 5 March 1887 (which was played at Crewe), Aston Villa met West Bromwich Albion at Kennington Oval in their first final. Dennis Hodgetts scored their first goal in the final and Villa went on to take the FA Cup with a 2–0 victory.

First League match.

One of the founder members of the League, Aston Villa faced local rivals Wolverhampton Wanderers on 8 September 1888 in their first League game and, thanks to a goal by Tommy Green, drew 1–1. A week later, Villa notched up their first win in the League with a 5–1 victory over Stoke and a fortnight after that Albert Allen scored their first League hat-trick in Villa's 9–1 victory over Notts County.

First League championship.

Aston Villa finished in fourth place in both the 1891/2 and 1892/3 seasons when Sunderland took the title but in 1893/4 Villa pushed Sunderland into second place, taking their first League championship by a six-point margin. In 1894/5, Sunderland took the championship again as Villa slipped to third place but in 1895/6 Villa won the title back and a year later when they landed both League and FA Cup to achieve their first 'double'.

First League Cup game.

One of the few top-flight clubs to enter the first Football League Cup competition, Villa beat Huddersfield Town 4–1 on 12 October 1960 (Ron Wylie scoring the first goal) and progressed to the first ever final. The first leg of the final at Rotherham ended 2–0 to the Yorkshire side but Villa won the second leg 3–0 at Villa Park to become the first club to win the competition.

First UEFA Cup tie.

On 17 September 1975, Villa played Antwerp in their first game in the competition and crashed 4–1, Ray Graydon scoring their goal. They recorded their first win in the competition on 14 September 1977 when they beat Fenerbahce 4–0.

First European Cup tie.

On 16 September 1981 Aston Villa scored an easy first victory over Valur Reykjavik when Tony Morley opened the scoring en route to a 5–0 win. Further victories followed and on 26 May 1982, Villa line up against Bayern Munich in their first final. Peter Withe scored the only goal of the match to give Villa the trophy at the first time of asking.

Sheffield Wednesday FC

Sheffield Wednesday FC came into being on the evening of 4 September 1867 when the Wednesday Cricket Club (founded in 1820) formed a football section. The name 'Wednesday' had been adopted by the cricketers, simply because on that weekday afternoon they took time off from work to play sport.

SHEFFIELD WEDNESDAY

Ron (right) and Peter Springett pictured before facing one another in an FA Cup tie at Hillsborough. (Syndication International)

The meeting to form the football section was held at the Adelphi pub, a building eventually demolished to make way for the Crucible Theatre, scene of many recent sporting dramas in the shape of world snooker championships.

Wednesday's footballers were the city's leading club within ten years of their formation, having dominated local club football almost since their foundation. In 1880, they entered the FA Cup for the first time and scored a sensational win over Blackburn Rovers. A year later, Wednesday reached the semi final and in 1896 won the trophy for the first time.

By this time the club were established members of the Football League and three years later moved to Hillsborough, then known as 'Owlerton'. Wednesday's first permanent home had been at Olive Grove, a ground alongside the Midland Railway near Queen's Road, which they leased from the Duke of Norfolk. Before that they had led a nomadic existence, playing some games at Bramall Lane.

Apart from one season at the end of the 19th century, Wednesday enjoyed First Division football until after the First World War. They lifted the League championship in successive years (1903 and 1904) and after winning back their First Division place in 1926, the Owls went on to take two more consecutive championships (1929 and 1930). They won the FA Cup again in 1907 and 1935, and that last Cup win proved to be Wednesday's most recent major honour.

A post-war period of ups and downs culminated in relegation to Division Three for the first time, in 1975. Happily, the Owls bounced back into Division One and Hillsborough is still one of the world's major football venues.

First game.

Wednesday played their first game way back on 31 December 1867 against nearby Dronfield, when they won 1–0. The identity of the goalscorer has never been established but Dronfield scored four 'rouges' — that is to say, they put the ball through an 'outer' goal four times. Wednesday, however, scored through the 'inner' goal which was worth any number of rouges and consequently took the game.

First FA Cup game.

Blackburn Rovers figured prominently in Wednesday's early FA Cup games and were their opponents on 18 December 1880 in their first game in the competition. Bob Gregory scored Wednesday's first goal and they won the game 4–0. The following season, on 6 March 1882, Blackburn Rovers were again their opponents when Wednesday reached their first FA Cup semi final and, this time, the score went Blackburn's way as after drawing 0–0 at Huddersfield, they hammered Wednesday 5–1 in the replay at Manchester. No prizes for guessing Wednesday's first FA Cup Final opponents on 29 March 1890 — yes it was Blackburn Rovers! The game was played at the Kennington Oval and ended in a 6–1 defeat for Wednesday. Six years later, Wednesday won the FA Cup for the first time by beating Wolverhampton Wanderers 2–1.

First League game.

Wednesday were elected to the First Division of the Football League in 1892 and met Notts County in their first League match. Tom Brandon scored the only goal to win the game for Wednesday.

First League championship.

After finishing at the foot of the First Division table at the end of the 1898/9 season, Wednesday stormed back to the First Division by winning the Second Division title the following season. Three seasons later, Wednesday won the Football League championship for the first time one point ahead of Aston Villa and Sunderland, and retained the title the following year with an increased margin of three points.

First Football League Cup match.

It was not until the sixth year of the competition that Sheffield Wednesday played in the Football League Cup for the first time when they lost 1–0 to their local rivals Rotherham United. A year later, Wednesday scored their first victory in the competition struggling to a 5–3 win over Third Division Stockport County.

First European competition.

On 12 September 1961 Wednesday first ventured into European competition when they met Olympique Lyonnais in the first round of the Inter Cities Fairs Cup. Keith Ellis opened the scoring for them but they lost the tie 2–4.

First exchange transfer of two brothers.

Brothers Ron Springett and Peter Springett were the first brothers to be involved in an exchange transfer when Ron returned to QPR with Peter moving to Hillsborough from Loftus Road. A cash adjustment saw Wednesday pay £40 000 for the younger Springett and receive £16 000 for the older man, who had cost them £9000 when he first signed from QPR in 1957/8.

Manchester City FC

Manchester City was formed in 1880 by the young men of St Mark's church, West Gorton. Then, not surprisingly, called St Mark's FC, they initially played on a field off Clowes Street before moving to the Kirkmanshulme Cricket Ground for a brief spell. The cricketers, however, were not at all happy when they realized that their pitch was being damaged by the footballers and soon gave St Mark's FC their marching orders. Without a regular ground to play on, the club all but wound up until, in 1884, they resumed play as Gorton FC playing at Clemington Downs, a piece of waste ground at the back of a factory. The club then moved to another field off Pink Bank Lane where they played until 1887 when they went to yet another site in Bennett Street. This land was owned by a railway company, the Manchester, Sheffield and Lincolnshire Railway (better known locally as 'The Mucky, Slow and Late') and became the club's first fully enclosed ground. Situated next to the main Manchester to Hyde road, it quickly became known as 'The Hyde Road Ground' and remained the club's home for 36 years.

At the same time that the club moved to the new ground, the name 'Ardwick FC' was adopted and it was under that name that the club joined the Football Alliance in 1891. In 1892, the Football Alliance was absorbed into the Football League as the 'Second Division' and Ardwick FC finished their first season in a respectable fifth place. The following season, things began to go disastrously wrong, both on and off the field, when the club finished in 13th position and virtually collapsed into bankruptcy. Joshua Parlby, together with a number of other enthusiastic members of the Manchester Football Association, took the bull by the horns, formed a new limited company to run the club and changed its name to Manchester City FC.

Since then Manchester City have spent most of the time in the First Division, but acquired a reputation as the 'quick-return' boys of the League when, being relegated to the Second Division on a number of occasions, they won their way back immediately! Their yo-yoing between the First and Second Divisions has recommenced in recent years after a particularly long uninterrupted spell in the First Division.

Manchester City's 1936/7 championship-winning team. (Colorsport)

First game.

Manchester City's first game took place on 13 November 1880 against another church side, Macclesfield Baptists FC and this ended in a 1–2 defeat for City. The scorer of City's goal was a Mr Collinge, whose first name is not known.

First FA Cup match.

City's first game in the FA Cup brought them up against Liverpool Stanley FC and was a very one-sided affair with City achieving a thumping 12–0 victory. Davie Weir scored their first goal and, although City (then still known as Ardwick FC) looked destined for a fine FA Cup run they were drawn against Halliwell in the next round and scratched to give their opponents a walk-over into the next round.

First League match.

Bootle were their opponents on 3 September 1892 when they played their first League game and they achieved a comfortable 7–0 victory. Joe Davies scored the first League goal and, indeed, went on to grab a hat-trick. Further victories followed and it was not until 8 October 1892 (their seventh game) that they suffered their first defeat, losing 1–3 to Darwen.

First FA Cup final.

After defeating The Wednesday 3–0 in their first FA Cup semi final on 19 March 1904, City faced Bolton Wanderers in their first FA Cup Final at the Crystal Palace on 23 April 1904. Football wizard Billy Meredith, City's marvellous Welsh international player, scored the only goal of the game to give City the trophy for the first time.

First League championship.

City won the Second Division championship by a six-point margin in 1898/9 and went on to win their first League championship in 1936/7. The following season they achieved the dubious distinction of becoming the first reigning champions to be relegated when they finished in 21st position!

First League Cup game.

Joe Hayes scored City's first League Cup goal to set them *en route* to a 3–0 victory over Stockport County on 18 October 1960 but Portsmouth ended their hopes of glory when, two months later, they beat City 2–0.

First League Cup final.

1970 proved to be an exceptional year for City when they appeared in two finals in the space of seven weeks. The first of these was against West Bromwich Albion in the League Cup and Tony Doyle scored their first goal in their 2–1 victory.

First European final.

Seven weeks after defeating West Bromwich Albion in the League Cup Final detailed above, City faced Gornik Zabrze in the European Cup-Winners Cup Final in Vienna and won this, too, by the same 2–1 margin.

18 | *MORE CUP FIRSTS*

The Welsh Cup

The Welsh Cup is one of the oldest established competitions still in existence and was first held in 1877. The very first tie was played on 13 October 1877 between Newton and the Druids (the first Welsh club to be founded in 1870). The game ended in a 1–1 draw and the Druids won the replay on 5 February 1878, 1–0. They eventually went on to play Wrexham in the first final at Acton Park, Wrexham on 30 March 1878. James Davies of Wrexham scored the first and only goal of the match to give his side a 1–0 victory. No trophy was awarded until 1879 and the first holder was Newtown Whitestars who beat Wrexham 2–1 at Oswestry on 1 April 1879.

The Irish Cup

In relative terms, football arrived a little late in Ireland. Cliftonville was the first Irish club to be founded on 11 October 1879, just under a year after the first soccer match had been played in Belfast (an exhibition match between the Scottish clubs Queens Park and Caledonia, which ended 3–1) and the Irish Cup was started in 1880. The first final took place in 1881 between Moyola Park and Cliftonville and ended in a 1–0 victory for Moyola Park.

Controversy soon reared its head, when in 1885/6 the Cup was withheld after Distillery had beaten Limavady in the final and in 1899 Linfield were awarded the trophy after their opponents, Glentoran, had walked off before the final game had finished! Four years earlier, Linfield had beaten Bohemians 10–1 to become the first British club to reach double figures in a cup final and in 1921/2 they became the first British club to complete a grand slam by winning every competition entered.

Inter-League games

The first inter-League match was played at Sheffield on 20 April 1891 between the Football League and the Football Alliance, but as the two bodies amalgamated the next year, this match is no longer regarded as being an official tie.

The first official game was between the Football League and the Scottish League and was played at Pike's Lane, Bolton on 11 April 1892. This game finished level at 2–2 and before the Football League discontinued inter-League fixtures in 1976, a further 62 matches were played between the two sides.

Other leagues subsequently participated in matches of this type and for a short while Italy, Denmark, Belgium and Eire were also involved.

Bishop Auckland's Bob Hardisty proudly displaying the FA Amateur Cup after his club's victory in 1954/5. (*Book of Football Champions*)

FA Amateur Cup

The Amateur Cup was first contested in 1893 and the first final in 1894 was between Old Carthusians and Casuals. Old Carthusians (who had won the FA Cup in 1880/81) won the match 2–1 and became the first (and in the strictest sense of the word – the only) club to win both trophies.

The competition ceased in 1974 when the FA withdrew official recognition of 'amateur' status, and was replaced by the FA Challenge Vase. In the first final of the new trophy, Hoddesdon Town FC beat Epsom FC 2–1.

FA CHARITY SHIELD

Originally founded in 1898 as 'The Sheriff of London's Charity Shield', this competition traditionally starts the English football season. For the first ten year's of its life the match was between a top professional and a top amateur club. In 1908 the match became known as the FA Charity Shield and it is now played between the FA Cup-winners and the League Champions.

The first game between Sheffield United and the Corinthians ended 2–2 and, after a replay had ended with the same score, the shield was retained for six months by each club. The following year, Queens Park of Glasgow held Aston Villa to a draw and adopting the same sharing method as the previous year, became the first and only Scottish holders.

Manchester United FC became the first team to win

Kevin Keegan and Billy Bremner (minus shirts) leave the Wembley pitch after being sent off during the 1974 Charity Shield game. (Colorsport)

the shield after the change of name to FA Charity Shield in 1908 when they beat Queens Park Rangers 4–0 after a 1–1 draw.

Always regarded as a friendly showcase for English soccer, the first of the matches to be played at Wembley on 10 August 1974 proved to be anything but friendly. Liverpool FC won the game against Leeds Utd FC 6–5 on penalties after the score had been tied 1–1 at the final whistle and Kevin Keegan and Billy Bremner became the first Britons to be sent off at Wembley.

South American Cup

This competition began in 1960 and is the South American equivalent of the European Cup. Throughout the years, although many moments of superb football have emerged from this competition, there have been too many instances of aggressive if not downright brutal play and incompetent refereeing, for Europeans to regard the contest other than cynically. It must be said, however, that this is the most stable and by far the most popular international tournament of its kind in South America.

Penarol of Uruguay beat Olimpia Asuncion of Paraguay 1–0 on aggregate in the first final.

Michel Platini holds aloft the European Nations Trophy on 27 June 1984, after France had beaten Spain 2–0. On 8 December 1985 he became the first European to win the 'man of the match' award, when Juventus beat Argentinos Juniors in the World Club Cup Final in Tokyo. (Allsport)

World Club Championship

This competition, between the winners of the European Cup and the South American Cup, was first contested in 1960 and until 1980 was played as a two-legged, home-and-away event.

Penarol of Uruguay played Real Madrid of Spain in the first competition and after a 0–0 draw in Uruguay, Real Madrid won the trophy with a 5–1 victory in Spain. Pele, playing for Santos in the 1962 game against Benfica, became the first player to score a hat-trick in the competition as his side won both home and away matches. The following year Santos again won (by beating AC Milan) and became the first club to retain the title. In 1971 and 1973 Ajax declined to compete, despite having won the European Cup and the losing finalists took their place.

In 1980 the first of a series of one-legged matches was staged in Tokyo when Nacional of Uruguay beat Nottingham Forest 1–0.

Texaco-Cup/Anglo-Scottish Cup/Group Cup/ Football League Trophy

The above competitions were virtually one and the same.

In 1970 Texaco sponsored a competition between Scottish and Football League clubs based on the idea of a British Cup. Wolverhampton Wanderers FC beat Heart of Midlothian FC in the first final and up to the time that the competition was succeeded by the Anglo-Scottish Cup in 1976 no Scottish club won at all.

Fulham FC beat Middlesbrough FC 5–1 on aggregate in 1976 and it was not until 1980 that a Scottish club (St Mirren FC) managed to win. The Scottish clubs withdrew in 1981 and the competition was renamed the Group Cup for one season until it was changed to the Football League Trophy in 1983. In 1984, it was replaced by the Associate Members Cup (being then restricted to Third and Fourth Division sides) and in 1985 became the Freight Rover Trophy – an event which in itself created a number of firsts.

The Freight Rover Trophy

This was the first Wembley final for associate Football League members and the first final at Wembley for which the teams were invited to train on the 'hallowed turf'.

Most important of all, the match was the first final at Wembley to specifically provide a SAFE (Soccer as Family Entertainment) enclosure with concessionary tickets. (This must surely set a trend for future soccer attendances and will undoubtedly help to bring back the crowds to the game.) Wigan Athletic FC beat Brentford FC 3–1 in the first final.

Watney Cup

This competition, sponsored by the brewery, was

started in 1970 and was played before the start of the season between the top scoring sides from each division of the Football League. Its main claim to fame lies in the innovative use of the penalty 'shoot out' in the event of a tie. On 5 August 1970 this was first used when Manchester United FC beat Hull City FC 4–3 on penalties after their semi-final match was tied 1–1 at full-time. Derby County FC won the first competition by beating Manchester United FC 4–1 and the sponsorship and the competition ceased in 1973.

Dryborough Cup

This competition was the Scottish equivalent of the Watney Cup and was contested for a total of six seasons between its instigation in 1971 and its abandonment in 1981. Although it proved to be a greater crowd-puller than the Watney Cup, it too suffered from lack of interest or support. Aberdeen beat Celtic 2–1 in the first final in 1971 and although Celtic went on to appear in five of the six finals, they took the trophy only once.

Anglo-Italian Cup/Anglo-Italian League Cup-Winners Cup/Anglo-Italian Tournament

The origin of these competitions is very closely tied up with the need to give Swindon Town FC an additional reward for winning the League Cup in 1969, as they were excluded from participation in the Fairs Cup because of their Third Division status.

For two seasons both the Anglo-Italian Cup and the Anglo-Italian League Cup-Winners Cup were contested and Swindon Town FC were the first winners of both competitions. In 1969 they beat AS Roma 5–2 on aggregate to win the first Anglo-Italian League Cup-Winners Cup and in 1970 beat Napoli 3–0 in the Anglo-Italian Cup (this match was abandoned after 79 minutes, but the result stood). In 1976 the competition ceased and the Anglo-Italian Tournament for leading non-League sides took its place. Monza beat Wimbledon 1–0 in the first final of the new competition.

FA Challenge Trophy

This competition was established in the 1969/70 season for the major professional and semi-professional sides other than the members and associate members of the Football League. In the first final which was played at Wembley in 1970, Macclesfield Town FC beat Telford United FC 2–0.

Super Cup

In 1972/3 this somewhat contrived competition between the winners of the European Cup and the winners of the European Cup-Winners Cup was started. The first two competitions were both won by the European Cup winners Ajax of Holland when they defeated Rangers FC and AC Milan respectively. Liverpool FC became the first British

winners in 1977 when they defeated Hamburg of West Germany 7–1 on aggregate and, in 1983, Aberdeen FC became the first Scottish club to win when they, too, defeated Hamburg 2–0 on aggregate.

(Above) Supporters of both Wigan Athletic and Brentford enjoy the Freight Rover final in the hugely successful SAFE Family enclosure. (John Maiden)
(Below) Chelsea's David Speedie and Colin Lee celebrate their club's success in beating Manchester City 5–4 in the first ever Full-Members Cup Final at Wembley on 23 March 1986. Speedie scored a hat-trick and Lee scored the other two Chelsea goals. (ASP)

Page numbers in italics are illustrations.
Losing teams will not be found in the
    index.
There may be more than one reference
    per page number: search carefully.

MORE
SUPERLATIVE SOCCER TITLES
FROM GUINNESS BOOKS

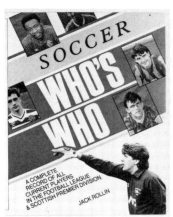

£5.95

£5.95

£3.95

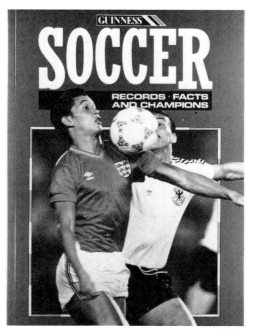

£8.95

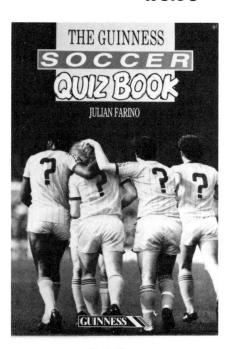

£4.95

THE AUTHOR

John Robinson is a Fellow of the Chartered Association of Certified Accountants and has spent much of his life as a partner in an accountancy practice. He is now the Co-Editor of *The Footballer*, the widely acclaimed journal of Soccer History, and owns a publishing company which specializes in soccer books.

In 1982 he published his first book *The Supporters' Guide to Football League Clubs* and, firmly established as a favourite with the fans, this is now in its 6th edition. Since completing the first edition of Guinness *Soccer Firsts* in 1986, he has written both *The FIFA World Cup 1930–1986* and *The European Championship 1958–1988*, and is currently researching another major soccer publication.

Acknowledgements

I would like to place on record my sincere thanks to the following soccer devotees without whose assistance I would have been unable to complete this book:
George Thomson for his initial idea; John Burt; Cliff Butler; Peter Cogle; Ray Goble; Stephen Hill; Keith Littlewood; Robert McElroy; Andy Porter and Patrick Woods.

In addition, I wish to thank my wife Glenys for withstanding my daily bombardment of soccer anecdotes.